buildings
that changed history

buildings
that changed history

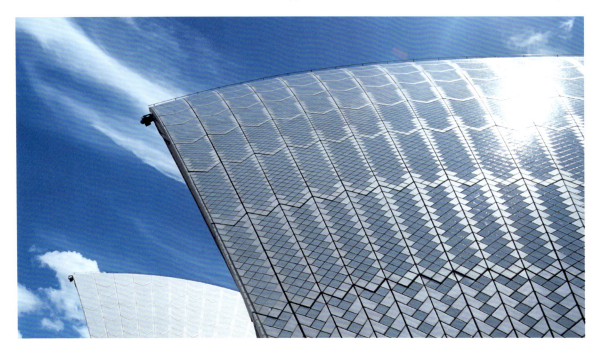

Contents

Looking at Buildings	6	**Angkor Wat** Angkor, Cambodia	56		
		Abbaye de Ste-Madeleine Vézelay, France	60	**Belém Tower** Lisbon, Portugal	112
Great Pyramid Giza, Egypt	16	**Krak des Chevaliers** Near Homs, Syria	64	**Château de Chambord** Loire Valley, France	116
The Parthenon Athens, Greece	20	**Borgund Stave Church** Lærdal, Norway	68	**St. Basil's Cathedral** Moscow, Russia	120
Colosseum Rome, Italy	24	**Chartres Cathedral** Chartres, France	72	**Villa La Rotonda** Vicenza, Italy	124

2500 BCE–1100 | 1100–1500 | 1500–1700

Pantheon Rome, Italy	28	**Burghausen Castle** Burghausen, Germany	78	**Himeji Castle** Himeji, Japan	128
Hagia Sophia Istanbul, Türkiye	32	**Florence Cathedral** Florence, Italy	82	**Masjid-i-Shah** Isfahan, Iran	132
Temple of the Inscriptions Palenque, Mexico	38	**Alhambra** Granada, Spain	88	**Taj Mahal** Agra, India	136
Bulguksa Temple Jinheon-Dong, South Korea	42	**Doge's Palace** Venice, Italy	94	**Royal Palace** Amsterdam, Netherlands	142
Palatine Chapel Aachen, Germany	46	**Temple of Heaven** Beijing, China	98	**Palace of Versailles** Paris, France	146
Borobudur Magelang, Java, Indonesia	50	**King's College Chapel** Cambridge, UK	102		
		Ducal Palace Urbino, Italy	106		

REVISED EDITION
Senior Editors Laura Sandford, Janashree Singha
US Editor Lori Hand
Managing Editors Gareth Jones, Soma B. Chowdhury
Senior Production Editor Andy Hilliard
Production Controller Nancy-Jane Maun
Jacket Designer Tanya Mehrotra
Pre-production Coordinator Tarun Sharma
Jackets Editorial Coordinator Priyanka Sharma
Creative Head Malavika Talukder
Publishing Director Georgina Dee
Art Director Maxine Pedliham
Managing Director Liz Gough

WRITTEN BY
Philip Wilkinson

FIRST EDITION

DK LONDON
Senior Editor Angela Wilkes
Senior Art Editor Gillian Andrews
Editor Anna Kruger
Designer Phil Gamble
Production Editor Tony Phipps
Production Controller Mandy Inness
Picture Research Sarah Smithies, Roland Smithies
Jacket Designer Mark Cavanagh
Managing Editor Stephanie Farrow
Managing Art Editor Lee Griffiths
US Editors Kate Johnsen, Shannon Beatty

DK INDIA
Senior Editor Kingshuk Ghoshal
Senior Art Editor Rajnish Kashyap
Editors Shatarupa Chaudhuri, Esha Banerjee
Art Editors Pooja Pipil, Vikas Chauhan
DTP Designers Shanker Prasad, Arjinder Singh
Managing Editor Saloni Talwar
Managing Art Editor Romi Chakraborty
DTP Manager Balwant Singh
Managing Director Aparna Sharma

Melk Abbey Melk, Austria	154			**Guggenheim Museum, Bilbao** Bilbao, Spain	222
Blenheim Palace Woodstock, UK	158	**Chrysler Building** New York City, USA	194	**Jean-Marie Tjibaou Cultural Centre** Nouméa, New Caledonia	226
Amalienburg Pavilion Nymphenburg, Germany	164	**Villa Savoye** Poissy, France	198	**Jin Mao Tower** Shanghai, China	230
Monticello Charlottesville, USA	168	**Fallingwater** Pennsylvania, USA	202	**Seattle Central Library** Seattle, USA	236

1700–1900

1900 TO PRESENT

Houses of Parliament London, UK	172	**Sydney Opera House** Sydney, Australia	208	**Palace of the Arts** Valencia, Spain	238
Neuschwanstein Castle Bavaria, Germany	176	**Brasília Cathedral** Brasília, Brazil	212	**MAXXI** Rome, Italy	240
Sagrada Familia Barcelona, Spain	180	**Pompidou Centre** Paris, France	216	**Yusuhara Wooden Bridge Museum** Kōchi, Japan	244
Hôtel Tassel Brussels, Belgium	186	**National Gallery of Canada** Ottawa, Canada	220		
Grand Palais Paris, France	188			**Glossary** **Index** **Acknowledgments**	246 250 255

Previously published as *Great Buildings*
This American Edition, 2025
First American Edition, 2012
Published in the United States by DK Publishing,
a division of Penguin Random House LLC
1745 Broadway, 20th Floor, New York, NY 10019

Copyright © 2012, 2025
Dorling Kindersley Limited
25 26 27 28 29 10 9 8 7 6 5 4 3 2 1
001–345219–July/2025

All rights reserved.
Without limiting the rights under the copyright
reserved above, no part of this publication may be
reproduced, stored in or introduced into a retrieval
system, or transmitted, in any form, or by any means

(electronic, mechanical, photocopying,
recording, or otherwise) without the prior
written permission of the copyright owner.
DK values and supports copyright. Thank you
for respecting intellectual property laws by not
reproducing, scanning or distributing any part of this
publication by any means without permission.
By purchasing an authorised edition, you are
supporting writers and artists and enabling DK to
continue to publish books that inform and inspire
readers. No part of this publication may be used or
reproduced in any manner for the purpose of training
artificial intelligence technologies or systems. In
accordance with Article 4(3) of the DSM Directive
2019/790, DK expressly reserves this work from
the text and data mining exception.

Published in Great Britain by Dorling Kindersley Limited
A catalog record for this book
is available from the Library of Congress.
ISBN 978-0-5939-6676-1

Printed and bound in China

www.dk.com

This book was made with Forest
Stewardship Council™ certified
paper – one small step in DK's
commitment to a sustainable future.
Learn more at www.dk.com/uk/
information/sustainability

Looking at Buildings

Buildings are among the largest structures made by human beings, and the most ubiquitous. Apart from agriculture, no human activity has changed the face of the Earth more than architecture. All around the world there are buildings from across the ages, some dating back thousands of years. Fascinatingly diverse, they range from simple wooden churches to magnificent Gothic cathedrals, and from grandiose palaces to minimalist modernist villas.

The astonishing variety of buildings stems in part from the different cultural traditions that have developed around the world. Western architecture, with its succession of styles from classical to Gothic, is one of the most prominent traditions, and its influence has spread far and wide, but the buildings of other civilizations—those of China, Japan, or Islam, for example—are equally fascinating. *Great Buildings* takes an in-depth look at some of the most distinctive buildings produced by these different traditions. It also explores innovative buildings of the 20th and 21st centuries, designed by architects who have broken with tradition and work internationally.

Looking at architecture is a personal experience, but one that is enriched by broader knowledge—the more you know about buildings, the closer you look, and the more you notice and enjoy. Like a helpful guide standing next to you, this book takes you on a visual tour of 53 of the world's great buildings—outstanding examples of architecture that are typical of their period or style. The book suggests a way to look at every building—taking it in as a whole, then looking slowly around the outside before going inside to explore the interior and take a close look at details. This approach highlights how one room leads to another in a carefully managed, almost theatrical country house, or how one space merges seamlessly into the next in the organic architecture of Frank Lloyd Wright. It helps you to understand how the spaces in a Buddhist temple embody the essence of the faith, and how contemporary architects have planned the interior of an art gallery or an office block. By understanding the parts of buildings, you can appreciate them as a whole—their history and purpose, their use of space and form, and the fascinating details that make them unique. To do so makes you marvel at the skill of the architects, builders, and artisans who created these great buildings.

External form

Every building exists in three dimensions, and when you look at it from the outside, you see a solid object. This three-dimensional quality of a structure is often called its form, and the form of a building has a huge impact on how you perceive it. Whether a building dominates its setting or blends into it, whether it is tall or hugs the ground, whether its façades are symmetrical or irregular, whether it has an internal courtyard or not—all of these are different aspects of a building's form.

COMPACT OR EXTENDED FORMS

Even two buildings with a similar purpose—two country houses, for example—can take radically different forms because their owners and architects had different priorities. Some houses, such as Palladio's villas, have a compact, symmetrical form focused on a central feature—a portico or a dome perhaps. Although houses like this can be grand and formal, they are also self-contained, occupy relatively modest sites, and were designed to accommodate just a small number of people. There are, however, country houses that take a very different form— vast, sprawling buildings that extend for thousands of feet, incorporating service wings, courtyards, gatehouses, and other elements. This kind of house— the Palace of Versailles outside Paris is a famous example—has long and complex façades, and entrance courtyards that spread out over a huge area. These different approaches suggest contrasting ways of living—a cultured country retreat in the case of the villa, a lifestyle on the most lavish scale at Versailles, with a sizable household and staff. The villa looks out over the landscape; the palace, however, seems to take over and monopolize the landscape with its all-embracing form.

FORM AND FAITH

Religious buildings show similar contrasts of form. Mosques often combine a spacious prayer hall, sometimes roofed with a dome, with one or more slender minarets; a major mosque may also have a courtyard leading to various other rooms and buildings. Many Christian churches, especially large cathedrals and abbeys, combine upward-pointing spires, turrets, and pinnacles with a layout that places an emphasis on length. Buildings associated with eastern religions, such as Buddhist shrines, are usually more centralized structures and, although they may rise to a point, they do not have the tall, slender, spires of Gothic cathedrals. The form of different kinds of religious structures has evolved from the way they were used. A mosque needs to accommodate a group of people at prayer and to provide a place from which the call to prayer is made. A cathedral, with its spires and grand west

◀▲ **CONTRASTING HOUSES** While the Villa La Rotonda, Italy (left), has a compact, self-contained plan centered on its dome, Blenheim Palace in the UK (above) extends over an enormous site and is visible from far across its vast park. Both the houses however, have formal, symmetrical façades and use elements of classical architecture to create a sense of grandeur.

▲▶ **STUPA AND SPIRE** The terraces of the Buddhist stupa at Borobodur (above) rise up and narrow toward the center. By contrast, Christian churches, such as Chartres (right) have spires at one end to emphasize the building's height.

front, directs the visitor's gaze up toward heaven but also points the way to the front door and the cavernous processional spaces inside. A Buddhist shrine or temple, on the other hand, might consist of a series of shallow terraces that symbolize the journey toward enlightenment. As pilgrims ascend on foot, they look at the carvings of the Buddha and meditate on his teachings.

FORM AND EFFECT

It is always worth walking around a building before entering, since this can tell you a lot about its form and what its builders wanted to achieve. On most buildings every façade is different. The shape and texture of each of them can be surprising—and the back often looks very different from the front where the entrance is. Every part of a building's exterior contributes to the overall effect. Both a castle tower and a skyscraper, for example, dominate their site and are designed to make people stop and marvel at the status of the people who had them built. They achieve this effect in different ways. The protruding turrets and balconies of a castle tower create much of its impact; the dramatic effect of a skyscraper is enhanced by its setbacks—the way in which the tower is stepped back in stages toward the top. Features such as classical porticos, the design of doorways and window openings, or supporting arches, also add interest. They break up the form, and sometimes, as with the windows on a skyscraper or the rows of buttresses on a medieval cathedral, create a rhythmic repetition that gives the exterior additional visual variety. Such features are all aspects of a building's form and add to its character.

◀▶ **TOWERS** A tall, late-medieval building, such as the Belém Tower (left), has a series of protrusions that make its solid form more complex and decorative. By contrast, the classic skyscraper form is a tall tower with setbacks creating a tapering effect. Pioneered by the builders of towers such as New York's Chrysler Building (right), this form was adopted for countless other skyscrapers around the world.

Interior space

Architects often think of a building as a series of spaces: when designing a new building, they start with the functions that the structure needs to fulfill, design spaces for those functions, and then define the spaces using walls, windows, and roofs. The character of an interior, therefore, varies immensely from one building to another.

SIMPLE AND COMPLEX SPACES

Some buildings are relatively simple in spatial terms. When you open the door and walk inside, you can take in the whole interior in one glance. This is the case with some religious buildings, including many temples or cathedrals. It is also true of ancient structures such as medieval hall houses. In these simple buildings virtually the entire life of the inhabitants—eating, working, and sleeping—took place in a single room. Most buildings, however, are made up of multiple spaces that are either separate rooms or distinct areas linked by arches or similar openings. The most complex buildings are grand palaces, such as Versailles, which have hundreds of rooms arranged in a very particular, formal manner. Suites of rooms are designed to lead from one space to another. The first room is often the grandest and most formal, such as an audience chamber, and the last is the smallest, most intimate room, where the owner would receive close friends and colleagues. The proportions of all these spaces contribute to their impact. In classical architecture rooms often have the proportions of a cube or double cube. Others take the form of perfect circles or have dimensions based on classical formulas, such as the golden section. This underlying geometry gives rooms a formal, ordered character, as opposed to the informality of a small house or cottage.

ORDER AND REPETITION

Another way of arranging space is to use repeating elements of the same size and shape, such as the arches, piers, and windows in a church or cathedral, which combine structural strength with a sense of formality. Arches, in particular, add a different dimension to an interior—a sense of interest or even

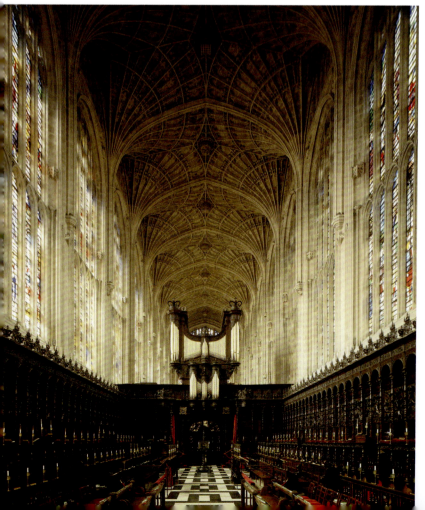

◄▲ **SINGLE AND MULTIPLE SPACES** At King's College Chapel in the UK (left), almost the whole interior, from the great expanse of the fan-vaulted ceiling to the carved stalls below, is visible at a single glance, even though a wooden screen divides the space in two. The interior decoration may be intricate, but the building is very simple in terms of space. In a grand palace such as Versailles in France (above), many of the rooms are small by comparison with the Chapel interior, but they interconnect, giving visitors tantalizing glimpses of the neighboring rooms. A splash of vivid color or the hint of a portrait through a doorway makes people want to explore further.

mystery. When you see an arch inside a building, you instinctively want to go through it to find out what is on the other side. Arches in Byzantine and Gothic buildings open up new vistas and lead to different spaces—to the aisles or side chapels in a cathedral, for example, which fulfil different purposes. If the interior of a cathedral is complex, there will always be a dominant axis that leads to the altar. In many churches this axis is accentuated by elongating the interior, directing your eyes past ranks of arches and piers toward the altar, as at Vézelay or Chartres, both in France. Another way of organizing this kind of space, is to centralize the interior. Many ancient churches, including Hagia Sophia in Istanbul, have a huge central dome, as do some modern places of worship, such as the cathedral at Brasília.

In all these examples the interior space of the building is arranged in a very obvious way. In some structures, however, space is exploited in a more fluid fashion, and this is often the case with contemporary buildings. Le Corbusier wanted his houses to be open-plan, so that one space flowed naturally into another—an approach that Frank Lloyd Wright also adopted in many of his house designs. Interconnecting spaces, gentle ramps, and big balconies or roof terraces that link the exterior and interior of the building are typical features of houses like these, and the interiors of some modern public buildings are arranged in a similar way. By stretching the concept of what a room is, the fluid interior spaces of these buildings remind us how innovative and exciting architecture can be.

◄ **FLOWING SPACE**
Rome's MAXXI art gallery has walkways and bridges that appear to flow across its interior. The building also seems to rise and dip around its oddly shaped site. These features, combined with the pale, curving interior walls, create a sense of fluid space quite unlike that of a traditional gallery with rectangular rooms.

▲ ► **SPATIAL ORGANIZATION** The repeated arches of the abbey church at Vézelay, France (above), direct your eyes toward the main focus of the building—the high altar. The arches frame the space, making it formal and regular. The lateral arches also open up vistas of the side aisles and chapels, creating the impression that this large building is in fact a collection of complex and interesting spaces. The cathedral at Brasília (right) also has strong repeating forms, notably the concrete ribs that form the main structural elements of the building. These work in the opposite way from the arches at Vézelay, converging on a central crown and emphasizing the immense scale of the centralized interior space.

Architectural detail

"God is in the detail." This assertion is often attributed to the German modernist architect Ludwig Mies van der Rohe. It meant that every aspect of a building is important, right down to the smallest detail. Put simply, having a great idea is not enough: an architect has to give his or her idea form by making sure that every slab of masonry is correctly positioned, every glazing bar properly finished, every door handle exactly the right shape—and that all these details harmonize with each other and with the building of which they are a part. This idea of the building as a whole, in which every detail has to work, has always been a key part of architecture.

ILLUSTRATING BELIEF

For the visitor, examining architectural details—whether they be arches, carved capitals, window catches, stained glass windows, or frescoes—can be hugely rewarding. They offer fascinating clues to how a building's creators thought about the structure, how it was used, and what the needs, lives, and beliefs of the people who first used it might have been. Gothic cathedrals provide some of the best examples of the richness of architectural detail because the master masons and artisans of the Middle Ages poured their skills and devotion into these amazing works of art, turning them into what they saw as images of heaven on Earth. Carvings around doorways and capitals, stained glass windows, wall paintings, and choir stalls fill these buildings with imagery designed to bring the Christian story to life and provide an inspiring place for worship. Hindu temples and some Buddhist shrines have a similar wealth of imagery. Although some religious or cultural traditions, such as Islam, do not permit representative art, a major mosque adorned with tiles decorated with arabesques and inscriptions from the Qur'an is just as rich visually as a Christian cathedral or a Hindu temple.

STYLE AND SUBSTANCE

Secular buildings, from houses to palaces or seats of government, can be equally lavish in detail. A palace may be full of paintings that glorify its royal patron, or have imagery, carvings, or plasterwork that portray the owner's interests, be they heraldry

▲ **CAPITAL** At the Pantheon in Rome, the architectural style is immediately apparent in details such as this Corinthian capital. They indicate that the building is in the classical tradition, drawn from ancient Greece and passed on to architects all over the world.

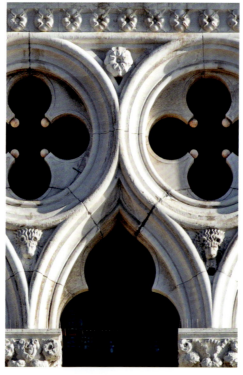

▲ **GOTHIC ARCHES** These arches on the front of the Doge's Palace in Venice are in a highly ornate and richly carved style of Gothic unique to the city. This kind of lavish ornament reveals a great deal about the wealth of Venice and its rulers.

▲ **KHMER RELIEFS** The relief carvings that adorn Khmer temples, such as Angkor Wat in Cambodia, portray figures and episodes from Hindu mythology. They reflect the idea of a building as a physical representation of an entire belief system.

ARCHITECTURAL DETAIL

◀ **IRONWORK** In the 19th century cast iron was widely used both structurally and for decoration. Here, curves and scrolls of ironwork run up the vast posts and trusses that support the roof of the Grand Palais in Paris, a building rich in Art Nouveau detail.

or hunting. Many of these details, from classical columns to rococo plasterwork, also reveal the sources and interests of their architects. Some followed the strict principles of classical architecture, while others adopted the more fluid approach of the baroque style. Ornamental styles also reveal the attitudes of architects to the kind of building they considered appropriate for a particular purpose. In the 19th century, for example, many people believed Gothic to be the ideal style for churches, and the classical style more suitable for the civic or national values embodied in a public building such as a town hall. Details associated with these styles could be used to conjure up images of piety or civic pride. At the end of the 19th century architects in Europe turned their backs on the past and created Art Nouveau ("New Art"). Unlike the revivalist styles popular at the time, Art Nouveau was based on non-historical details such as sinuous plant forms and whiplash curves. Modernist buildings went further, sometimes eliminating ornamentation completely. Even these restrained structures, however, include telling functional details, from carefully designed bathroom fittings to perfectly proportioned and aesthetically pleasing doors and windows.

From a humble floor tile to a carved stone boss at the apex of a high, vaulted ceiling, architectural details can easily be overlooked, but they are worth seeking out. They remind us not only that great buildings are extraordinary works of art, but of the countless builders, architects, and artisans who worked long and hard on their creation. From the grand sweep of a vast façade to the tiniest carving or image in a window, buildings are an endless source of fascination and pleasure.

◀ **MIHRAB** Intricately decorated, this niche in the Masjid-i-Shah mosque in Iran indicates the direction of Mecca so that those attending prayers know which way to face.

▲ **STAINED GLASS** Color is an important element in most buildings. In Chartres Cathedral, France, the richness of the medieval stained glass floods the interior with dazzling light.

- **GREAT PYRAMID**
  Giza, Egypt

- **THE PARTHENON**
  Athens, Greece

- **COLOSSEUM**
  Rome, Italy

- **PANTHEON**
  Rome, Italy

- **HAGIA SOPHIA**
  Istanbul, Türkiye

- **TEMPLE OF THE INSCRIPTIONS**
  Palenque, Mexico

- **BULGUKSA TEMPLE**
  Jinheon-Dong, South Korea

- **PALATINE CHAPEL**
  Aachen, Germany

- **BOROBUDUR**
  Magelang, Java, Indonesia

2500 BCE – 1100

Great Pyramid

c. 2560 BCE ■ ROYAL TOMB ■ GIZA, EGYPT

ARCHITECT UNKNOWN

The first great monumental structures in the world, the pyramids of Egypt were built as tombs for the rulers of the Old and Middle Kingdoms between about 2600 and 1800 BCE. The most imposing pyramids are those at Giza, west of Cairo, which were made for kings Khufu, Khafra, and Menkaure. The largest of the three is Khufu's tomb, known as the Great Pyramid.

No one knows for sure why the ancient Egyptians chose the form of the pyramid for their pharaohs' tombs. It may have been because the shape represented the spreading rays of the sun and was therefore a symbol of the Egyptians' revered Sun God. The pyramid may also have represented a symbolic stairway, up which the deceased ruler made his journey to heaven, or the shape may have recalled the primal mound that was the scene of one of Egypt's creation myths. Whatever the reason, the pyramid shape clearly meant a lot to the pharaohs, who deployed huge resources moving millions of stone blocks—some of which weighed 15 tons—to build structures up to 450ft (146m) high that contained little more than a tiny chamber for the royal sarcophagus. The builders laid out these enormous structures with extraordinary precision—the Great Pyramid's base is level to within 1in (2.1cm).

The Great Pyramid was originally part of a large funerary complex, much of which has long since disappeared. This consisted of a temple near the Nile River, where the king's body was received, a causeway to the tomb site, a mortuary temple, small pyramids for the ruler's wives, and the king's vast pyramid itself. Inside, as well as the burial chamber at its heart, the pyramid contains a number of other chambers, passages, and shafts, all of which are expertly constructed and positioned, but their intended use is unknown. Although it looks simple in form, this enormous building looming up from the desert retains its essential mystery.

KHUFU

c. 2609–2560 BCE

Pharaoh Khufu was the second ruler of the Egyptian 4th Dynasty and the son of its founder, Sneferu, who had ruled for almost 50 years and built three pyramids at Meidum and Dahshur. Khufu came to the throne when he was about 20 years old and probably ruled for around 23 years, although the exact dates of his reign are not known for certain. He had a reputation as a ruthless ruler, but little is known about his life except that he probably led military campaigns in areas such as Nubia and Libya. Khufu's name is short for Khnum-khuf, meaning "the god Khnum is his protection"—Khnum was the deity who controlled the flooding of the Nile. During the river's annual inundation, which lasted for about three months, no agricultural work was possible so Khufu ordered around 100,000 farm workers to Giza, where he provided accommodation while they labored on his pyramid.

Visual tour

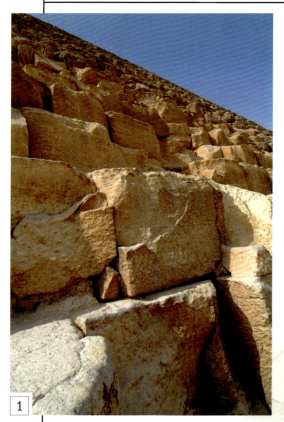

1 ▲ **MASONRY** The core of the pyramid consists of massive blocks of limestone. This stone came from local quarries, and the average weight of the blocks is around 2.5 tons. The exact figure is uncertain because it is not possible to measure the size of blocks hidden deep inside the solid structure's heart. The builders laid the roughly shaped blocks in horizontal patterns and used gypsum mortar to hold them together and fill any gaps between them.

2 ▲ **LIMESTONE CASING** Most of the pyramid's white outer casing has disappeared and was recycled for use in other buildings. This high-quality stone came from Tura, which was to the south of Giza and on the other side of the Nile River (between modern Cairo and Helwan). To mine the stone at Tura, quarry workers had to dig deep underground, but the quality of the stone justified the additional labor. The builders probably used sleds to drag the stone to the site, and devices such as ramps and levers to maneuver the heavy blocks into position.

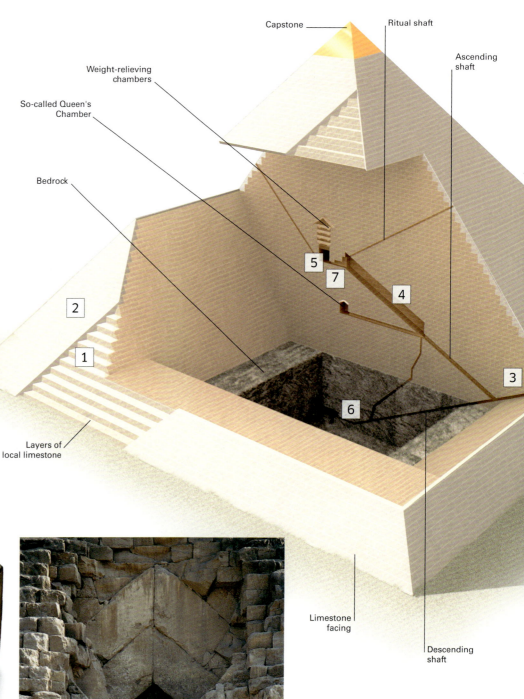

3 ◀ **ENTRANCE** The pyramid entrance is topped with two pairs of huge stones to support the weight of the masonry above. Although now clearly visible, this doorway would have been hidden from view once the pharaoh's burial had taken place. The entrance is situated 24ft (7.3m) east of the central axis of the pyramid. From it a narrow passage leads down through the pyramid's core and into the bedrock beneath, toward the subterranean chamber where the builders might have originally planned to place the pharaoh.

GREAT PYRAMID ■ EGYPT

ON DESIGN

One of the great mysteries of this pyramid is the purpose of the narrow, straight shafts that lead up toward the outside world from the King's Chamber and from the abandoned burial chamber, sometimes called the Queen's Chamber, beneath it. Both chambers have pairs of shafts running in similar directions, but those from the abandoned chamber stop before they reach the outside. The shafts are very narrow—around 8in (20cm) square—and Egyptologists once referred to them as "air shafts." Scholars now believe that the shafts had a ritual purpose since they are oriented toward specific stars. They may have been there to offer the king's soul an escape route for the final journey to heaven.

▲ **GRAND GALLERY** The approach to the King's Chamber is via a narrow ascending passage that opens out dramatically into the Grand Gallery, an awe-inspiring space 26ft (8.74m) high and 153ft (46.7m) long. The side walls are corbeled inward so that the space tapers at the top. A series of holes along the gallery's sides probably held wooden beams that supported massive stone blocks. Once the pharaoh was entombed, workers removed these beams, letting the blocks slide down to seal the ascending passage.

▲ **KING'S CHAMBER** The pharaoh's burial chamber is lined with huge blocks of red granite, including nine granite slabs that span the roof, which is 18ft (5.5m) across. Cracks appeared in these ceiling slabs while the pyramid was being built, so the masons arranged a series of weight-relieving chambers directly above. At one end of the room stands the pharaoh's sarcophagus, also of red granite, but thieves removed the rest of the chamber's contents.

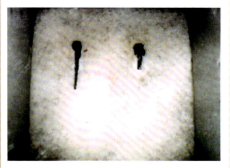

▲ **Blocked shaft**
When researchers sent a robotic camera up one of the shafts leading out of the abandoned chamber, the shaft was obstructed by a limestone block containing two copper pins. The purpose of the block is unknown.

ON SITE

The gently sloping limestone plateau at Giza was ideal for building large structures. It provided a convenient source of stone for construction and a base that was not too difficult to level before building could begin. The pharaohs of the 4th dynasty and their architects planned their three large pyramids with meticulous care. The sides of the pyramids are oriented almost exactly with true North, and the pyramids, mortuary temples, and other buildings nearby reveal other careful alignments that may have had cosmic significance. Their meaning is as yet unknown.

▲ **SUBTERRANEAN CHAMBER** This chamber, with painted hieroglyphs that are said to show the name of Khufu, is cut deep into the bedrock beneath the pyramid some 98ft (30m) below ground level. Access is through a descending passage that runs straight for a total of 192ft (58.5m), first through the pyramid's limestone core then through the bedrock. Near or below ground level was the usual position for the pharaoh's tomb in a pyramid at this time, and the pyramid's builders probably originally intended the subterranean chamber to be Khufu's final resting place. It was never finished.

▲ **PORTCULLIS** When Khufu's entombment was complete, workers carefully sealed the King's Chamber to deter grave robbers. They achieved this by sliding down three heavy granite slabs, which then blocked the way between the Grand Gallery and the chamber. These granite slabs were held in place using grooves above the entrance to the King's Chamber, and the workers must have lowered them into place using ropes.

▲ **Pyramid complex**
Because they are perfectly aligned, the pyramids at Giza catch the sunlight in the same way, producing an awe-inspiring effect of light and shade on a monumental scale.

The Parthenon

447–438 BCE ■ TEMPLE ■ ATHENS, GREECE

KALLIKRATES AND IKTINOS

By the middle of the 5th century BCE Athens was the most powerful city in Greece and one of the major cultural centers of the ancient world. In 447 BCE, the Athenians began to rebuild the temples on the Acropolis (the hill overlooking Athens), which had been badly damaged during wars with Persia (modern Iran). The largest new structure was the Parthenon, a temple to Athena, the city's patron goddess. At the heart of the building, in the shrine known as the cella, was a huge statue of the goddess made of ivory and gold.

Prized for its proportions and outstanding set of decorative carvings, the Parthenon quickly became the most famous Greek temple, and its architecture was widely admired and imitated. Architects Kallikrates and Iktinos modified Doric, the simplest of the Greek orders (see p.23), by introducing a sculptural frieze around the building, an unusual feature in a Doric structure. They also employed optical tricks to make the building appear perfectly proportioned. The platform on which the temple stands is convex, and the columns lean slightly—both effects that are said to trick the eye into seeing the building as perfectly straight.

The Parthenon was not always used as a temple. In 1687, the Turks, who ruled Greece, used it to store arms and explosives during their war with Venice. The Venetians attacked the temple and blew it up, making off with some of the sculptures from the building. In the early 19th century, British ambassador Lord Elgin controversially removed many others, which remain in the British Museum. The Greeks built a dedicated museum for them in 2009, and have demanded their return.

ON SITE

The Acropolis had been a major religious site for about 1,000 years before the Parthenon was built. Other than the Parthenon, which dominates the site, the Greeks built three other major buildings in the 5th century BCE—two temples, the Erechtheum and the temple of Athena Nike, and the Propylaea, a great ceremonial gateway. These buildings occupied a site that was central to Greek history and myth—some of the older structures, wrecked by the Persians, were left untouched, and the Erechtheum was built on the very spot where, according to legend, Athena and Poseidon fought over who should be the patron deity of Athens.

▲ **The Acropolis**, dominated by the Parthenon

Visual tour

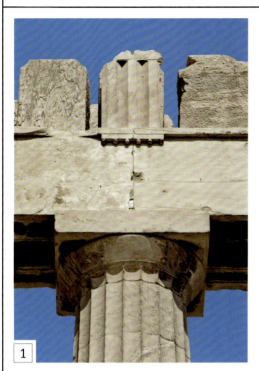

▲ **DORIC ORDER** The Parthenon's outer columns are Doric, the order that tops fluted columns with an unadorned square slab called an abacus. The simple shapes of the architecture catch the sun beautifully, making the design clear in the strong Mediterranean light. Above the abacus are the horizontal bands of stone that make up the entablature: first the plain band called the architrave, then the more ornate band known as the frieze.

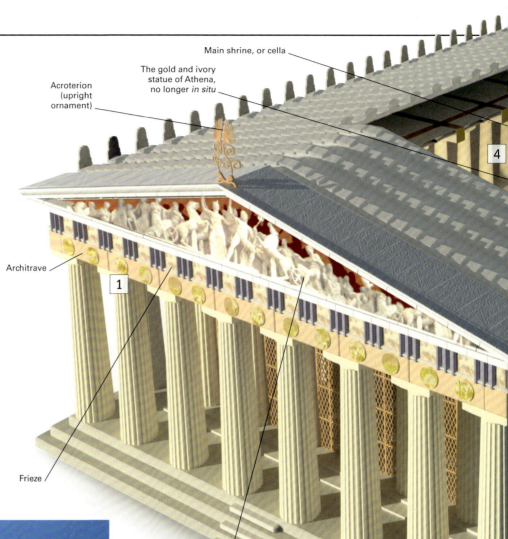

▲ **SOUTHERN FRIEZE** The temple's friezes are made up of triglyphs (simple patterns of three vertical bands) alternating with sculptures in low relief known as metopes. Although many of the metopes have been removed, a few remain, including the one above. This is part of a series depicting a battle between a Greek people called the Lapiths and the centaurs, mythical beasts that were part-human, part-horse. Carvings such as these were meant to show the triumph of Greek civilization over barbarism. They were the work of the great Athenian sculptor Phidias, or of those working under him.

▼ **WEST METOPE** The metopes on the temple's west end depict a legendary battle between the Athenians and the Amazons, a mythical race of warrior women. This subject was especially important on a temple dedicated to Athena because the scene was also shown on the shield carried by the goddess. The defeat of the Amazons is another example of Greek triumph.

THE PARTHENON ■ GREECE 23

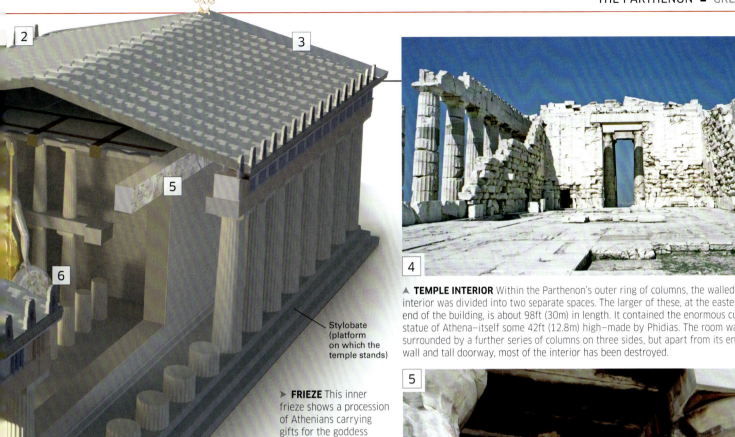

Stylobate (platform on which the temple stands)

▲ Reconstruction of the Parthenon, showing the position of the cella, cult statue, and sculptures that are no longer present.

▶ FRIEZE This inner frieze shows a procession of Athenians carrying gifts for the goddess Athena. This event probably represents part of the Great Panathenaic Festival, which was held in Athens every four years and involved religious sacrifices, games, and cultural events. Some of the participants in the procession have brought a special robe made by the women of Athens, to place on the statue of the goddess in the temple.

▲ TEMPLE INTERIOR Within the Parthenon's outer ring of columns, the walled interior was divided into two separate spaces. The larger of these, at the eastern end of the building, is about 98ft (30m) in length. It contained the enormous cult statue of Athena–itself some 42ft (12.8m) high–made by Phidias. The room was surrounded by a further series of columns on three sides, but apart from its end wall and tall doorway, most of the interior has been destroyed.

▲ COLONNADE The columns at the corners are spaced slightly more closely together than the rest of those in the Parthenon colonnade. This slight irregularity in the design gives the temple façades more variety and rhythm than they would otherwise have.

ON CONSTRUCTION

The ancient Greeks developed a series of style variations called the orders, which they used to design columns, together with the structures supported by them, on their temples, monuments, and other buildings. There were three orders, and each provided a series of guidelines for these architectural elements. The orders were highly influential and were adopted and extended by the Romans and later civilizations.

The simplest and earliest of the orders is the Doric, which has fluted columns topped very plainly with two stones–the tapering echinus and square abacus. The Ionic order is slightly more ornate, and its capitals are adorned with spiral volutes. The last and most decorative of the three orders is the Corinthian, which has capitals featuring the curling leaves of the acanthus plant. Both the Ionic and Corinthian orders have a base, a wider section between the column and the ground, while the Doric usually lacks a base.

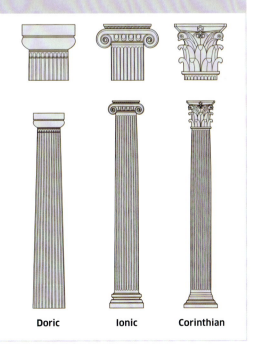

Doric   Ionic   Corinthian

Colosseum

69–81CE ■ AMPHITHEATER ■ ROME, ITALY

ARCHITECT UNKNOWN

In ancient Rome, perhaps the most popular entertainments were the gladiatorial games, in which men fought one another to the death or wrestled with wild animals such as lions and tigers. These games were held in amphitheaters, often vast structures with rows of tiered seats surrounding the arena, the central combat area named after the sand used to cover the surface and absorb the victims' blood. The construction of the greatest of these amphitheaters, the Colosseum in Rome, was begun during the reign of emperor Vespasian (69–79CE) and completed during that of his son Titus (79–81CE).

The Colosseum probably got its name from the nearby colossal statue of the emperor Nero, but the name could also refer to the building's size—the enormous elliptical structure measures 617 by 512ft (188 by 156m) and seats up to 55,000 spectators. From the outside, the amphitheater's huge ellipse, with a travertine façade, is made up of three rows of 80 arches with a plain wall above them. The lower row of arches leads into a large network of entrance passageways and stairs beneath the vaults that support the amphitheater's stone seats. The whole building was designed so that the huge audience could get to their seats quickly and would have an uninterrupted view of the spectacle once they were seated.

Constructing the Colosseum was a formidable task. As well as some 3.5 million cubic feet (100,000 cubic meters) of travertine for the façade, the builders used great quantities of concrete for the foundations and vaults, together with bricks and tufa for some of the concealed walls. Although only about half of the outer walls have survived intact, together with many of the entrance passages and the area under the arena, these are enough to reveal the magnificent scale of the building and the great engineering skill that went into the construction of its walls, arches, and vaults.

VESPASIAN

c.9–79CE

A successful military commander, Vespasian became famous for taking part in the Roman invasion of Britain in 43CE and for defeating the Jewish rebellion in 66CE. While Vespasian was in Jerusalem in 68CE, the tyrannical emperor Nero committed suicide and a series of weak emperors took over for a few months. In the following year Vespasian won the support of the army and Senate and was made emperor. A down-to-earth man, he was an enthusiastic builder who completed the construction of the Temple of Claudius and built the Temple of Peace in Rome. He was a shrewd politician who understood the importance of keeping the people of Rome happy and built the Colosseum as an entertainment center on the site of the artificial lake next to one of Nero's palaces—the location sent a message that Nero's hated tyranny was over. When Vespasian died, the crown passed to his son, Titus, who completed the amphitheater.

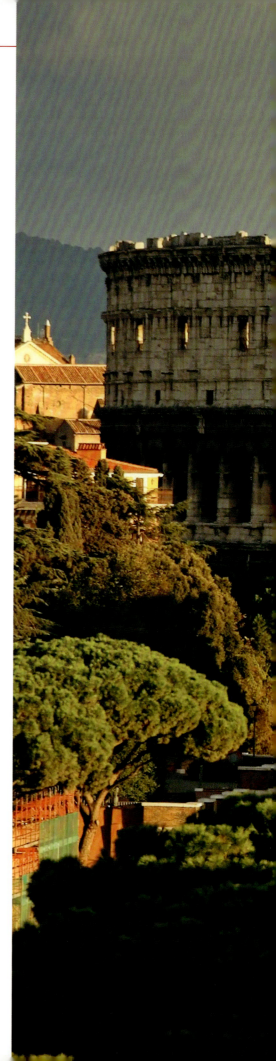

Visual tour

▲ **FAÇADE** The semicircular arches on the outside of the Colosseum are flanked by half columns in different classical orders—the simple Tuscan order (an invention of the Romans) at the bottom, Ionic in the middle, and the ornate Corinthian, with its capitals of carved acanthus leaves, at the top. This approach follows the hierarchy of orders common in most classical buildings (see p.23), in which the plainest order is at the bottom, and the most decorative order at the top. Statues originally occupied the arches on the two upper levels.

▲ **POCK MARKS** The amphitheater's builders employed iron clamps (using some 300 tons of iron in total) to hold together the stone blocks used on the façade and elsewhere on the building. Later, in the Renaissance, much of this stone was removed for reuse. The many holes and scars on the structure show where the clamps were originally positioned.

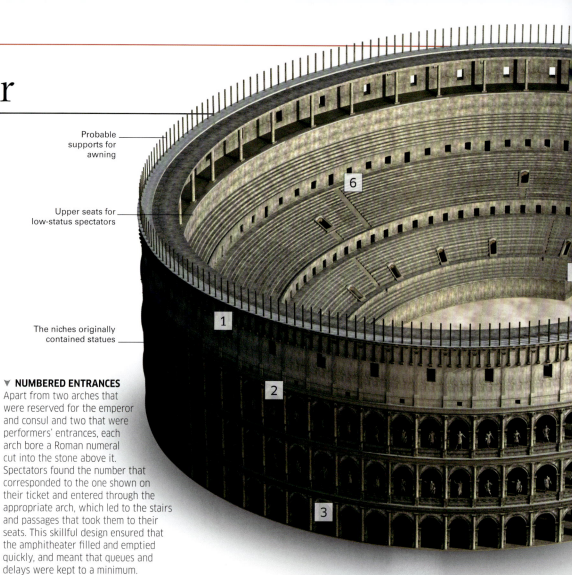

▼ **NUMBERED ENTRANCES** Apart from two arches that were reserved for the emperor and consul and two that were performers' entrances, each arch bore a Roman numeral cut into the stone above it. Spectators found the number that corresponded to the one shown on their ticket and entered through the appropriate arch, which led to the stairs and passages that took them to their seats. This skillful design ensured that the amphitheater filled and emptied quickly, and meant that queues and delays were kept to a minimum.

▶ **CIRCUIT CORRIDORS** Four circulation corridors run around the Colosseum beneath the seating, linking the various passages and stairs. These corridors contain vast arches—the Romans did not invent the arch, but they were one of the first civilizations to use it to its full potential in large-scale engineering projects ranging from aqueducts to amphitheaters. The Colosseum arches support the huge weight of the audience and rows of seating above, while leaving plenty of floor space in the corridors below. The generous space provided by these circuit corridors enabled the organizers of the games to route spectators through the building along the most efficient paths.

Corinthian columns
Ionic columns
Tuscan columns

IN CONTEXT

Archaelogists believe that the large area beneath the Colosseum's arena contained machinery for lifting cages so that the animals could be released straight into the arena. There were also winches that controlled the trapdoors and raised scenery. At Capua Vetere in southern Italy an amphitheater survives with the arena floor and trapdoors largely intact. Some of these trapdoors are located above corridors and would have been used by the gladiators; others were linked to the lifts for caged animals.

▲ **Amphitheater at Capua Vetere**
This structure had 64 trapdoors altogether; the Colosseum probably had even more.

▶ **STAIRWAY** Many of the access stairs form an integral part of the structure beneath the seating, so have remained intact. This well-preserved example leads directly to a tier of seating, through one of the openings or access points that were known as *vomitoria*. The term suggests the rapid exit of the audience from the amphitheater and has nothing to do with vomiting.

▶ **SEATING** None of the original seating survives, but archaeologists have found many fragments, which have enabled them to recreate a few rows of one segment of the *maenianum secundum immum*, the second main level of seating. Each seat is 17in (44cm) high and 24in (61cm) wide, and the stone blocks are stepped on the far side of the segment for ease of access. Roman senators sat on the podium, the lowest level of the Colosseum, close to the arena. Unlike the rest of the amphitheater, the podium did not have stone seats, but was a platform on which senators could place their own stools or chairs.

◀ **BENEATH THE ARENA**
This lower level contains a network of passages and small rooms, or cells, where the gladiators waited their turn to appear in front of the spectators. There are also 32 small, vaulted chambers, which are thought to have been used as cages for the animals. The masonry of these structures also supported the arena floor, which was probably made of wood. The structures beneath the arena were modified several times during Roman times, but for much of the period there were probably devices for raising trapdoors and powering other machinery, together with various ramps and stairs for the gladiators.

Pantheon

c.110–124CE ▪ TEMPLE ▪ ROME, ITALY

ARCHITECT UNKNOWN

The best preserved of all Roman temples is the Pantheon in Rome. It is famous for its massive entrance portico and colossal circular dome, which was the biggest such structure of its time and is still the largest unreinforced concrete dome in the world. The Pantheon was built on the site of a temple that had been destroyed in a fire. Historians used to attribute the Pantheon to the emperor Hadrian (reigned 117–138CE) and his architects. Recent archaeological work shows, however, that some of the bricks used in its construction are from an earlier period, so the work may have begun under the emperor Trajan (reigned 98–117CE) and been finished under Hadrian.

Most Roman temples were rectangular and surrounded by columns in a similar way to Greek buildings such as the Parthenon (see pp.20–23). The Pantheon is, however, different. Its portico leads to a rectangular vestibule, and beyond this is a rotunda (a circular chamber) perfectly proportioned so that its diameter and height match—both stand at 142½ft (43.4m), which equals 150 Roman feet. The reason for the building's unusual design is unknown, but the spherical shape may symbolize unity, since the Pantheon was a temple dedicated to all the gods.

Remarkable for its unique proportions and the engineering achievement of its dome, the Pantheon is also unusually well preserved. It became a church in the Christian era, and as a consequence the building was cared for. Features such as the marble cladding of the interior, for example, were not removed and recycled elsewhere, as was the case with most Roman buildings. The Pantheon survived to influence the designers of countless other buildings roofed with domes and fronted by classical porticoes.

ON **CONSTRUCTION**

The dome of the Pantheon is built of concrete, a material that the Romans used widely, especially for structures such as vaults, domes, and curving walls. The result is one of the most stunning roofs in all ancient architecture, plain and purposeful from the outside and elegant within.

The architect carefully designed the dome so that its shell is thick around the edge and much thinner towards the top—the upper part is only about 4ft (1.2m) thick. The builders also made the dome's structure lighter toward the top by mixing the concrete with tufa and pumice instead of the tufa and brick in the lower part. This ingenious construction reduces the weight of the dome and minimizes the strain on the supporting walls. At the very top is a circular hole, the oculus, which is open to the sky, letting natural light into the heart of the building.

▲ **Dome** The stepped profile and oculus are clearly seen from above.

Visual tour

1 ▲ PORTICO Eight Corinthian columns front the Pantheon's portico. The shafts of these columns are 39ft (12m) tall, the equivalent of 40 Roman feet. The columns support a simple entablature, above which is the large triangular pediment. This looks very plain now, but would have originally housed some form of sculpture. This may have featured an eagle set inside a wreath and was possibly made of gilded bronze to match the bronze doors below, which survive to this day.

2 ◀ CAPITAL Although the capitals of the portico are badly worn, they still bear the acanthus leaves of the Corinthian order, which was invented by the ancient Greeks and imitated by the Romans. This delicate decoration complements the rather severe treatment of the rest of the façade, providing relief for the eye as well as an elegant termination for the tall granite columns.

- The oculus is 27ft (8.2m) across and lights the interior
- The dome is thinner toward the top to reduce the weight
- The upper level of the walls helps to buttress the dome, which appears saucer-shaped from the outside although hemispherical within
- The floor is covered in slabs of granite, marble, and porphyry
- The temple was originally raised above the surrounding ground and could be reached via a flight of steps

3 ◀ RELIEVING ARCHES The walls of the Pantheon's rotunda are made of a combination of concrete and brick. Although they form a very simple circular shape, these walls are built in a complex way on very deep foundations in order to cope with the stresses and strains generated by the enormous dome above. One feature that strengthens the wall is the series of large, brick relieving arches that can be seen at different levels around the building. The upper level of the wall, where these arches are most clearly visible, conceals and strengthens the lower part of the Pantheon's dome.

PANTHEON ■ ITALY

▶ **INTERIOR DOME** The temple rotunda, with its coffered dome and patterns of niches and openings around the walls, is the best preserved, large-scale Roman interior. The internal walls reveal a perfect marriage of architecture and engineering: the niches and semi-domes are both visually elegant and a key component of the structure, helping to buttress the walls and support the weight of the dome.

▲ **DOME COFFERING** Five rows of square indentations called coffers extend around the dome's inner surface. These set up a satisfying architectural pattern and provide a way of reducing the dome's weight. The center of the dome was originally embellished with stucco ornaments.

▶ **WALL NICHES AND ALTAR** Eight niches, one of which forms the entrance, surround the rotunda. A pair of marble Corinthian columns flanks each one. Originally, the niches probably housed statues of the Roman gods. Later, they were transformed into Christian altars.

ON DETAIL

The Romans were famous for their beautiful inscriptions in capitals, the styles of which still influence typographers and stonemasons. These inscriptions are outstanding for the subtle variations in the widths of their strokes, making them visually attractive and easy to read. Inscriptions in Roman capitals appear on gravestones, monuments, triumphal arches, and civic buildings. The Pantheon inscription, which runs along the entablature of the portico, commemorates the previous temple on the site, erected by the general and politician Agrippa in the 1st century BCE. Hadrian and Trajan saw their work as rebuilding the temple, so did not claim the building as their own.

▲ **Portico inscription**
In inscriptions such as the one commemorating Marcus Agrippa on the Pantheon, the Romans perfected the capital letters that we still use today.

IN CONTEXT

The Romans' use of concrete helped them create all kinds of structures, not only large domes such as the one roofing the Pantheon, but also arches and vaulted ceilings. A structure they often used in large buildings was the barrel vault, a vault with a semicircular cross section. This kind of ceiling proved effective in large public or imperial buildings, where the architect wanted to create a sense of grandeur. Concrete vaults were especially useful for bathhouses, where a wood-framed roof would have been badly affected by the damp atmosphere.

▲ **Baths of Caracalla**
The baths built in the 3rd century CE by the emperor Caracalla had many domed and barrel-vaulted ceilings.

HAGIA SOPHIA ■ TÜRKIYE

Hagia Sophia

c.532–37 CE ■ CHURCH ■ ISTANBUL, TÜRKIYE

ISIDORUS & ANTHEMUS

After the fall of Rome in the 5th century CE the eastern part of the Roman empire survived and was ruled by a succession of Christian emperors based in the capital city of Constantinople (modern Istanbul). This realm became known as the Byzantine empire after another early name of its capital, Byzantium. A distinctive style of architecture developed in this region, seen most memorably in its churches. Some of these were aisled basilicas on the Roman model, but many were domed buildings with stunning central spaces, walls covered in marble, and ceilings decorated with glittering mosaics.

The largest of these churches was Hagia Sophia, the church of the Holy Wisdom in the heart of Constantinople, built for the emperor Justinian I in 532–37 CE. Its most remarkable feature is its dome, some 107ft (32.5m) in diameter and an engineering wonder of the ancient world. This dome is flanked by a pair of semi-domes with a similar diameter that help create a vast space supported only by buttresses on the exterior and rows of columns and arches within.

This remarkable structure was repaired after an earthquake in 558 CE, and much of it survives, together with the rich marble cladding of its walls and decorative details such as the finely carved capitals of its columns. The building's fine series of mosaics, however, only survives as fragments. Those that do remain, showing Jesus Christ, the Virgin Mary, Christian saints, and prominent members of the imperial family, are of the highest quality, and they reveal how the building's architects exploited light entering the windows to create magical effects in the domes and upper walls. This marriage of breathtaking interior space and decorative detail makes Hagia Sophia one of the world's greatest buildings.

JUSTINIAN I

483–565 CE

From humble beginnings Justinian rose to become emperor and was crowned jointly with his wife, Theodora, in 527 CE. He chose good military leaders and was successful in war, building a huge empire, but his greatest achievement was to rework Roman law, which had an influence on nearly all the countries in Europe. Justinian was a notable builder, and several churches in Constantinople and in the Italian city of Ravenna were constructed during his reign. For Hagia Sophia, he chose as architects the Greeks Anthemius of Tralles and Isidorus of Miletus, both of whom were renowned for their ability in mathematics and especially geometry—skills that proved invaluable in the design and construction of Hagia Sophia's complex domed structure.

▲ **Justinian** The emperor holds a model of Hagia Sophia.

Visual tour: exterior

◀ **CENTRAL DOME** This consists of large bricks from 24-27in (610-686mm) square and about 2in (50mm) thick. These are held together with mortar and laid to create a shallow dome that rises just 50ft (15.2m) above the supporting masonry. The semi-domes on either side help to buttress this enormous and heavy structure.

One of four minarets added after the building became a mosque in the 15th century

Mass of buttressing masonry

Domed baptistry

▲ **SMALL DOMES** Around the edges of the church and in the precincts are various smaller structures, mostly added later, also roofed with domes. These later domes show the enduring influence of Byzantine construction on Islamic architects, who built many mosques with domed roofs and who favored domes for roofing a range of structures from tombs to bathhouses.

▶ **EAST END** This view from the east shows how the church is made up of a series of structures, from the apse in the foreground to the vast dome beyond, each of which is wider and taller than the previous one, and each of which buttresses the next. This careful construction of the building's masses and masonry allowed the architects to include plenty of windows, which would weaken the structure if it were not so carefully balanced. All the windows have semicircular tops, similar to the windows in the Roman buildings that influenced the architects.

◀ **IMPERIAL DOOR** One of the main entrances to the church is through a pair of magnificent bronze doors into the southwestern porch. Although not original, these doors come from the Byzantine period and bear monograms from the 9th century. Their decoration consists of bands of ornaments—studs, serpentine curves, stylized flowers, and the key-pattern design much used by the ancient Greeks—around plain central panels. This combination of ornaments is unique.

HAGIA SOPHIA ▪ TÜRKIYE   35

ON **ALTERATIONS**

In 1453, the forces of the Muslim Ottoman empire, under its ruler Mehmet II, conquered Constantinople. The city became the Ottoman capital, and Hagia Sophia was turned into a mosque. As a result, the Ottomans made several alterations to the building.

These changes took place over a long period and included the addition of four minarets, the removal of furnishings used in Christian worship, and the construction of a *mihrab*, which is the niche that indicates the direction of Mecca. The Ottomans also covered over most of the mosaics, although they did this surprisingly slowly—some of those in the vaults are still visible in illustrations from the 18th century. The building remained a mosque until 1934, when Kemal Atatürk, the father of modern Türkiye, secularized it and turned it into a museum. Since then, a number of the mosaics have been uncovered, although some of the elements of the mosque, including the impressive pulpit, have been allowed to remain.

This crescent finial replaced the original cross

The shallow dome was partially rebuilt after a collapse in 558 CE

The semicircular apse marks the church's east end

▲ **Inscriptions**
When the building became a mosque, the Ottomans added boards bearing Qur'anic inscriptions, which they set high up on the piers around the nave.

▼ **MASONRY DETAIL** Although much of the brickwork at Hagia Sophia was designed to be hidden under plaster, it is very skillfully made, with bricks carefully laid in neat designs and held together with good-quality lime mortar mixed with brick dust. The construction is generally much better than in many late Roman buildings in which brickwork was often thrown together in random designs covering an inner core of rubble.

◀ **BUTTRESSES** All around the building, buttresses prop up the walls, transferring to the ground the stresses and strains produced by the dome. Many of these buttresses consist of an arch that connects a mass of masonry to the wall. This type of structure is called a flying buttress, a form often said to have been invented by the Gothic masons of medieval western Europe, but pioneered here several centuries earlier to support Hagia Sophia's unusual structure.

Visual tour: interior

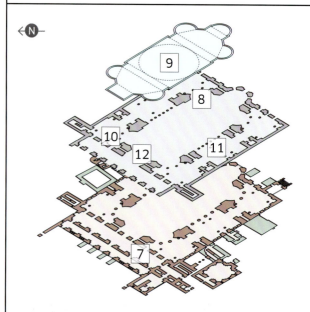

▲ **NARTHEX** Visitors enter the church through the narthex, a long vestibule that runs along one entire side of the building. This space has a ceiling vaulted in a series of compartments above a marble-clad wall, and doorways with simple classical cornices.

▼ **INTERIOR FROM THE GALLERY** Upper galleries run along the south, west, and north sides of the church, providing extra accommodation for church council meetings and opening up views of the large central space. From here worshippers would get a good view both of the ceremonies taking place below and of the mosaics that originally adorned the walls and the dome.

▲ **NAVE INTERIOR** The enormous nave is dominated by the dome, together with the semi-domes and the arches beneath. At the base of the dome is a ring of small windows, and only the ribs of masonry between the windows link the dome to the pendentives (the triangular masses of stonework below). Contemporaries, such as the Byzantine historian Procopius, marveled at the way the dome seemed to float above the lower masonry, with very little means of support.

HAGIA SOPHIA ■ TÜRKIYE

ON DESIGN

Hagia Sophia was originally decorated with non-figurative mosaics and contemporary writers said that the interior glistened with gold. From the 9th century onwards, it became fashionable in the Byzantine empire to decorate churches with figurative subjects. Artists began to adorn churches with mosaics showing religious subjects and members of the imperial family. Mosaics were added over the centuries, but after the building became a mosque, they were plastered over because of the Islamic ban on figurative art.

Later scholars, however, have uncovered some of the Christian mosaics. The subjects include the Virgin and Child, saints such as John Chrysostom and Ignatius Theophorus, and emperors Justinian and Constantine. Imperial costumes and jewellery, as well as saintly attributes such as crosses and Bibles, are portrayed in rich colours. The most beautiful mosaic is the Deisis (prayer or supplication), which portrays Jesus Christ, the Virgin Mary, and John the Baptist, using tesserae (small cubes) that allow subtle gradations of light and shade. The mosaic-makers often angled the gold tesserae slightly so that each piece caught the light in a different way, adding to the glittering effect.

10

▲ **RAMPS** As in many Byzantine churches, gently sloping ramps link Hagia Sophia's upper galleries to the ground floor. These ramps, neatly vaulted in brick, provided easy access to the upper areas for the Byzantine clergy in their long robes. When Ottoman Sultan Mehmet conquered Constantinople in 1453, he is said to have ridden his horse up one of the ramps in a grand gesture of victory.

▲ **Virgin and Child** flanked by an emperor and empress

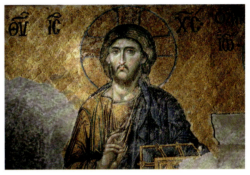

▲ **Jesus Christ** from the Deisis mosaic in the South aisle

11

▲ **UPPER-LEVEL ARCHES** Round columns made of gray marble support the arches in the galleries. These columns have paler capitals with intricate carving that exemplify the skill of Byzantine masons. The capitals vary in design, but most have decoration consisting of small scrolls and stylized foliage made up of a mixture of curvaceous leaves and fronds. The masons cut this decoration deeply, so that there is a strong impression of light and shade.

12

▲ **EMPRESS'S LOGE** The gallery at the western end of the church is a long vaulted space that runs directly above the narthex. Reserved for the empress and her companions, it is sometimes referred to as the empress's loge. The space provides the best view of the east end of the church—the focus of worship where the altar and iconostasis (screen) were originally placed.

Temple of the Inscriptions

c.615–683 ▪ TEMPLE ▪ PALENQUE, MEXICO

ARCHITECT UNKNOWN

Long hidden in the Mexican rainforest, the Temple of the Inscriptions is one of the best examples of religious architecture from the Classic period (c.250–900) of the Central American Maya civilization. This large step pyramid rises steeply to about 68ft (21m) high and is crowned by a temple building. The pyramid consists of nine tiers with a central staircase running up one side to the temple on top. Although it has lost most of its original decoration, which would have been in brightly colored stucco, the pyramid is nonetheless a very striking building, dominating one of the central plazas in the ancient city of Palenque.

The most remarkable part of the building, however, is hidden from view. Deep inside it lies the tomb of Palenque's ruler K'inich Janaab' Pakal, who reigned over the city for nearly 70 years until his death in 683. The king's sarcophagus was protected by a heavy, lavishly carved stone lid, and the tomb contained artifacts, including jade jewelry. The monument was begun toward the end of Pakal's reign and was completed by his son and successor, K'inich Kam B'alam II.

Like most Maya pyramids, the Temple of the Inscriptions is very tall. Archaeologists believe that its builders wanted to make it visible from afar and to raise the temple up to the sky. The carved reliefs on the piers (supports) that flank the five doorways to the temple and the inscriptions inside, which chronicle Pakal's reign and give the building its name, are just some of the features that make this such an outstanding structure.

ON SITE

Palenque went into gradual decline after about 800, and the surrounding jungle grew over the site. The city was known only to locals until it was rediscovered in the 1560s by a priest, Lorenzo de la Nada. Archaeologists began to survey the site in the 18th century. They found the Temple of the Inscriptions near a large building, thought to be the royal Palace, on one of the main plazas. Other temples, houses, and a court for the Maya ball game were nearby. The proximity of the Temple of the Inscriptions to the Palace signifies just how important it was. Some scholars have suggested that the king looked out at the temple from the Palace tower, a vantage point that would have enabled him to watch the rising sun align with the temple at the winter solstice.

▲ Palenque

Visual tour

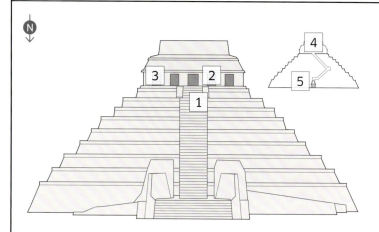

▼ **PIERS** Four of the piers at the front of the temple were originally richly decorated with stucco reliefs. Now badly worn, the reliefs seem to show standing figures, each of which holds the image of a deity that has one leg in the form of a snake. Thought to depict ancestors, the standing figures are presenting images of the Maya god of lightning, K'awiil, who could transform his leg into a serpent and who symbolized royal power and regeneration. As Maya rulers were considered divine, this was fitting imagery for a temple that housed the king's tomb.

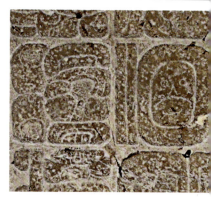

▼ **STAIRCASE** The broad stone steps make the steep ascent from ground level to the temple at the top of the pyramid. Although the steps are wide, it is unlikely that they were used by large numbers of people. The temple, which has five entrances, was a sacred space that was probably the preserve of Maya priests and the royal family. The size and prominence of the staircase was more to do with emphasizing the importance of the building and to provide a suitably grand setting for the priests as they made their ceremonial ascent.

◀ **INSCRIPTION** The largest inscriptions in the temple are found on three huge stones on the inner walls. Carved in shallow relief, they are written in the Maya script, which is made up of semi-pictorial characters known as glyphs. The texts contain more than 600 glyphs and are the longest legible Maya inscriptions known. It is not easy to translate them because they are worn, but the texts describe the life of Pakal. He became king when just 12 years old after Palenque was attacked and damaged by a rival Maya army. Pakal rebuilt the city and oversaw its expansion during his long reign. The inscriptions end with the news of the king's death followed by the name of his heir, Kan B'alam II, who continued Pakal's great building projects.

▼ **ENTRANCE TO THE TOMB** A narrow stone staircase descends from the temple, through the solid rock of the pyramid, all the way to the tomb at its base. This steep staircase, flanked by roughly finished walls, was designed for use only during the royal entombment. Once the king was buried, it was sealed beneath a slab in the middle of the temple floor. The stairs and tomb were only uncovered in 1952, when an archaeologist noticed that several holes had been drilled in the slab and then blocked with stone plugs. After Pakal was entombed, workers must have lowered the slab carefully into place using ropes looped through the holes. When the slab was positioned securely, they plugged the holes, and the tomb was left completely undisturbed for over a thousand years.

ON DESIGN

Constructing a Maya pyramid and tomb was a huge enterprise involving hundreds of laborers and masons, as well as skilled artists. Several specialists were also employed: carvers, who made inscriptions, carved the sarcophagus lid, and cut decoration into the stonework; workers in stucco, who created the relief panels and made sculptures that have been found on the site; and painters, who decorated the temple in bright colors, traces of which remain. There is also great artisanship in Pakal's remarkable death mask (below), which was fashioned from pieces of jade on a wooden frame and had eyes made of shell and obsidian. The same talented artisan may also have made the jade bracelets and necklace that were placed on the king's body.

▲ Pakal's death mask

◀ **TOMB** This small chamber at the base of the pyramid was the king's final resting place. The sloping sides and solid roof were carefully designed to withstand the enormous weight of the stone above. After Pakal had been laid in his stone sarcophagus, it was sealed with a massive stone slab decorated with an image of a young man. Scholars have interpreted this image in various ways, but the consensus is that the young man represents the king portrayed in the likeness of a god and shown on his journey to the next world. Part of Pakal's entombment ceremony involved sacrificing five of his attendants, whose bodies were left in the tomb before the entrance was blocked with offerings of jade, shell, and pottery, and the stairway filled with rubble and sealed.

IN CONTEXT

The city of Palenque had been destroyed in a war in 599 and still needed a great deal of rebuilding work when Pakal came to the throne. The king began this task, and it was continued by his son, who completed the Temple of the Inscriptions and oversaw the construction of the tomb with its elaborately carved sarcophagus. He also boosted the city's power through alliances and conquests, giving him the resources to continue rebuilding and to finish most of the monuments.

▲ Cast of carved sarcophagus lid

Bulguksa Temple

c.751–774CE ▪ TEMPLE ▪ JINHEON-DONG, SOUTH KOREA

KIM DAESEONG

The Temple of the Buddha Land is a masterpiece of Korean architecture. It was built in the 8th century during the reign of the Silla kings, a dynasty of rulers who had unified the whole Korean peninsula by 668CE. Bulguksa was one of the main Silla building projects in the capital, Gyeongju, and is a complex of predominantly wooden buildings, together with some structures made from stone. Its architecture was influenced partly by the design of Chang-an, the capital of the Chinese T'ang Dynasty, and partly by images of palaces depicted in paintings of the Buddhist Pure Land or Western Paradise—a beautiful region where followers attained enlightenment or hoped to be reborn on the final stage of the journey.

Bulguksa's many buildings include wooden prayer halls, stone pagodas, and a number of structures that are known as bridges but are staircases. It is constructed around a series of courtyards, one of them containing the main prayer hall, Daeungjeon, the Hall of Great Enlightenment. These halls are low, wood-framed structures with overhanging, upturned tiled roofs and are similar in form to traditional Chinese buildings. They are brightly painted and have broad openings that allow easy access. Like many Korean temples, they were built without nails—the beams have interlocking joints that hold them in position, but the buildings can also be dismantled and relocated to another site. Many ancient wooden buildings in China, Japan, and Korea, like Bulguksa, have been partially rebuilt over the centuries according to the original design and layout. For this reason they are still considered structures of great antiquity that demonstrate the traditional woodworking skills and decorative flair of the originals.

IN CONTEXT

Bulguksa is a temple of the Mahayana Buddhist faith, the branch of Buddhism practiced most widely in China, Japan, and Korea. Devotees of this faith follow the teachings of the Buddha, but the various forms of Mahayana Buddhism also revere a number of other enlightened figures, including some whose images appear in the temple architecture. Among them are disciples of the Buddha, and Bodhisattvas—individuals who have postponed their own transition towards enlightenment to remain on the earthly plane and help others along the Buddhist path. Prominent among these is the Bodhisattva of Compassion, Avalokiteshvara, whose image appears in one of the temple's halls, the Gwaneumjeon. The temple complex also has shrines to Vairocana (a celestial figure who is sometimes known as the "Supreme Buddha") and Amithaba (known as the "Buddha of Infinite Light"). There is also a rich tradition of gods and mythical figures: some appear as carvings on the temple buildings and include a group of protective deities called the Four Heavenly Kings and other guardian figures.

▲ **Jiguk-cheonwang**, or watcher of the lands, is one of the Four Heavenly Kings.

Visual tour

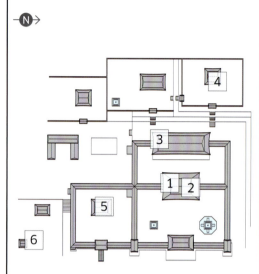

▶ **DAEUNGJEON** The Hall of Great Enlightenment is the central building of the temple complex and one of the main prayer halls, celebrated for its statue of the Buddha. From the outside, the building is marked by its sweeping, upturned roof, which has a substantial overhang on each side of the structure of wooden posts and plainly finished screen walls that encloses the interior. The hall is raised up on a stone platform, which gives it additional height and prominence.

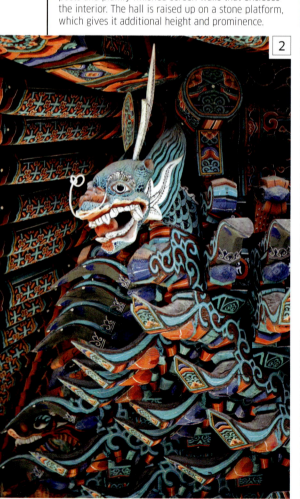

◀ **DAEUNGJEON ROOF DECORATION** On the exterior of the Daeungjeon, the most lavish decoration is reserved for the underside of the overhanging roof—typically the most ornate part of traditional Korean temple buildings. Both the surfaces of the roof itself and the wood posts that support it are covered in abstract patterns. The paintwork on the supporting posts is especially eye-catching and the designs emphasize the undulating structure. At the corners are carved dragons, finished in the same color scheme. Dragons were thought to be able to change shape and exist on more than one plane of being, so artists often used them to represent the nature of the Buddha.

▶ **MUSEOLJEON** The name of this building means "Hall of No Words," in recognition of the belief that the Buddha's message cannot be taught using words alone. Around the outside of the hall is a colonnade with red-painted supporting posts laid out on the same grid as the posts that hold up the hall itself. Although many of the structures that make up Bulguksa have been rebuilt over the centuries, the Museoljeon is said to be one of the oldest halls on the site, dating back to the 7th century.

BULGUKSA TEMPLE ■ SOUTH KOREA   45

ON CONSTRUCTION

Bulguksa contains two pagodas, called Seokgatap and Dabotap, constructed from stone, both dating from 751CE. The two are very different. Seokgatap has a very simple design on a square plan, with the upper stories decreasing in size as they rise. Dabotap is more complex—there is a square base with staircases and a quartet of square columns at the bottom, and a series of more ornate octagonal stories, one supported by stone columns in the shape of bamboo poles, above. The differences in construction reflect the Buddha's teachings, which appear complex but contain an essential unity.

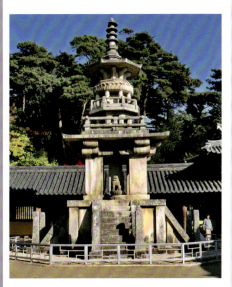

▲ **Dabotap Pagoda**
With its series of delicately carved upper stories, this 34ft (10.4m) pagoda has a design that is unusual in Korean Buddhist architecture for its complexity.

▲ **GWANEUMJEON** This is a shrine dedicated to Avalokiteshvara, the Bodhisattva of Compassion. Although it is smaller than some of the other halls, the Gwaneumjeon is set on the highest part of the site, and its elevation is further increased by its substantial stone platform. The deeply overhanging roof also helps the building stand out.

◀ **ROOF DETAIL** Like many traditional Korean buildings, Bulguksa has roofs made of clay tiles in a combination of round and curved shapes. The round tiles cover the joins between the lines of curved tiles, resulting in a pattern of pronounced ridges that run along the roof and form intricate shapes at the corners.

ON CONSTRUCTION

Bulguksa's bridges—effectively platforms accessed from stone staircases—form the approaches to many of the temple's buildings. Some of them, which date back to the 8th century, are plain; others feature beautiful designs, such as lotus flowers. Symbolic content is hidden within these structures—the 33 steps of one of the staircases, for example, reflect the number of stages, or heavens, on the path to enlightenment specified in particular Buddhist texts.

▲ **Cheongungyo and Baegungyo**
The Cheongungyo (Blue Cloud Bridge) and Baegungyo (White Cloud Bridge) together form the entrance to the temple complex.

▲ **BELL PAVILION** The complex has a number of open-sided buildings, such as the pavilion that houses the temple's bell. This is built like the prayer halls, but without the thin, non-structural screen walls between the upright posts. The pavilion combines a sturdy wooden framework, strong enough to support the large bell, with an overhanging roof of great delicacy.

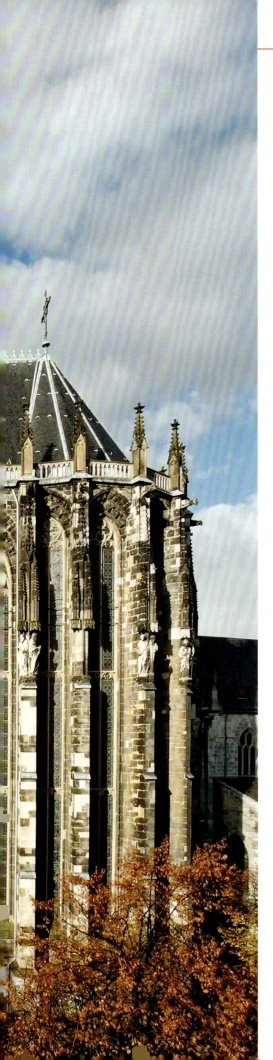

Palatine Chapel

c.792–804 ■ CHAPEL ■ AACHEN, GERMANY

ODO OF METZ

Commissioned by Charlemagne, the king of the Franks (later Holy Roman Emperor), as part of his great palace complex at Aachen (also known as Aix-la-Chapelle), the imposing Palatine Chapel became the emperor's final resting place and the site of successive royal coronations. Charlemagne's palace has not survived, but the chapel remains (albeit with extensions from the 14th and 15th centuries) as one of the best examples of European architecture from the so-called "Dark Ages."

Charlemagne and his architect—probably Odo of Metz, who is mentioned in an early inscription—chose an unusual plan for the chapel, which has 16 sides converging on an octagonal dome. This dome-centered plan was influenced by Byzantine churches, such as Hagia Sophia (see pp.32–37) in Constantinople (Istanbul) and San Vitale in Ravenna, Italy. By imitating the building projects of the Christian rulers of the Byzantine (eastern Roman) Empire, Charlemagne was reinforcing his own claim to the title of Emperor: he was crowned by the pope on Christmas Day in the year 800.

Although the chapel draws on the influence of the great Byzantine churches, it is not a large building—the dome measures just 47.5ft (14.5m) across. The architect used a simplified version of the Byzantine style, which also draws on earlier Roman models. Barrel and cross-vaults roof the 16-sided ambulatory, and the dome in the center also has a cross-vault. The decoration of these spaces displays a rich but sober quality that complements this simplicity. The polychrome masonry of the arches and the colored marble lining the walls enhance the effect, as do mosaics in the vaults and sumptuous bronzework and gold fittings. The richness of the decorations, which glowed in the light from the windows and candles, created a glittering, magical interior.

CHARLEMAGNE

c.742–814

Charlemagne was the ruler of the Franks, a Germanic people originally from the Rhineland, who, from the 5th to the 8th centuries, expanded their territory to occupy much of what is now France, Germany, and the Netherlands. He defended his territory, against attack from eastern peoples, such as the Saxons, whom he defeated in battle, and annexed large territories in northern Italy to create the greatest European empire since the Romans. Conquests in Italy then made him the protector of the pope, who crowned him emperor. Although the empire did not survive for long after Charlemagne's death, it was hugely influential: in the following centuries many German rulers took the title of Holy Roman Emperor and aspired to wield pan-European power.

Visual tour

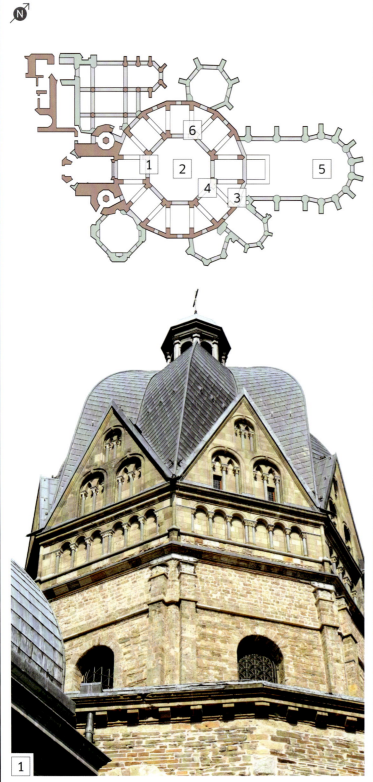

▲ **DOME** The octagonal form of the dome rises above the 16-sided ambulatory that surrounds it. These outer walls of the chapel are very plain. On the lower levels are simple round-topped windows and pilasters (slight vertical protrusions) at the corners. The gables above are more ornate, but still follow the same style, with rows of blind, round-topped arches and very small window openings. This exterior simplicity is typical of early Christian architecture, which covered highly ornate interiors in very plain outside walls: builders considered the exterior "worldly" and kept it distinct from the sacred space within.

▲ **DOME INTERIOR** A series of eight marble-clad piers hold up the polychrome arches that support the weight of the dome. This space is very high, and the architect based its proportions and dimensions on the description of the New Jerusalem in the Book of Revelation. The distance from the floor to the top of the dome is 118ft (36m).

◀ **PULPIT** The pulpit was a gift to the chapel from Emperor Henry II, who was crowned here in 1002. Henry's entitlement to the imperial crown was at first disputed, and he probably donated the pulpit as a gesture of thanksgiving for the support that enabled him to be appointed emperor. It is made of gilded copper and studded with precious items including ivory reliefs, crystals, and semi-precious stones.

PALATINE CHAPEL ■ GERMANY

6

▲ **VAULTING** The ambulatory surrounding the central space is roofed with simple cross-vaults, each with four roughly triangular compartments covered in decorative mosaics. Natural light from the round-topped windows originally made the golden tesserae (cubes) of these mosaics glitter brightly, but this effect was reduced by the addition of smaller chapels that cut down the amount of natural light.

5

▲ **SHRINE** The shrine that contains the remains of Charlemagne's body has been dated to the late 12th century. It consists of an oak chest just over 6.5ft (2m) long, covered with silver and gilded decorations, including golden statues of the Virgin Mary, Charlemagne, and many successive emperors.

◀ **COLUMNS AND CAPITALS**
The semicircular arches are divided by slender vertical columns topped with crisply carved Corinthian capitals in the classical style. These columns are not significant structurally but serve an important symbolic purpose. Some of them are made of porphyry, and Charlemagne had them brought to his chapel from Ravenna and Rome. In the ancient world porphyry was used only for imperial buildings, and, by employing it, Charlemagne claimed a link with the rulers of the Roman empire.

4

ON CONSTRUCTION

By the 14th century the chapel had the status of a cathedral, and frequently there was not enough space for the crowds who flocked to Charlemagne's shrine or to attend imperial coronations. To increase capacity, the cathedral commissioned a large new choir (a long space with an apse, or a semicircular end) in the Gothic style. Stained-glass windows line the sides and the apse, and the entire space is topped with a pointed stone vault. The windows are 89ft (27m) tall and reach almost to the stone vault. The jewel-like setting they create makes a fitting home for the gilded shrine of the emperor, which medieval pilgrims visited in huge numbers.

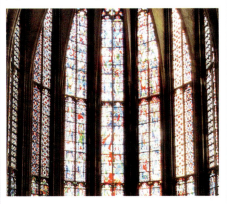

▲ **Stained glass**
The glass in the choir windows was installed after the building suffered bomb damage during World War II, but the effect is similar to the original.

IN CONTEXT

The model for the Palatine Chapel and other round and polygonal churches is thought to be San Vitale, Ravenna, which was begun in 526. An octagonal building crowned by a dome supported on arches, it is richly adorned with mosaics. Ravenna, the capital of the western Roman empire after the fall of Rome, was later a focal point of the Byzantine empire. It was natural that the builders of the Palatine Chapel should look to San Vitale for inspiration.

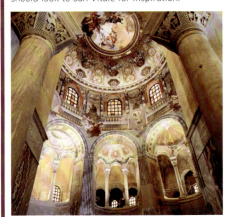

▲ **San Vitale, Ravenna, Italy**
Although details such as the round columns and capitals differ, San Vitale has a similar style and plan to Charlemagne's chapel.

BOROBUDUR ■ INDONESIA

Borobudur

c.825CE ■ TEMPLE ■ MAGELANG, JAVA, INDONESIA

ARCHITECT UNKNOWN

The world's greatest Buddhist monument, Borobudur is a vast 9th-century temple that combines a stupa (shrine to the Buddha), a pilgrimage site, and a three-dimensional symbol of Buddhist beliefs. Built on a hill, it is an enormous pyramid adorned with elaborate carved reliefs and houses statues of the Buddha.

No one knows when Borobudur was built or by whom, but construction seems to have been completed around 825CE under the Sailendra dynasty, a family of powerful rulers who promoted Mahayana Buddhism. Their architects took an existing Buddhist form, the stupa, and developed it.

A traditional stupa is a mound containing sacred remains. At Borobudur the stupa is the size of a small hill and consists of a series of open stone terraces or galleries, which divide the monument into levels. Each level symbolically represents the realms or states of existence in Buddhist cosmology. The building's base symbolizes the realm of desires where most mortals live. The next five levels, made up of terraces on a square plan, represent the world of forms, a place attained by Buddhists who have overcome desire. This section bears carved reliefs narrating the story of the Buddha's life and other subjects from Buddhist scriptures. The three circular galleries make up the final level, which denotes the formless realm—the state of nirvana to which Buddhists aspire. This part houses 72 statues of the Buddha kept beneath pierced stone canopies, each in the shape of a stupa.

Pilgrims followed a set route, walking around the lower levels, looking at the carved reliefs, and absorbing the story of the Buddha before rising to the higher levels. The changing galleries and the simplification of the sculpture gave pilgrims a sense of the spiritual development needed to ascend from the realm of desires to higher levels.

ON **CONSTRUCTION**

Borobudur does not have an interior. It consists of an earth mound supporting open-topped terraces. To construct these terraces, the builders quarried a vast amount of local stone. They shaped the blocks individually to fit together like jigsaw pieces, laying them without mortar. At some stage, the design was modified. The monument's lowest level, the base, extends some distance out from the main structure and was added later. In the late 19th century restorers discovered an original base, decorated with relief carvings, buried beneath the later stonework of the lowest level. No one knows why this was hidden. It may have been because the structure needed strengthening or because there was some religious imperfection in the original work.

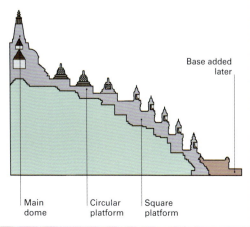

Visual tour

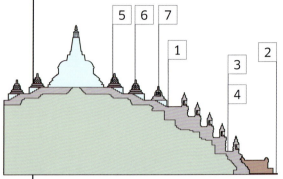

▼ GUARDIAN LION Borobudur has several carved lions, which stand as guardians on and near the temple. Although extensively carved, the statues are not very realistic–lions were not indigenous to Indonesia, and the carvers, who may never have seen real ones, produced stylized portrayals. Lions were symbols of bravery. They were also linked to royalty and appear on some of the thrones shown in Borobudur's relief sculptures. Buddha was sometimes said to have had the voice of a lion.

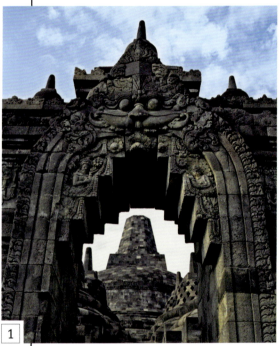

▲ ARCH OF KALA This gate takes the form of the face of Kala ("time"), a complex being who appears in both Hindu and Buddhist mythology. In Buddhism Kala is said to devour the obstacles that stand in the way of enlightenment. In Hindu mythology Kala is also identified with a demon called Rahu, who stole the elixir of life from the gods and was decapitated by Vishnu but lived on because he had already drunk the magic potion. He is therefore a symbol of immortality, and the jewels and ornaments on his face represent the elixir. The face of Kala often appears on *mandalas*, sacred diagrams based on circles and other shapes, which are used in meditation and spiritual teaching. Seen from above, with its combination of circles, squares, and other shapes, Borobudur bears a close resemblance to a *mandala*.

► LIFE OF BUDDHA A series of reliefs on the lower levels of Borobudur show episodes from the life of the Buddha. They tell the story of Prince Siddhartha's birth and early life, his renunciation of his royal life, his travels as a wandering monk and searcher for truth, and his eventual enlightenment. In this panel he is teaching some of his disciples. Many of the reliefs illustrate the events against a vivid background of trees and plants, all of which are beautifully carved.

BOROBUDUR ■ INDONESIA

▼ **BUDDHA STATUE** All the carvings of the Buddha at Borobudur look similar, but there is some variation in the *mudras* (symbolic hand gestures) of the figures. The statues on the upper levels show the Buddha making a gesture that symbolizes the "turning of the wheel of the doctrine." This is the *mudra* associated with the Buddha's preaching of his first sermon, which, according to some traditions, was delivered from the top of Mount Sumeru. The use of this *mudra* is a reminder that understanding his words and following his path will lead his followers toward salvation.

▲ **UPPER LEVELS STUPAS** The top levels of the monument are ringed with small bell-like stupas with diamond-shaped openings that reveal the Buddha statues inside. At the very top is a single large stupa, similar in form to some in India. This pinnacle recalls Mount Sumeru, the great mountain at the center of the world of Mahayana Buddhism. It is a reminder that Borobudur is a symbol of the cosmos and that its builders were the Sailendra kings, known as "Lords of the Mountain."

▼ **STUPA REMOVED** Some of the openwork stupas on the upper levels no longer survive, allowing visitors to see the Buddha statues more clearly. The removal of these structures also reveals how the masonry fitted together with the help of the holes carved in the circle of stones at the stupa's base.

▲ **SHIP** The reliefs depict many details of contemporary life, from the furniture and decoration of the royal palace to the life of the forest and the sea. Intricate carvings of sailing boats show the kind of water transport available when Borobudur was built. This ship, carved on the main wall of the first gallery, has several sails and an outrigger, like many vessels used in Southeast Asia.

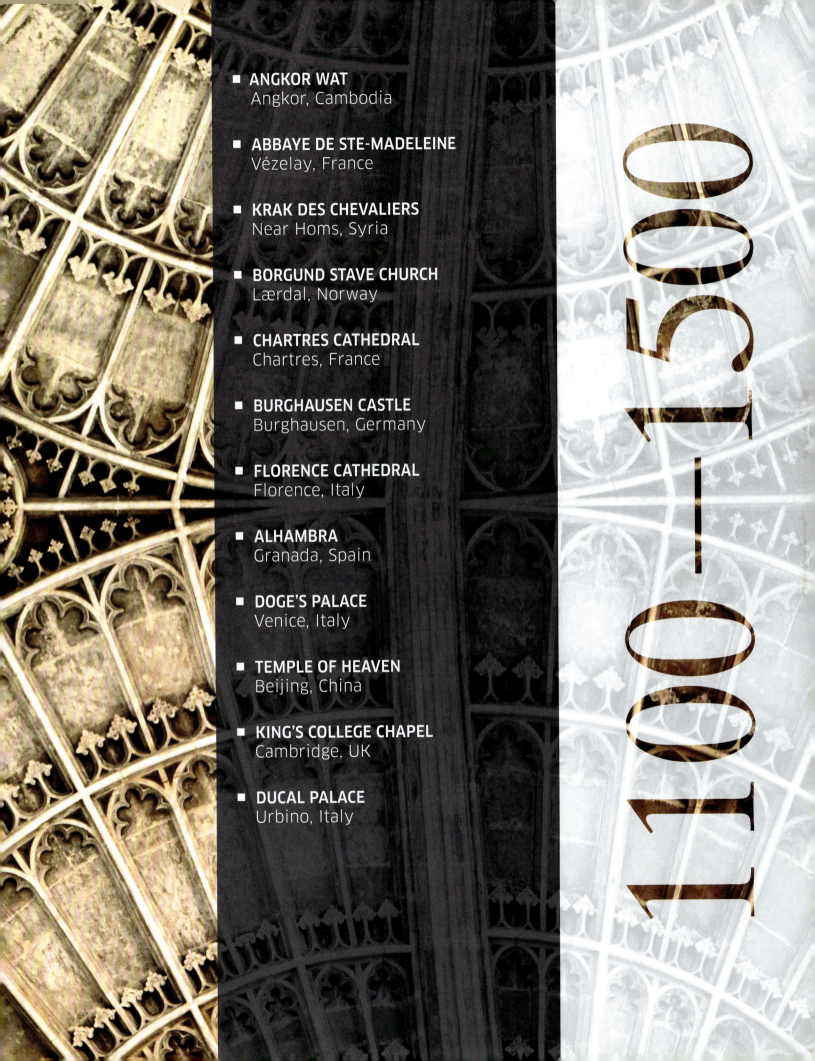

- **ANGKOR WAT**
  Angkor, Cambodia

- **ABBAYE DE STE-MADELEINE**
  Vézelay, France

- **KRAK DES CHEVALIERS**
  Near Homs, Syria

- **BORGUND STAVE CHURCH**
  Lærdal, Norway

- **CHARTRES CATHEDRAL**
  Chartres, France

- **BURGHAUSEN CASTLE**
  Burghausen, Germany

- **FLORENCE CATHEDRAL**
  Florence, Italy

- **ALHAMBRA**
  Granada, Spain

- **DOGE'S PALACE**
  Venice, Italy

- **TEMPLE OF HEAVEN**
  Beijing, China

- **KING'S COLLEGE CHAPEL**
  Cambridge, UK

- **DUCAL PALACE**
  Urbino, Italy

1100–1500

Angkor Wat

c.1150 ■ TEMPLE ■ ANGKOR, CAMBODIA

ARCHITECT UNKNOWN

A vast and magnificent temple complex at the heart of Angkor, the capital of the powerful Khmer dynasty that ruled Cambodia from the 9th to the early 14th century, Angkor Wat is one of the largest religious structures ever built. The Khmer dynasty was a distinctive civilization that reached its height during the 12th century under King Suryavarman II, who extended the borders of his kingdom and built large cities and enormous temples. During his reign, the city of Angkor grew to become probably the biggest pre-industrial city in the world. The construction of Angkor Wat began in about 1120. Originally built as a temple dedicated to the Hindu god Vishnu, it served as a shrine to the Khmer "god-king," Suryavarman, and was also intended to be his mausoleum. Its design, with five distinctive lotus-bud spires that rise above tiered platforms, was heavily influenced by the

Hindu architecture of India. Like many Indian temples, those of the Khmers are centered on a shrine topped with a tall, pointed roof that represents the sacred mountain, Meru, the home of the gods. But at Angkor Wat, the sheer scale and the arrangement of the buildings are distinctly Khmer. In addition to the central pointed roof there are four smaller roofs, which together represent the peaks of Meru. Three sets of galleries enclose the temple, and a wall and moat surround the complex, enclosing a structure that is around 4,920ft (1,500m) long.

The Khmer sculptors covered the complex with carvings showing episodes from the great Hindu epics and images illustrating the cosmology of the Khmers. The galleries alone contain thousands of such carvings, and a visitor walking around them to view all the reliefs would cover a total of around 13 miles (21km).

IN CONTEXT

After the Khmer empire declined during the 14th century, many Khmer cities and monuments disappeared beneath the encroaching jungle vegetation. Wooden houses were destroyed, but the ruins of many stone temples survived, and the massive structure of Angkor Wat was preserved, largely owing to its broad protective moat. The temple was virtually unknown in the West until the arrival of French explorer Henri Mouhot in the mid-19th century. Mouhot published descriptions of the site, and his writings encouraged both European and Cambodian scholars to investigate Angkor, preserve the temple, and study the history of the Khmers. At last the temple, which had long been a national symbol for Cambodia, became known all over the world.

▲ **French explorer** Louis Delaporte arrives at the ruins of Angkor in this 1874 image from *L'Illustration*.

Visual tour

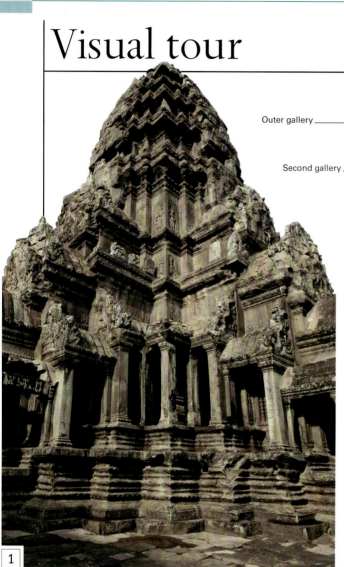

Outer gallery
Second gallery
Stairs to central courtyard
Library

▼ **VISHNU** The two Hindu deities most revered by the Khmers were Shiva, the destroyer and re-creator, and Vishnu, the preserver, who was responsible for maintaining the balance between good and evil. Suryavarman II favored Vishnu, and the god's statue was originally installed in the central shrine at Angkor Wat. Later, when the temple became a sacred Buddhist site, its guardians moved this statue of Vishnu to one of the building's corner towers.

▲ **TOWER** The temple's five elaborately carved towers, which give the temple its distinctive silhouette, rise to tall roofs shaped like elongated pyramids. The builders constructed these roofs using a technique called corbeling, in which each set of stone blocks is offset slightly so that the structure gets narrower as it rises. The tower structure is 141ft (43m) high but because it is set on a platform, its top is some 213ft (65m) above ground level.

▼ **LIBRARY** This building, a long structure built on a platform surrounded by steps, is known as a library. Most temples had a single library, but Angkor has a pair set in opposite corners of the outer courtyard. No one knows for sure exactly what these "libraries" were used for: they may have served as subsidiary shrines or housed collections of religious writings.

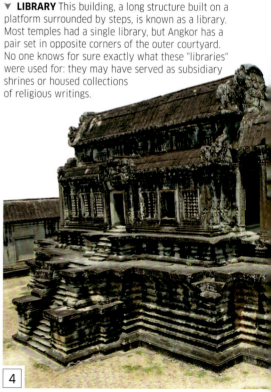

▲ **INNER COURTYARD** Angkor Wat is designed as a series of courtyards, each accessed by gateways and often with short towers or turrets at the corners. Around each courtyard there are covered galleries with one side open and one side walled. These structures are raised above the courtyard level on steps and pillars to create a sense of separation. Pilgrims visiting the temple would walk around these galleries, admiring the relief carvings along the walls.

ANGKOR WAT ■ CAMBODIA

Corner tower

Pathway to building entrance

▲ **CRUCIFORM GALLERY** Situated near the entrance to the complex, this gallery is a smaller, more intimate space than the long galleries of the main courtyards. Like the other galleries, its walls are decorated with relief carvings. One unusual feature is the stone baluster rails covering some of the openings. These look as if they have been turned on a lathe.

▶ **APSARAS AND DEVATAS** Many of Angkor's relief carvings feature *apsaras* and *devatas*, supernatural female figures and gods from Hindu mythology. In the Angkor Wat reliefs, *apsaras* wear complex headdresses and are often shown dancing. Although both figures appear in Hindu writings such as the Vedas and the *Mahabharata*, they are often treated differently in Cambodian art, as decorative or "guardian" figures on the walls and columns of temple galleries and shrines. *Apsaras* are depicted as dancers, while *devatas* stand still and act as guardians.

◀ **HINDU LEGEND** Relief carvings in one of the galleries depict a famous story featuring Vishnu. They show how gods and demons churned the sea of milk, using the king of serpents, Vasuki, as a rope wrapped around a mountain, Mandarachal. Pulling on Vasuki made the mountain turn rapidly, but when it started to sink, Vishnu, in his incarnation as the turtle Kurma, supported the mountain on his back.

ON **ALTERATIONS**

Toward the end of the 12th century, the Khmer empire went into decline, and with it the Hindu beliefs and reverence of King Suryavarman II that had inspired the construction of the temple. Angkor Wat was, however, neither abandoned nor demolished. Under Jayavarman VII (c.1181–1215), who had adopted the Buddhist faith, it became a Buddhist shrine. The statues of Vishnu were removed or moved to less central positions, and people set up images of the Buddha. After Jayavarman's reign Hinduism was revived, and many Buddhist statues were defaced, but in the 14th century Buddhism became the main faith in Cambodia again, and since then, Angkor Wat has remained a Buddhist temple.

▶ **Buddha** The branches of a tree grow over the smiling face of the Buddha, testimony to the endurance of the faith at Angkor.

ON **DESIGN**

The Khmers built their temples from stone but their houses and other buildings from wood. The latter have perished, so our knowledge of Khmer architecture is mainly derived from temples. For most of their history, the Khmers built these as towerlike sanctuaries within walled and galleried courtyards. Monumental structures, the temples were planned symmetrically, oriented to the four cardinal compass points, and set in landscapes with much use of water. After the construction of Angkor Wat, the temples became still more ornate and complex, but the building methods remained fairly simple: in many cases mortar was not used, and the structures were held together by the sheer weight of the stone and the precision of the masonry.

▲ **The Bayon, Angkor** This ornate temple from the early 13th century is covered with carved Buddha heads. Its original plan featured six inner chapels and many towers.

Abbaye de Ste-Madeleine

c.1120–38 ▪ CHURCH ▪ VÉZELAY, FRANCE

ARCHITECT UNKNOWN

The basilica of St. Mary Magdalene, Vézelay, is one of the greatest examples of Romanesque architecture, a style influenced in part by Roman buildings and fashionable in Europe during the 11th and 12th centuries. In creating this style masons drew several elements from the Romans and the early Christian builders who followed them.

Foremost among these was the idea of the basilica, consisting of a long nave with side aisles separated from it by rows of semicircular arches. From the same tradition they also took round-topped windows without tracery and plain vaulted ceilings, adding elements of their own, including a separate sanctuary at the east end to house the high altar. This eastern end of a Romanesque church often featured an apse, and sometimes had an ambulatory (passage) off which were a number of side chapels. This combination of a high nave and sanctuary with a lower ambulatory and chapels produced two different kinds of space, one high and spacious, the other low and intimate. Romanesque buildings are also known for their rich sculptural decoration, with carved capitals and doorways. Burgundy is particularly rich in such sculpture—both the basilica at Vézelay and the cathedral at Autun are famed for their beautiful carved decoration.

St. Mary Magdelene was rebuilt in 1096 when the monks were given a collection of relics said to be from the tomb of Mary Magdalene. In 1120 the building was damaged by fire, and reconstruction was carried out over the next two decades. Although the basilica suffered war damage in later centuries, a major restoration in the 19th century—under the French scholar and architect Eugène-Emmanuel Viollet-le-Duc—skillfully preserved the glorious spaces and fragile carvings of this magnificent building.

IN CONTEXT

The Romanesque style was used widely across Europe, especially in church architecture, where its spread was partly due to the growth of monasticism in the 11th and 12th centuries. France is especially rich in buildings from this period. As well as the notable churches of Burgundy, there are elaborately carved churches in the south and more austere buildings in the north, such as the two Norman abbeys in Caen. After the conquest of 1066, the Normans also took the style to England. Cathedrals such as Durham and Peterborough show English Romanesque architecture (often called Norman architecture) at its best, with careful treatment of piers and arches, which often display complex moldings and abstract carvings. Builders of small churches in England also adopted these patterns. In Germany cathedrals such as Worms and Speyer show the style on a much larger scale, with multiple towers and spires creating dramatic skylines and exterior walls decorated with rows of blind semicircular arches.

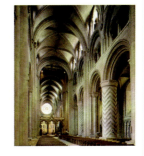

▲ **Durham cathedral**
The nave arches are supported by boldly carved piers.

Visual tour

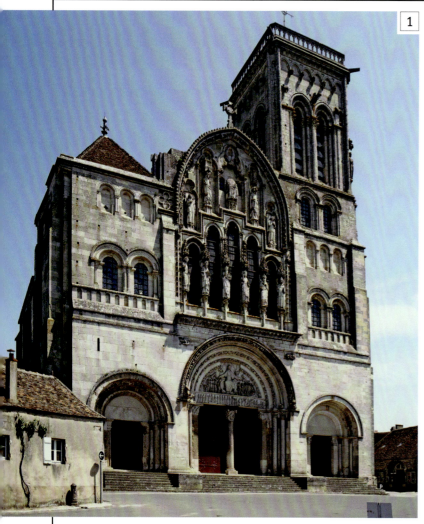

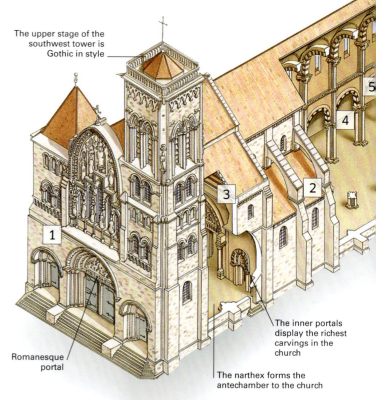

◀ WEST FRONT The church has been much altered and repaired since it was built: some of the details of the west front are in the Romanesque style (round arches), while others are in the later Gothic style (pointed arches). The Romanesque details include the three doorways, two pairs of windows above them, and groups of three blind arches higher still. The lower portion of the tower is original, but the upper section is Gothic, as is the upper central section of the façade with its five narrow windows and statues. Many medieval cathedrals exhibit this fusion of styles.

The upper stage of the southwest tower is Gothic in style

Romanesque portal

The inner portals display the richest carvings in the church

The narthex forms the antechamber to the church

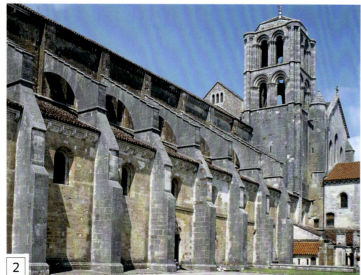

▲ NAVE WINDOWS In the 12th century, windows were usually very small, as is the case with those lining the sides of the church at Vézelay. In this period glass was very expensive, and masons had not yet developed the highly complex buttressing systems that were required to support buildings with bigger windows and heavy stone vaults. The 12th-century builders relied mainly on very thick walls and small buttresses to hold the structure together.

▶ NAVE PORTAL The inner portal of the nave is encrusted with carving, which is particularly lavish in the tympanum (the semicircular panel above the door). The sculpture here centers on the figure of Jesus Christ. Rays of light fall from his outstretched arms onto the Apostles at his sides. In the two quarter-circle bands above the Apostles are reliefs showing peoples of the world. In the outer ring are roundels depicting signs of the zodiac and typical activities for each time of year—for example, the grain harvest next to Leo (July to August) and the grape harvest next to Libra (September to October).

ABBAYE DE STE-MADELEINE ■ FRANCE

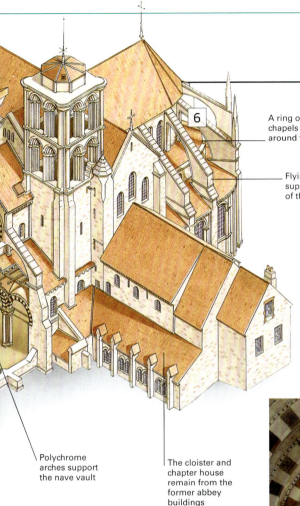

A ring of small chapels is arranged around the apse

Flying buttresses support the roof of the choir

Polychrome arches support the nave vault

The cloister and chapter house remain from the former abbey buildings

▼ **NAVE CEILING ARCHES** This close-up from a high viewpoint shows the row of transverse semicircular arches that support the nave vault. Made of alternate white and dark brown stones, they produce a dazzling striped effect that is unusual in French medieval architecture. Just visible above each arch is a much thinner band of carved stone, its delicacy contrasting with the boldness of the stripes.

ON DETAIL

The piers of the nave and aisles are topped with almost 100 capitals, each of which is carved with a unique scene. The subject matter includes stories and characters from the Bible—from Adam and Eve to the lives of the Apostles—with a strong emphasis on portrayals of Old Testament figures such as Noah, Isaac, Jacob, David, and Moses. There are also symbolic carvings, such as fighting devils and a basilisk, a mythical beast that probably represented evil or death. Many of the capitals show entire biblical stories. A powerful example is the capital showing Moses, who has come down from Mount Sinai holding the Commandments carved on stone tablets to find his people worshiping a golden calf.

▲ **Moses**
Holding the tablets of the law, Moses strikes the golden calf, and a demon flees from the calf's mouth.

▲ **NAVE INTERIOR** The arches on either side of the nave are very simple in form, with none of the complex moldings seen in many later churches. The piers supporting them, on the other hand, are much more decorative and feature clusters of small shafts, some of which rise the whole height of the church to support the larger arches in the ceiling of the nave.

◀ **CHOIR AND APSE** Slightly later in date than the rest of the church, the choir, apse, and ambulatory (the passage behind the high altar) are in the early Gothic style, with narrow, pointed arches, round piers, and a ribbed vault. The windows here are larger than those in the nave—Gothic masons saw the light of the sun as an embodiment of God's light and strove to build churches with ever larger windows to admit the sun's rays.

Krak des Chevaliers

c.1142-92 ▪ CASTLE ▪ NEAR HOMS, SYRIA

ARCHITECT UNKNOWN

High on a rocky outcrop overlooking the Homs Pass in the Syrian desert stands the formidable Krak des Chevaliers, one of the finest and best preserved castles of the Middle Ages until it was damaged from shelling during the Syrian civil war. Between the 11th and 13th centuries the rulers of Europe embarked on the Crusades, a series of unsuccessful attempts to recapture the Holy Land from the ruling Muslims, ostensibly to make Jerusalem safe for Christian pilgrims arriving there from the West. During these expeditions the Crusaders built a series of castles as military bases in areas that are now in Syria, Lebanon, Israel, and Jordan. Krak des Chevaliers was one of these strategic outposts, defending the Homs Pass on the main route from the Mediterranean Sea to the Holy Land.

There had been a castle on the site since about 1030. The Crusaders captured the stronghold on two separate

occasions, finally handing it over in 1142 to the Knights Hospitaller, a military, religious order set up to defend conquered lands in Southwest Asia (the Middle East) and protect European pilgrims to Jerusalem. The Knights occupied the castle until 1271, when, after numerous sieges, it was finally captured by the Mamluk Sultan Baibars.

During their tenure, the Knights Hospitaller rebuilt the castle, extending it, strengthening the fortifications, and providing accommodation for a large force of up to 2,000 men. The resulting building is one of the best surviving examples of a medieval concentric castle, one that has two rings of defensive walls. These massive stone walls, the huge towers, and the castle's lofty site, commanding views in every direction, made it almost impossible to take. T. E. Lawrence (Lawrence of Arabia) called Krak the "most wholly admirable castle in the world".

IN CONTEXT

The first stone castles, built by the Normans in the 11th century, were based around a single large tower called a donjon. Later castle builders, especially the Crusaders, realized that even the largest donjon was vulnerable to attack, so they added more defensive features—rings of outer walls, strong gatehouses, wall towers, as well as barbicans (outer fortifications)—to make the castles more difficult to attack.

The builders understood the importance of choosing a good site, so they set their castles on hills and outcrops, from which defenders could see enemies approaching. Among the Crusaders military orders such as the Knights Hospitaller (the builders of Krak, Silifke, and Margat) and the Teutonic Knights (lords of Montfort) were especially skilled at castle building.

▲ **Kerak** This well-defended, square-towered castle in Syria fell after an eight-month siege.

Visual tour

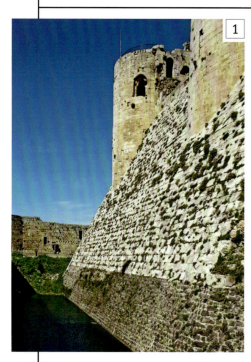

1 ◀ TALUS Many of Krak's outer walls are thicker at the base than at the top, giving them a smooth, sloping profile called a talus (French for "slope"). This made them stronger, and less vulnerable to attack by weapons such as siege towers. Defenders could also hurl heavy rocks down the talus onto enemies below. These sometimes broke into sharp fragments, injuring attackers and impeding their progress.

The warden's tower provided accommodation for the Grand Master of the Hospitallers

Defending archers could shoot from the wall walk

An aqueduct brought in fresh water from outside

The cistern formed a defensive moat and stored water for the castle

◀ CONCENTRIC WALLS The two rings of defensive walls protected the castle from attack. Enemies had to penetrate both sets of walls to reach the living quarters within the castle. This was an almost impossible task, especially as they came under attack from rows of archers who stood behind each set of walls, which gave them a huge range of fire. The protruding wall towers made it possible for the archers to shoot in different directions— to aim at attackers at the base of the walls, for example.

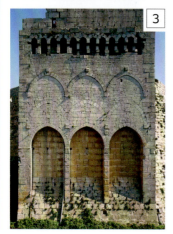

3 ◀ TOWER OF THE KING'S DAUGHTER This tower provided an excellent vantage point at one corner of the castle. The lower part of the tower, with its pointed Gothic arches, was built by the Crusaders. The castle's later Mamluk occupiers built the upper section of the tower.

▶ INNER WARD The courtyard, or inner ward, the best protected part of the castle, contained some of the most important buildings. These ranged from the Knights' meeting hall, chapel, and apartments to those that were vital for the castle's military success—a vast building used to store supplies and a stable block that could accommodate up to 1,000 horses.

KRAK DES CHEVALIERS ■ SYRIA

The dark entrance passageway has a hairpin bend to impede attackers and make it easy for defenders to ambush them

The talus protected the wall from siege weapons

▼ **GREAT HALL** This imposing Gothic interior next to the cloister in the inner ward was probably used both as a meeting room and a reception room where the Master of the Hospitallers would receive visiting dignitaries. In European houses rooms like this often had a wooden roof. The Great Hall, however, has a stone vault, which helped protect the building from attack by fire but was also proof of the Knights' superior social status.

▲ **VAULTED LOGGIA** The Hospitallers built their castle in the Gothic style, with the pointed arches and stone vaults seen in European cathedrals (see pp.72-77). The finely carved vault ribs and the opening flanked by delicate shafts in areas like this vaulted passage indicate the high quality of the craftmanship. It is clear from such architectural details that Krak des Chevaliers was intended not only to protect its occupants, but also to reflect their social standing.

ON CONSTRUCTION

Almost everything about the castle, from its hilltop position to its tall towers, was designed to make the building strong and easy to defend. The concentric walls are up to 80ft (24m) tall and very thick—some are said to be 100ft (30m) thick at the base. They have arrow slits in them, through which archers could take aim, and are topped with crenellations so defending archers could take cover between shots. At the top of many of the walls there are machicolations, protrusions that protected defenders while enabling them to drop missiles on enemies below. Anyone who managed to force an entry into the castle had to find his way along tortuous, winding passages, some of which had holes in the ceiling, through which defenders could shoot at him. Attackers stood little chance of survival.

▲ **Machicolations**
The upper parts of some of the towers, such as the one on the left above, jut out, making it easier for defenders to drop rocks or pour boiling water through the machicolations onto attackers below.

Borgund Stave Church

c.1180 ■ CHURCH ■ LÆRDAL, NORWAY

ARCHITECT UNKNOWN

The stave churches of Norway are masterpieces of architecture, built almost entirely of wood. The finest examples of them are tall buildings with multiple tiered roofs, such as the one at Borgund in southwestern Norway. Stave churches first appeared following the arrival of Christianity during the reign of King Haaken the Good (c.934–61CE). Most buildings of the time in Scandinavia were made from wood, and the builders of the region's first churches used their traditional material to create places of worship with a unique atmosphere.

At first, Norway's early Christians built their churches by constructing walls made of rows of upright posts rammed into the earth. By the 12th century, however, they had evolved a more sophisticated form of building, in which a wooden framework was set on a low base of stone (foundation), to isolate it from the damp ground and prevent the wood from rotting. These buildings, called stave churches because of the staves (the vertical boards) used to construct them, often have steeply pitched roofs topped by wooden spires.

The stave church at Borgund dates back to the late 12th century. It is notable for its tall nave, which rises in several stages to a slender spire, for the fine carpentry of its posts and staves, and for ornate details such as the carved dragon's-head finials that adorn its roof. Although it is based on a conventional church plan, with an aisled nave plus an apse at the east end to house the altar, the vertical emphasis, wooden construction, and style of ornament make Borgund and similar stave churches in Norway quite unlike other Christian churches in both appearance and atmosphere.

IN CONTEXT

During the early Middle Ages there may have been thousands of stave churches in the Nordic countries, but only a few remain– around 30 in Norway and a handful elsewhere. Many of these survivors are "single-nave" churches. These are simple buildings, planned along the lines of many European stone churches, with a nave and smaller chancel, which are both rectangular. They are not usually very tall, although they sometimes have spires.

The second group consists of more elaborate buildings, such as Borgund and Heddal. Much taller than the single-nave churches, these have many long, upright posts that support the main roof. Lean-to constructions with lower roofs, containing the aisles, abut on to the main structure. Builders used local pine in the form of trunks with the bark removed for the posts, planks for the upright wall boards, and small split pieces for the roof shingles. They are stunning examples of the versatility of the carpenter's craft.

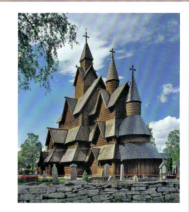

▲ **Stave church** at Heddal, Norway

Visual tour

▲ **ROOFS** The shingle-covered roofs of the church are at once beautiful and practical. Most of the shingles are diamond shaped, creating a scalelike appearance, but the builders used shingles with rounded ends at the edges of the roofs to give them a decorative, scalloped border. The shingles overlap tightly to keep out water, and all the roofs have a generous overhang so that rain and snow fall well clear of the church's wooden walls and aisles, helping to keep those dry too.

▲ **DRAGON'S-HEAD FINIALS** At four prominent places on the roofs, these finials, which are similar to those on the prows of Viking ships, are survivors from the local pagan culture, adopted by the Christian missionaries. They were probably intended to protect both the church and the worshipers from evil spirits. Like the grotesques on Gothic cathedrals, they may also have been symbols of the secular world that Christians leave behind when they enter the holy space of the church.

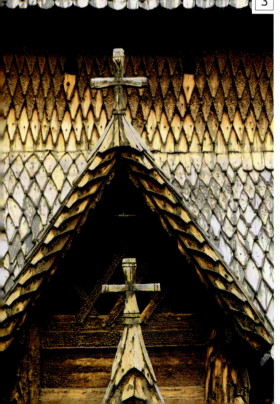

◀ **GABLE** The north, south, and west sides of the church have gables over the three entrances to the building, which echo the larger ones above them. The small gables show how the building was extended slightly at one time to create three porches. These gave worshipers a dry place of shelter as they entered the church in the rain or snow. The shingles are wrapped around the edges of the gables to create a decorative finish and are topped with crosses.

Wooden spire

The gable end is covered with wooden shingles

Protruding western porch

▶ **WEST DOORWAY** The wooden walls on either side of the main entrance to the church display a riot of carving. There is an abstract design around the semicircular arch, and above this and on either side of the doorway is a relief featuring stylized birds and beasts, including elephant heads, which the carvers must have known only from books. The creatures are surrounded by an intricate tangle of swirling foliage.

◀ **ANIMAL CARVING** As well as the carved reliefs around the doorways, there are some striking animal carvings. This example, standing proud on a shaft next to the south doorway, may well represent a 12th-century Norwegian carver's idea of a what a lion looks like.

The east end of the church has a round end, or apse

The outer part of the church forms the ambulatory around the nave

South doorway

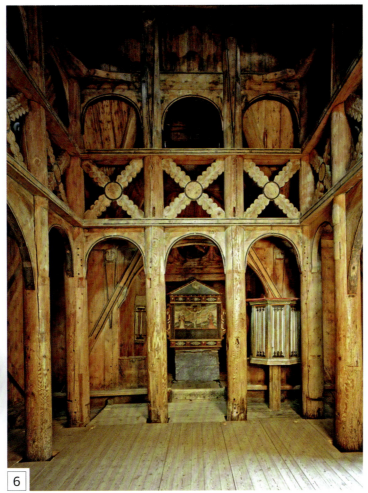

▲ **NAVE** At the heart of the interior is the nave, where the upright posts that form the main structural beams of the building soar from the floor up toward the roof. They are braced with crossbeams and joined by semicircular arches, all of which give the framework extra strength and rigidity. Beneath the floorboards the posts rest on horizontal wooden sills that join them together at the bottom and provide more strength. The sills themselves rest on stone foundations.

▲ **ROOF AND WALL CONSTRUCTION** Looking up toward the roof, you can see how the areas between the big upright posts are either bridged by arches or filled in with the beams that make up the walls. There are few windows, just tiny, round "wind-eyes" that let a little light and air into the church. At the top the posts are again tied together by horizontal beams, on which the roof rests. The framework of the roof is clearly visible.

1100–1500

Chartres Cathedral

1194–1223 ■ CATHEDRAL ■ CHARTRES, FRANCE

ARCHITECT UNKNOWN

During the night of June 10, 1194 disaster struck the northern French city of Chartres when a fire swept through its streets. Much of the walled city was destroyed, and the cathedral sustained severe damage—only the west front and crypt survived. The task of rebuilding it according to the original ground plan began almost immediately, and the new cathedral was largely complete by 1223. It subsequently survived major conflicts, including the French Revolution, but the various restoration works that have taken place over the years have not altered the essential unity of its design. The building remains an outstanding example of a medieval cathedral.

The architecture of Chartres is Gothic, the style that evolved in France in the 12th century and remained popular in various forms until the end of the 15th century. Gothic is typified by pointed arches, large windows, and its emphasis on height. The spires and high vaults of Chartres and other Gothic churches seem to soar upward, as if toward heaven, and the large windows fill the interior with light—a symbol, in the minds of medieval builders and congregations, of God's presence.

Although following the Gothic style of their predecessors, the builders of Chartres were innovative in approach. They incorporated enormous upper windows, giving the stained-glass artists maximum scope. The masons of Chartres also excelled in sculpture: the carvings, especially those on the building's three main entrances, are among the finest and most extensive of those on any medieval cathedral. All the elements of Chartres, from stone spires to statuary and stained glass, combine to form a magnificent and harmonious work of art.

IN CONTEXT

Set on an area of high ground next to the Eure River, the various buildings of the medieval city of Chartres, from churches to merchants' and artisans' houses, were protected by a solid stone wall. Although Chartres boasted several churches, the cathedral was by far the largest building, and it dominated the city. With its vast nave and tall spires, the taller of which measures 377ft (115m), the cathedral was visible from miles away across the fertile plain to the southeast. It was probably the biggest building that most of the inhabitants of Chartres had ever seen.

▲ **Chartres** Illustration from 1568 showing the medieval city

Visual tour: exterior

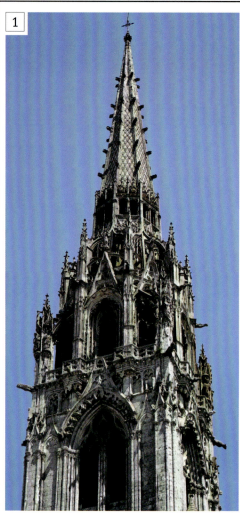

1 ▲ NORTHWEST SPIRE After a fire damaged the original northwest spire in 1503, work began on its replacement. The master mason, Jehan de Beauce, designed the spire in the late-Gothic "Flamboyant" style, with a lacelike network of pinnacles and buttresses.

2 ◀ SOUTHWEST SPIRE Here, the original spire survives. It is plain in comparison to the northwest tower. The simple octagonal structure rises out of a cluster of tall, narrow gables pierced by slender pointed arches, similar to those lower down on the west front.

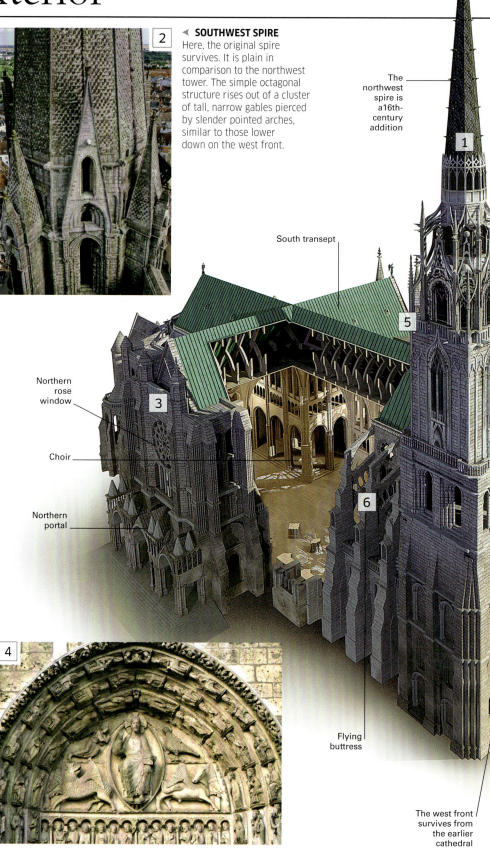

3 ▲ NORTH TRANSEPT Beneath the intricate tracery of the rose window, the north transept has a stunning porch with three doorways. These were carved in the early years of the 13th century, and much of the sculpture depicts the life of the Virgin Mary.

4 ▲ CHRIST IN MAJESTY The doorways of the west front survive from the 12th-century cathedral. Above the central doorway is a carved tympanum (the area immediately below the arch) depicting Christ surrounded by the symbols of the four Evangelists.

CHARTRES CATHEDRAL ■ FRANCE

The southwest spire dates from the 12th century

◄ **GARGOYLE** To prevent damage to the stonework, carved stone chutes direct rainwater well away from the cathedral's structure. Medieval masons traditionally carved these gargoyles in the form of grotesque monster heads—a touch of humor among the sacred carvings of the cathedral exterior.

ON DETAIL

The west front carvings, in the stately, rather stiff style of the mid-12th century, survive from the earlier cathedral. They show a range of figures from kings, queens, and rulers of the Old Testament to the Second Coming of Christ. On the north portal are 13th-century carvings of prophets and saints, while the life of Christ and the Apostles are featured on the south entrance.

▲ **13th-century sculpture** These figures (from left to right) are: Isaiah, Jeremiah, Simeon with the infant Jesus, John the Baptist, and St Peter.

► **12th-century sculpture** Statues of a queen of Judah and two Old Testament figures show the style of the earlier carvings.

ON CONSTRUCTION

In a Gothic cathedral, the insertion of large windows weakens the walls, which, as a result, need help in supporting the heavy stone vaults that make up the ceiling. The weight of the vault generates an outward thrust, which tends to push the tall walls away from each another and, without additional support, the structure would be unstable. To remedy the situation, medieval masons invented flying buttresses. These huge, arching masses of masonry prop up the building from the outside. At Chartres the flying buttresses are especially well built, each with three half-arches anchored by solid stone.

Western portal

▲ **FLYING BUTTRESSES** Running all the way along each side of the building and around the east end, these buttresses direct the outward thrust of the cathedral's heavy stone vault down to the ground (see box, right). Their delicate openwork masonry, built in the form of rows of small, connecting arches, reduces the bulk of the huge half-arches.

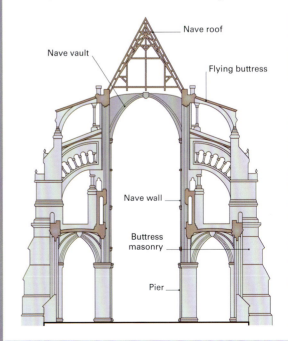

1100–1500

Visual tour: interior

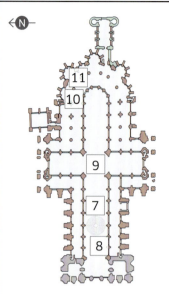

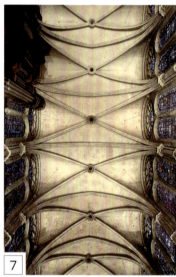

▲ **NAVE VAULT** Chartres has a quadripartite vault (curved stone ceiling), meaning that each bay or vertical division has four triangular sections. It is a simpler layout than the six-section vaults of many Gothic cathedrals. All the ribs of the vault spring from the uprights that separate each bay of the building, and there are large stone bosses (ornamental knobs) where the diagonal ribs cross.

▶ **THE NAVE** The overall impression created by the nave, with its soaring vault, is of sheer, dizzying height. All the verticals—piers (columns), lancet windows, and arches—draw your eye up to the ceiling, while the horizontal perspective focuses your attention on the high altar. The huge labyrinth, or maze, inlaid in the floor at the west end of the church symbolizes the pilgrim's journey to Jerusalem and the path of the soul to heaven.

CHARTRES CATHEDRAL ▪ FRANCE

ON DESIGN

Nearly all the magnificent, ancient stained glass from the original 12th-century cathedral has survived. The jewel-like windows portray biblical characters and saints, as well as the signs of the zodiac and scenes from daily life through the seasons. The figures depicted range from royalty and nobles to carpenters, wheelwrights, butchers, shoemakers, and apothecaries—a range that not only indicates the reach of the church to all levels of society, but also represents a slice of French medieval life. The rich colors of the designs were mostly achieved by adding metal oxides, probably in the form of ash, to the glass during their manufacture. As the sun shines through the enormous windows, the cathedral interior glows with shafts of colored light.

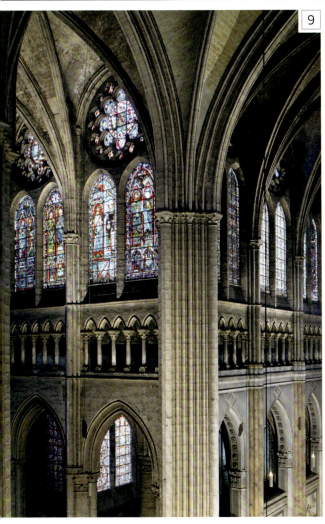

◀ **CLERESTORY**
The amount of color and light in a Gothic church depends partly on the clerestory, the row of windows above the arches in the nave and transepts. In many earlier French churches a tall gallery above the arches left space only for small clerestory windows. At Chartres, however, the gallery was omitted, and large clerestory windows extend upward from well below the base of the arches, thus giving the stained-glass artists space to include many portraits of saints and prophets.

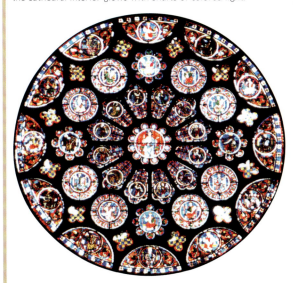

▲ **South rose window**
At the center of the window is the seated figure of Christ, encircled by 12 roundels showing angels. The larger roundels and semicircles depict the 24 crowned elders of the *Book of Revelation*.

◀ **AMBULATORY** A vaulted passage called the ambulatory curves all the way around the sanctuary and behind the high altar. This space was intended for the various processions that took place within the cathedral during services; it also gives access to the chapels and altars at the east end of the cathedral.

▲ **Zodiac window**
This window in the south ambulatory pairs the signs of the zodiac with seasonal activities. February (left) depicts a man warming his hands at a fire; the figures for September (right) harvest grapes.

▲ **AMBULATORY SCREEN** This elaborately carved stone screen, which separates the ambulatory from the choir, was begun in the early 16th century to a design by the master mason Jehan de Beauce. Its 41 tableaux depict scenes from the lives of the Virgin Mary and Jesus Christ.

▲ **Noah window**
In the north aisle this window depicts Noah chopping wood to build the ark. One of his sons is carrying a tree trunk.

▲ **Incarnation window**
This window on the west front includes the nativity scene above, showing Mary, Joseph, and the swaddled infant Jesus.

Burghausen Castle

c.1255–1490 ▪ CASTLE ▪ BURGHAUSEN, GERMANY

ARCHITECT UNKNOWN

At just over a half-mile in length, this colossal Bavarian stronghold is the longest medieval castle in Europe and a fine example of late-medieval architecture. Constructed on the site of an earlier fortified wooden building, it was substantially altered during the Middle Ages, especially under the powerful Dukes of Bavaria-Landshut, who lived there from the 13th to the 15th century. Many of the castle's buildings date from this period and are in the Gothic style.

Burghausen Castle stands on a long, narrow ridge overlooking water on both sides. It is essentially a chain of enclosed spaces called courtyards—the main castle (the inner courtyard) and five outer courtyards. Each courtyard was originally separated from those adjoining it by moats, bridges, and portcullises to strengthen the castle's defense. In times of war attackers would have to penetrate each courtyard in turn to take possession of the ducal quarters in the inner courtyard at the far end of the vast complex. In peacetime each courtyard was allocated specific roles, such as stabling horses or supplying food and drink. This practical arrangement meant that the castle's community was completely self-sufficient, which was vital for its survival in case of siege by enemies.

The dominant style of Burghausen, with its typically high stone walls and watchtowers overlooking the surrounding countryside, is the Gothic of the Middle Ages. The lower walls, which are massive and virtually windowless, appear to rise organically from their rocky foundation. Over the centuries some Gothic features have been replaced and the small medieval windows have been enlarged, but the castle's original ring walls, its first line of defense, remain virtually intact.

ON SITE

The castle stands in a commanding position on top of a rocky ridge. It overlooks the river Salznach on one side and an oxbow lake, the Wöhrsee, on the other. Medieval castle builders liked sites near water because rivers and lakes not only formed effective defensive barriers but also provided useful arteries for transport—the easiest and most economical way of transporting the tons of heavy stone needed for a major castle in the Middle Ages was by boat.

Burghausen's elevated location not only made access difficult for enemies but also ensured that the building was eminently visible from the surrounding countryside. A building like this was a massive symbol of the might of the Bavarian dukes who ruled over a region 124 miles (200km) wide to the south of the Danube River.

▲ **Aerial view** The castle is set next to the town of Burghausen, with the Wöhrsee to the west.

Visual tour: interior

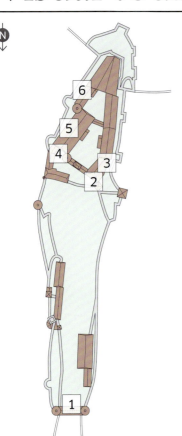

▼ **GEORG'S GATE** The bridge leading to Georg's Gate, the gatehouse of the castle's outer courtyard, spans a moat some 86ft (27m) across, with a drop of 16ft (8m) to the water below. In times of war a narrow bridge was easy to defend against attackers, who would be unable to advance in force. The round corner towers of the gatehouse gave defenders an excellent view of anyone approaching and a wide field of fire if anyone attempted to scale the walls.

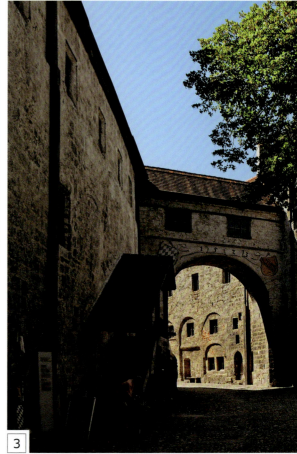

▲ **OUTER COURTYARD** This fortified enclosure leads to the main inner courtyard of the castle. The buildings here, which include the castle's brewery and bakery, have plain walls and pitched roofs. They originally had relatively few windows, to keep them more secure, but openings were added later and then enlarged after the Middle Ages to let in more light. The corner turret on the left and the square tower on the right are also defensive features, providing lookouts and firing positions. Sentries and soldiers could easily bar the small gateway to seal off this courtyard and protect the dukes' quarters beyond.

▶ **INNER COURTYARD** This courtyard at the heart of the castle contained the living quarters of the noble family, as well as the Knights' Hall, the women's rooms, and one of the castle chapels. This view shows the exterior stairs that lead up to the residential rooms on the first floor. The ground floor was traditionally used for storage, such as food stores and wine vaults, and sometimes for other services, such as workshops. The living quarters at top floor level are connected by a covered bridge so that people could cross from one building to the other without having to go down to the courtyard itself.

◀ **KEEP** Adjoining the northern end of the Knights' Hall, this great keep is the tallest tower in the castle and was probably used as a military headquarters in times of war. From the upper story the duke could keep a watch on the whole castle and the surrounding area and issue orders to his men. The keep also provided the final refuge if enemies managed to penetrate the outer walls and courtyards of the castle.

▼ **KNIGHTS' HALL** Located on the eastern side of the main courtyard, this was an assembly room and dining chamber for the knights and men-at-arms stationed at the castle. It is a plainly decorated but impressive room, with simple stone vaulting in an early Gothic style similar to that of St. Elisabeth's Chapel (below). A row of round, unadorned columns supports the stone ceiling, dividing the room into two parallel spaces.

ON CONSTRUCTION

Like many castles in Central Europe, Burghausen is a very long building on top of a crag. This rocky outcrop forms a secure foundation for the outer fortifications of the building and the inner walls that define the castle's courtyards.

Each of the five outer courtyards contained buildings planned for specific practical purposes. There were workshops, offices, and servants' rooms in the fifth and outermost courtyard; a chapel, garden, and gardener's house in the fourth; stables in the third; an armory in the second; and a brewery, bakery, and more stables in the first courtyard, the one closest to the main court of the castle with its ducal apartments. All the courtyards have thick walls and towers from which guards could keep a constant lookout over the surrounding area. A number of these towers, known as "pepperpots," were later converted into cannon emplacements.

▲ **Fortified walls**
Tall, sturdy stone walls with integral towers stretch along the sides of the second courtyard.

ON DETAIL

Medieval castles are usually thought of as utilitarian buildings, with plain stone walls for defense and spartan accommodation within. They were also, however, the homes of monarchs and nobles, and the buildings were partly intended to display their owners' identity and status. One way to do this was to use heraldry, and painted coats of arms can be seen on the castle walls at Burghausen. One of the pair of shields (below) on the Georg's Gate includes lions and a checkered pattern in blue and white—the arms of the Dukes of Bavaria. The other, bearing eagles, is that of the Polish royal family—Princess Hedwig of Poland married Duke Georg of Bavaria in 1475.

▲ **CHAPEL OF ST ELISABETH** One of two chapels in the castle, this one is close to the ducal apartments. It dates from the mid-13th century and has simple lancet (narrow pointed) windows in typical early Gothic style. The polygonal end of the chapel has a stone-vaulted ceiling, with vault ribs that spring from corbels (projections) between the windows. Beneath them are niches for statues of saints.

▲ **Coats of arms**
The arms of Duke Georg and Princess Hedwig are painted in niches in a wall near Georg's Gate.

Florence Cathedral

1296–1436 ■ CATHEDRAL ■ FLORENCE, ITALY

VARIOUS ARCHITECTS

Florence was one of the richest cities of late medieval Italy. At the end of the 13th century, the city council decided to replace the old church of Santa Reparata with a large new cathedral. They appointed an architect, Arnolfo di Cambio, and work began in 1296, but construction was interrupted when Arnolfo died in 1310. In the 1330s work on the building continued under a succession of different architects, including the great artist Giotto. In the following decades the cathedral slowly grew until most of the main structure was complete except for the dome.

Building the dome posed a huge challenge because it had to span a space some 138½ft (42m) across, and the plan allowed for no supporting buttresses. In 1418 the authorities announced a competition to find solutions to this problem, and the two main entrants were both goldsmiths—Lorenzo Ghiberti and Filippo Brunelleschi. Brunelleschi won, and he proposed building the dome with brick in such a way that no temporary supporting planks were needed during construction. His design is a triumph in terms of both engineering and visual brilliance, and the structure remains the largest brick dome in the world.

Florence Cathedral marks a transition between the Middle Ages and the Renaissance. The building was begun in an Italian version of the Gothic style, with pointed arches and stone vaults, but without the emphasis on height, pinnacles, and spires that French Gothic buildings display. In roofing the dome in this way Brunelleschi was adding a Renaissance element to the Gothic structure.

In the centuries that followed, work continued on adorning the cathedral in this harmonious marriage of styles. Renaissance artists Giorgio Vasari and Federico Zuccaro painted the dome's interior in the 16th century, while in the 19th, the west front of the building was refaced in the Italian Gothic style.

FILIPPO **BRUNELLESCHI**

1377–1446

Born in Florence, Brunelleschi first worked as a goldsmith and sculptor. He entered a competition with Lorenzo Ghiberti to design and produce bronze doors for the cathedral's baptistry. When both men's designs were accepted, Brunelleschi refused to work with Ghiberti, who was therefore given the job alone. In around 1418 Brunelleschi became involved in building the cathedral dome. He also remodeled a bridge in Pisa and designed the churches of San Spirito and San Lorenzo in Florence, as well as the city's Spedale degli Innocenti (Foundling Hospital), and the Palazzo di Parte Guelfa. Brunelleschi's buildings were hugely influential, especially the Spedale degli Innocenti, which historians sometimes call the first Renaissance building. The Palazzo became a model for homes for noble families in Italy, and the great dome of the cathedral inspired the dome of St. Peter's in Rome.

Visual tour: exterior

▲ **WEST FRONT** The cathedral's west front has the gabled outline seen on many late medieval Italian churches, with a central high portion and lower sides that reflect respectively the nave and flanking aisles within. Arched doorways, round windows, and small pointed openings (unlike the huge west windows of French or English cathedrals) are also typical Italian features. The original facing was left unfinished and later removed. The white, red, and green marble that now covers the west front was added in the 19th century, but harmonizes with the medieval walls of the adjacent bell tower.

▶ **BELL TOWER** Giotto designed the bell tower (campanile), which was built in 1334–59 and is an impressive 275ft (84m) in height. Giotto had intended to add a spire, but he died in 1337, and the design was subsequently modified. The top stage, which houses the bells, now ends with a flat parapet. The tower is still imposing—its four stages are marked by horizontal string patterns, its walls are clad in gleaming marble, and the openings on the three upper stages contrast well with the pale walls.

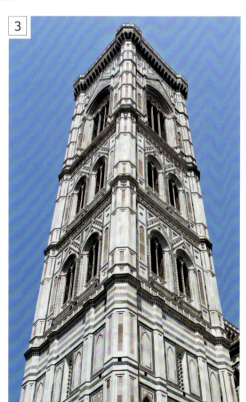

▲ **WHEEL WINDOW** The deeply set round windows on the west front have very simple tracery, consisting mainly of a central circle and radiating stone spokes similar to those of a wheel. French Gothic rose windows had more complex tracery, but Italian architects worked under the influence of Romanesque architecture with its plainer, more linear designs.

Parapet and roof where Giotto planned to add a spire

The belfry stage with large openings to allow sound to carry

The marble cladding was replaced in the 19th century

◀ **STONEWORK** A detail of the stonework on the cathedral's east end shows how different colored marbles are used to pick out a variety of architectural shapes. Some of this decoration involves the use of semicircular arches, another feature that both harks back to the era before Gothic and looks forward to the Renaissance. In some places the masonry inside the arches is divided by a pair of vertical bands, which produces a design similar to the semicircular "Diocletian" windows in Roman bathhouses and basilicas.

FLORENCE CATHEDRAL ■ ITALY

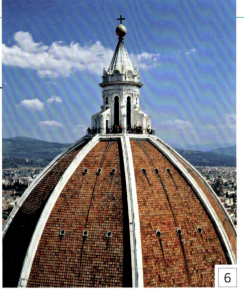

- The dome consists of inner and outer layers
- Concentric rings of stone strengthen the dome and prevent structural movement
- The crypt with tombs of Giotto, Brunelleschi, and numerous bishops
- Marble pavement
- The apse contains five side chapels

▲ **DOME** The masonry of the dome consists of brickwork between a number of stone ribs. Brunelleschi instructed the builders to lay the bricks in a herringbone pattern. This transferred the weight of the newly laid bricks to the adjacent stone ribs and meant that the builders did not need to erect temporary wooden supports for the masonry while the mortar was setting. At the top of the dome is a lantern that was completed in 1461 after Brunelleschi's death.

▼ **EAST END** The eastern part of the cathedral has a very unusual layout. Around the dome are three apses, each planned as a half-octagon and roofed with a semi-dome. Inside each apse are five small chapels lit by narrow Gothic windows, which are visible on the outside and surrounded by small pointed canopies. This layout gives the east end of the building a highly complex appearance, in which unity is provided by the repeating round-headed arches and the identical forms of the semi-domes.

ON DESIGN

As drawings and photographs show, the dome covers a vast space at the heart of the cathedral, but the structure's most ingenious features are hidden from view. A total of nine horizontal rings run around the dome, holding the structure in place like the metal hoops around a barrel. Each stone ring is about 2 x 3ft (60 x 90cm), and they work together to stop the dome's masonry from collapsing inward or moving outward and splitting the structure. Their inclusion meant that buttresses were not needed to hold the dome in place.

▲ **Dome cross section**
This drawing from 1610 by Ludovico Cigoli shows the dome in cross section, but does not reveal the reinforcing rings, which were unknown to the artist.

IN CONTEXT

A series of carved reliefs made for the campanile show a range of subjects, including episodes from the *Book of Genesis*, and scenes showing agricultural activities and crafts such as building and blacksmithing. There are also figures relating to classical scholarship, including Pythagoras, and the personifications of subjects such as Grammar. According to tradition, these beautifully carved hexagonal panels are the work of the great sculptor Andrea Pisano, although no one knows whether he carved them or provided the designs. Together, they were probably intended to sum up both the piety and the artistic sophistication of Florence.

▲ **Creation of Eve**
This is one of the biblical scenes from the campanile sculpture. The original is now in the Duomo Museum.

Visual tour: interior

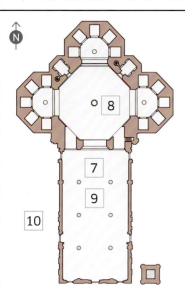

▶ **DOME** The interior of the dome has a huge surface, lit by the lantern in the center. Brunelleschi planned to decorate this with a mosaic that had golden tesserae (small cubes) to pick up the incoming natural light, but in the 16th century, Duke Cosimo I de'Medici rejected the idea and chose Giorgio Vasari to paint a fresco of the Last Judgment. The vast painting was finished by Vasari's successors.

▼ **CROSSING, SANCTUARY, AND ARCHES** Very plain pointed arches on massive piers support the dome, while smaller arches on more slender columns line the sanctuary beyond. Together with the pale stone interior walls, the uncomplicated vaulted ceilings, and numerous windows, these features increase the sense of light in the interior spaces.

◀ **MARBLE PAVEMENT** This was added under the patronage of the Medici family in the 16th century. At this time the unfashionable Gothic marble cladding of the west front was removed, and some of the stones were used in this pavement. This may have been the work of a member of the da Sangallo family, noted Florentine architects.

FLORENCE CATHEDRAL ■ ITALY

▶ PORTRAIT OF DANTE
One of the paintings in the cathedral is Domenico di Michelino's 1465 portrait of the poet Dante explaining his masterwork, the *Divine Comedy*. In the background is a view of Florence as it was in 1465, soon after the cathedral's dome—to the right of the poet—was completed.

ON **DETAIL**

The baptistry that stands to the west of the cathedral is an octagonal building older than the cathedral. During the 14th and 15th centuries the building was adorned with three remarkable sets of bronze doors, one set by Andrea Pisano and two by Lorenzo Ghiberti. Pisano's set and Ghiberti's first set show biblical scenes in high relief, enclosed in Gothic frames. Ghiberti's second pair of doors feature a series of low-relief panels showing Old Testament scenes with more realism.

▲ **The Israelites**
Moses' followers receive the law from the prophet in a scene on Ghiberti's second set of doors.

ON **DESIGN**

The mosaics in the baptistry ceiling, which date from 1225 and are the work of several artists, are earlier than the neighboring cathedral but show both the kind of treatment that Brunelleschi planned for the cathedral dome and some of the subject matter used in the cathedral frescoes. At the bottom of the mosaic is the figure of Jesus Christ in a roundel. On either side of this are panels depicting the Last Judgment, with the saved to Christ's right and the damned, tormented by demons, to his left. The rest of the mosaic, in concentric octagons around the central lantern, depicts angels and Old Testament scenes nearest the center, and New Testament scenes from the lives of Jesus Christ, the Virgin Mary, and Joseph toward the outer edges.

▲ **The mosaic ceiling** of the baptistry, Florence

Alhambra

1232–1390 ■ FORTIFIED PALACE ■ GRANADA, SPAIN

ARCHITECT UNKNOWN

The fortified palace of the Alhambra ("red fortress"), set squarely on a hill in the upland city of Granada, is one of the wonders of Islamic architecture. It was built by southern Spain's Muslim rulers, the sultans of the Nasrid dynasty, in the 13th and 14th centuries. Seen from a distance, its massive crenellated towers rising above the solid, red brick-and-stone walls that gave the palace its name, the Alhambra looks plain and forbidding. Yet inside, it is one of the world's most intricately decorated buildings, and its arcades, columns, ceilings, doors, and archways are testimony to the endless inventiveness of Islamic art and the phenomenal skill of its artisans.

The Nasrids, the last of Spain's Muslim dynasties, ruled a small part of southern Spain around Granada, Malaga, and Almeria. Because the country's Christian rulers were pushing down from the north and gradually reconquering their territory, it was vital for the Nasrids to create a secure fortified base, so the citadel of the Alhambra originally contained a whole spectrum of buildings—workers' houses, craft workshops, the royal mint, soldiers' quarters, public baths, several mosques, and the great palace itself—that formed a well-defended, self-contained community. Most of the subsidiary buildings are gone, some of them built over by later structures, such as the Renaissance palace of the Christian emperor Charles V, constructed in the 16th century just to the southwest.

The site's surviving Nasrid buildings are among the best examples of the carefully planned and highly ornate architecture of Muslim Spain. The Alhambra is arranged around several courtyards and gardens, watered by their own irrigation systems. These arched courtyards provide elegant, shaded areas with pools and fountains, where people could come and go in comfort. The arcades lead to beautifully designed rooms with decorative materials including plaster, ceramic tiles, and carved wood, as well as architectural features, such as capitals, with patterns of amazing complexity. Most stunning of all are the ceilings, some decorated with *mocarabes*—intricate plasterwork forms that hang like stalactites, magically catching the sun to create dappled patterns of light and shade.

Visual tour: exterior

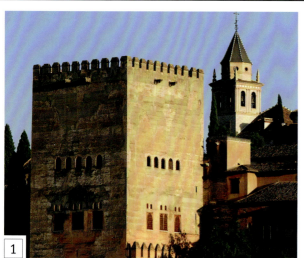

▲ **COMARES TOWER** At 148ft (45m) in height, the Comares Tower is the tallest building in the Alhambra and contains some of the most important rooms of the palace, including the Hall of the Ambassadors. The tower's thick stone walls made it strong and secure, and its height ensured that it was a good vantage point. Guards patrolling on the roof could look out from between the battlements, the ornate pointed tops of which were added in the 16th century.

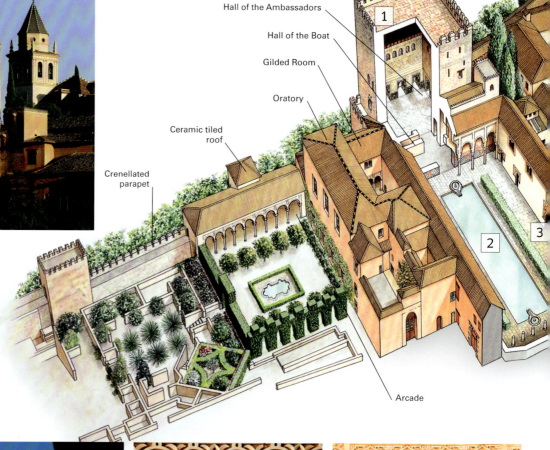

▲ **COURT OF MYRTLES** This long courtyard provides access to the family's private rooms. It is built around a large rectangular pool that is fed by two fountains and surrounded by a marble pavement. The water in the pool reflects the symmetrical arcades at either end, which feature slender columns, tall arches, and elaborately carved upper walls. The delicacy of these details is in marked contrast to the solid, crenellated walls of the massive Comares Tower beyond.

▲ **WALL DECORATION** The dazzling range of decorative detail in the Court of Myrtles includes inscriptions in flowing calligraphy set off by moldings, abstract symmetrical designs forming loops and curves, and row upon row of miniature arches. On exterior walls and beneath arcades, these patterns catch the strong natural light, giving the surfaces of the walls rich texture.

▲ **DOORWAY** The builders of Muslim Spain used several forms of pointed arch, such as this example from the Court of Myrtles, which has long straight sides rising to a shallow curving top. The most intricate carving is on the arch surround itself, where the filigree decoration breaks up the curve so that the edge of the arch seems to dissolve in a blur of fine detail.

ALHAMBRA ■ SPAIN

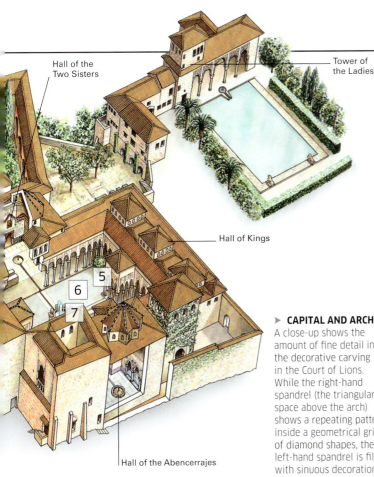

▶ **CAPITAL AND ARCHES**
A close-up shows the amount of fine detail in the decorative carving in the Court of Lions. While the right-hand spandrel (the triangular space above the arch) shows a repeating pattern inside a geometrical grid of diamond shapes, the left-hand spandrel is filled with sinuous decorations known as arabesques. Yet more intricate patterns cover the walls beyond.

▲ **COURT OF LIONS** This is the more ornate of the Alhambra's two main courtyards and adjoins a number of grand public rooms. The arcade, which surrounds all four sides, consists of multifoil arches— a typical Islamic form in which each side of the arch is split into a series of small curves. Clusters of slender columns support the arches, and these, together with the carved decoration that covers virtually every surface, give the court a shimmering quality.

▲ **FOUNTAIN** The Court of Lions is named for its central fountain surrounded by twelve stylized stone lions. From here four straight water channels flow toward the arcades, dividing the courtyard into four equal sections. This fourfold division is a fundamental element of the gardens of Islam, which were earthly representations of paradise as revealed in the Qur'an. The four watercourses represent the four rivers of life, flowing with water, wine, honey, and milk.

Visual tour: interior

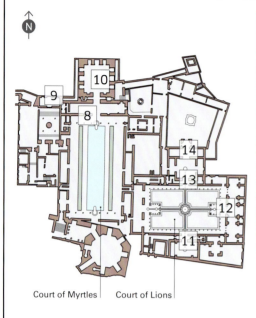

Court of Myrtles | Court of Lions

▲ **HALL OF THE BOAT** This room acquired its name owing to a confusion between the Arabic word *baraka* (blessing)—inscribed on the room's barrel-vaulted ceiling—and *barca*, the Spanish word for "boat." The room has window openings with flattened arches—a typical Islamic form.

▶ **HALL OF THE ABENCERRAJES** A group of knights from the Abencerrajes family was said to have been beheaded here—according to legend, a reddish stain on the floor marks the spot. The room contains one of the most remarkable ceilings in the whole palace. A dome made up of *mocarabes* covers a dramatic, star-shaped opening. Around the base of the dome are several small windows that cast light on to the gilded decoration, making it glitter and highlighting the exquisite details.

▲ **GILDED ROOM AND COURTYARD** Near one corner of the Court of Myrtles is the Gilded Room, an intimate space with a gold-painted wooden ceiling and ornate arches. The room looks out on to a small courtyard that is partly roofed over and partly open—another outdoor enclosure where the residents of the palace could find quietness, seclusion, and shade.

▲ **HALL OF THE AMBASSADORS** Inside the Comares Tower is the square Hall of the Ambassadors, the throne room of the Nasrid sultans. Under a ceiling made up of thousands of meticulously jointed pieces of wood, the ruling sultan sat surrounded by walls decorated with abstract patterns in shallow relief. Daylight enters the room through windows filled with pierced screens; these filter the light and reduce the glare of the sun.

ALHAMBRA ■ SPAIN

ON DETAIL

Each of the typical forms of Islamic decoration—arabesques, geometrical patterns, colored tiling, calligraphy, and foliate designs—appear all over the walls, ceilings, and arches of the Alhambra, and are further enhanced by the use of repeated three-dimensional forms, such as *mocarabes*. All these forms of adornment were designed and executed by highly skilled artists and artisans to take full advantage of any available light in the palace, whether it was direct sunlight, filtered light entering the rooms through pierced screens, or the light reflected from the Alhambra's pools of water.

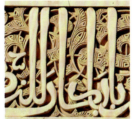

▼ **Pattern and color**
Many of the Alhambra's rooms have a tiled skirting with strong, colorful patterns that contrast effectively with the monochrome carvings on the walls above.

▲ **Calligraphy**
Even in a secular building such as the Alhambra, religious inscriptions from the Qur'an made up an important part of the decorative scheme.

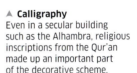

▲ **Foliate carvings**
Carved or molded plant forms, including delicate flowers, curling stems, and vines, seem to bring the lush gardens into the building.

◄ **HALL OF KINGS** This room makes up the eastern side of the complex around the Court of Lions. Named for its ceiling paintings that show the early rulers of the Nasrid dynasty, the hall is especially notable for its series of arches. These are substantial structures, but the intricate *mocarabe* decoration makes them appear less bulky.

► **HALL OF THE TWO SISTERS** The plain floor of this room has two particularly large flagstones, which give the hall its name. The walls are covered in fine plaster decorations, but the most striking feature of the room is the dome. Like the one in the Hall of the Abencerrajes, it is lit by a series of small windows that illuminate the *mocarabe* work to make patterns of light and shadow.

▲ **DARAXA'S MIRADOR** A small room that acts as a gazebo, this *mirador* (meaning "look-out") is an indoor space or viewing pavilion from which people can enjoy looking at the courtyard garden beyond. Although the garden was redesigned by the later Christian inhabitants of the palace, this *mirador* shows how the building's original designers worked to make links between the interior and exterior.

Doge's Palace

c.1309–1424 ■ PALACE ■ VENICE, ITALY

GIOVANNI & BARTOLOMEO BON

From the 7th to the 18th centuries the city of Venice was an independent republic with an elected nobleman, the Doge, as its head, advised by an assembly who made and passed laws. In 1297 a change in the law increased the number of noblemen in the legislative assembly, and the presiding doge decided to upgrade the Doge's Palace, near St. Mark's Square, so that the larger meetings could take place there. In 1309 work started on the new palace, a structure of shimmering beauty that is one of the world's great domestic buildings.

The first section of the palace to be completed fronted the lagoon, and the most famous part of the palace, which overlooked St. Mark's Square, was built in the following century. Alterations continued over the next few centuries, first in the Gothic and then in the Renaissance style.

The Doge's Palace is known above all for its Gothic façades and details. The Venetians developed their own version of Gothic, found in numerous palaces alongside the Venetian canals. It is a highly ornate style, featuring rows of pointed arches, rich decorative carving, masonry in different colors, and elaborate parapets at the top of the building. Loggias (open galleries) fronted with arches look out over the square and the canals and let both light and air into the interiors. Successive fires in the 16th century damaged the building, and although the Doge's Palace retained the Gothic exteriors, repairs to the interior reflected the Renaissance style.

The palace was not only a luxurious residence for the city's ruler, it also housed a magnificent meeting room for the assembly, a place where courts could be held, and even a prison. This multi-purpose building was, therefore, at the heart of Venetian life. Today, its intricate, lacelike façades and central position make it an enduring symbol of the city of Venice.

IN CONTEXT

Venice preserves many noblemen's houses on the banks of its canals. One of the most beautiful is the Ca' d'Oro, a house built in the 15th century for the Contarini family. The Ca' d'Oro has arches, loggias, and windows that are similar to those on the Doge's Palace, making it a building of incredible delicacy that seems to float on the Grand Canal. Venetian Gothic architecture was always admired and publicized by the writings of British critic John Ruskin and was much copied in 19th-century Europe.

To construct such palaces, the builders had to drive a small forest of wooden piles deep into the damp soil, topping them with a wood-and-stone platform to provide a foundation. On top of this they built the walls, which, with their numerous openings, were actually very light in weight. A level of non-porous stone, just above the water line, helped keep the building dry.

▲ **Ca' d'Oro** The main Gothic façade of this building overlooks the Grand Canal.

Visual tour

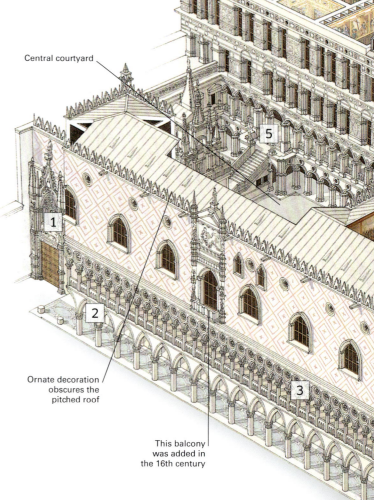

▲ **PORTA DELLA CARTA** This decoration, with Gothic windows, pinnacles, and carvings, is above the main entrance into the palace. Most of the details, which were the work of 15th-century Venetian architect and sculptor Bartolomeo Bon, have a delicacy typical of the city's Gothic architecture—especially the spiral shafts in the window, the filigree tracery, and the rich carving around the canopy. The winged lion is the symbol of St. Mark the Evangelist, patron saint of Venice.

▼ **CARVED CAPITALS** The Gothic masons of Europe often decorated capitals with rich foliate ornament. The capitals at the Doge's Palace are some of the most ornate of all. Many even include small human heads or figures half-hidden among the flowers and leaves. These figures are full of life—some carry pots, some shoot arrows, and others, like this example, are on horseback.

▲ **ARCHES AND QUATREFOILS** A close-up shows the care with which the architects designed the long rows of arches fronting the loggia. Each arch has an ogee (double-curve) outline held up on shafts with delicately carved capitals. Above the arches is a row of circles divided into four portions to form quatrefoils. These quatrefoil openings let more air into the loggia and cast a dappled pattern of light and shade onto the loggia floor.

DOGE'S PALACE ■ ITALY   97

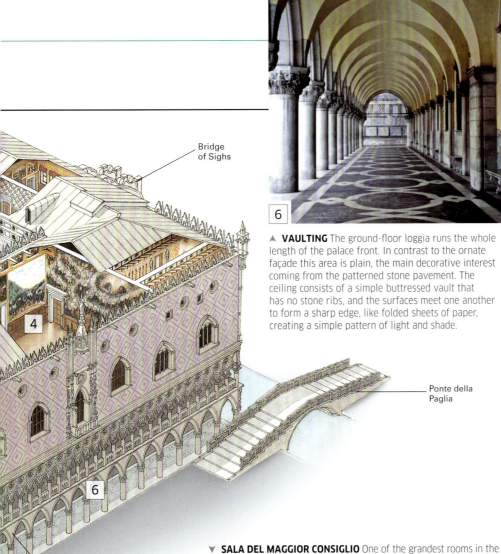

▲ **VAULTING** The ground-floor loggia runs the whole length of the palace front. In contrast to the ornate façade this area is plain, the main decorative interest coming from the patterned stone pavement. The ceiling consists of a simple buttressed vault that has no stone ribs, and the surfaces meet one another to form a sharp edge, like folded sheets of paper, creating a simple pattern of light and shade.

ON DESIGN

A covered stone bridge was erected in 1614 to link the newly built neighboring prisons with the rooms in the palace that housed the courts. It was popularly called the Bridge of Sighs. This name was first used in the 19th century by the British poet Lord Byron and referred to the sighs of the prisoners as they walked toward the prison. Designed by Antonio Contino and built in white limestone, the bridge is austerely classical, decorated mainly with simple moldings and scrollwork. Although it is relatively plain in design, the structure has an elegant shape, with the outline of its arch reflected by the line of its roof. This, together with the story about its name, has made the bridge famous.

▲ **Bridge of Sighs**
Prisoners passed to their cells via two narrow passages inside the bridge. Stone grilles secure the bridge's windows.

▼ **SALA DEL MAGGIOR CONSIGLIO** One of the grandest rooms in the palace, this chamber was the meeting place of the great assembly or council. At about 174ft (53m) long, it could hold up to 1,600 members of the Venetian nobility. After a fire in 1577 the room was rebuilt and two of the greatest Venetian artists, Veronese and Tintoretto, painted its frescoes. Veronese's *Deification of Venice* is on the ceiling, while the paintings on the walls include portraits of 76 doges by Tintoretto.

▲ **SCALA DEI GIGANTI** The giant statues of the Roman gods Mars and Neptune that guard the top give the staircase its name (The Giants' Staircase). The steps lead from the courtyard to the first floor, where the round-topped arches are in the Renaissance style. They show how the Venetian builders adapted this style of architecture, which was fashionable in the 16th century, by adding ornament that was as rich and complex as the carving of their Gothic predecessors.

Temple of Heaven

c.1420 ■ TEMPLE COMPLEX ■ BEIJING, CHINA

ARCHITECT UNKNOWN

One of the major religious complexes in Beijing, the Temple of Heaven was built by the emperor Cheng Zu in the 15th century. Although it is often referred to as a Taoist temple, Cheng Zu was also a devotee of Confucianism. This complex was the site where the emperor performed one of the most important and ancient rituals of the Chinese year: the annual prayer for a good harvest, which took place at the winter solstice. The temple, especially the central circular building called the Hall of Prayer for Good Harvests, is a masterpiece of Chinese architecture that allies traditional wooden building techniques with vivid decoration and powerful symbolic planning.

The Temple of Heaven consists of three main structures. The Hall of Prayer for Good Harvests, a triple-roofed building rising to a height of 125ft (38m), is the largest and the most imposing. The Imperial Vault of Heaven is a smaller and highly ornate round building, connected to the Hall of Prayer by a long raised walkway, the Vermillion Steps Bridge. Nearby is the third element, the Circular Mound Altar, an elaborately carved marble platform with three levels.

The main buildings on the site are round: in Chinese cosmology the circle symbolizes heaven. Expertly constructed from lumber, the posts, beams, brackets, and braces interlock in a complex fashion that is typical of traditional Chinese carpentry. The builders decorated these wooden components with painted and gilded designs of great intricacy and immaculate finish— appropriate qualities for a building used by the emperor. Fortunately, the traditional artisanship skills employed in these structures survived down the centuries in China, so when a lightning strike and fire in 1889 destroyed the Hall of Prayer, it was rebuilt in its original style.

CHENG ZU

1360–1424

Also known as the Yongle ("Perpetual Happiness") Emperor, Cheng Zu was one of the most influential rulers of the Ming Dynasty. He was prince of the area around Beijing and a skilled military leader, becoming emperor in 1402 after defeating his rival, Jianwen, in battle. Cheng Zu moved the imperial capital from Nanjing to Beijing, and began building the complex of palaces and government buildings that came to be known as the Forbidden City. His building projects in Beijing included the Temple of Heaven and a new imperial burial ground for himself and his Ming successors. Although a follower of Confucianism, he treated Taoism and Buddhism with equal respect. This attitude enabled him to win the political support of many, helping him to unify his huge realm and contributing to the survival of the Ming Dynasty for more than 200 years.

Visual tour

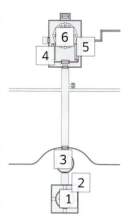

▶ **CIRCULAR MOUND ALTAR**
This is the three-tiered platform where the emperor prayed. It is constructed of finely carved marble, with curving walls that amplified the ruler's voice as he recited the prayers. The pillars and stones of the structure are arranged in multiples of the number nine, representing both the nine circles of Heaven and the emperor, who was seen as a divine being.

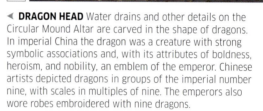

1

2

◀ **DRAGON HEAD** Water drains and other details on the Circular Mound Altar are carved in the shape of dragons. In imperial China the dragon was a creature with strong symbolic associations and, with its attributes of boldness, heroism, and nobility, an emblem of the emperor. Chinese artists depicted dragons in groups of the imperial number nine, with scales in multiples of nine. The emperors also wore robes embroidered with nine dragons.

4

▶ **HALL OF PRAYER ROOFS**
In Chinese architecture the color of roof tiles was often symbolic. Imperial palaces had yellow roof tiles, while the tiles covering the triple roofs of the Hall of Prayer are blue. This is the color of the sky and therefore represents heaven. Blue also dominates the painted decoration of the supporting beams beneath the eaves and the walls.

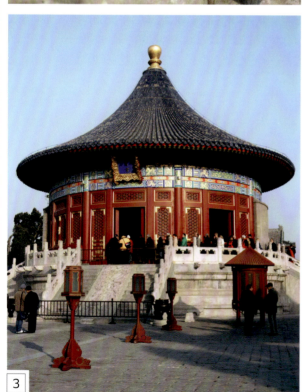

3

▲ **IMPERIAL VAULT OF HEAVEN** This is a small building with brick walls and a wooden-framed roof that spans the 51ft (15.6m) diameter of the structure without cross beams. Its original purpose was to store a collection of stone tablets, representing the gods, the elements, and natural forces such as rain and thunder. Officials took out these tablets for use during imperial ceremonies.

TEMPLE OF HEAVEN ■ CHINA

ON SITE

It soon becomes obvious to visitors that the planning of the temple's buildings is based on the circle, with its heavenly symbolism. The builders of the complex, however, also used the square. Each building stands on a square plot and squares also occur in the design of the structures. For the Chinese, the square represented the earth, and by placing these round buildings in square courtyards, the builders were emphasizing the unity of heaven and earth. This essential unity is embodied in the site as a whole, which has a boundary that is rounded at one end and square at the other.

▲ **Temple complex**
Looking down on the site, it is clear that the Circular Mound Altar is set within a round wall inside a square precinct.

▲ **HALL OF PRAYER EXTERIOR** Beneath the edge of each roof a series of protruding wooden beams and ornate brackets bears the weight of the roof structure. All these beams are meticulously painted, mostly in shades of blue and green. Below them, the walls bear images of dragons and beautiful abstract designs.

◀ **HALL OF PRAYER INTERIOR** Tall, round posts, decorated in red and gold with a foliage pattern, rise from the floor to support the roof of the Hall of Prayer. Up in the roof a network of beams links to these posts. Rather than cover the structure with a false ceiling, the intricate, exposed woodwork was brightly painted in celebration of the artisanship of the carpenters and decorators.

IN CONTEXT

Built over a period of 15 years, the Forbidden City was Cheng Zu's largest building project. It consists of a complex of around 900 separate buildings in a walled and moated compound at the center of Beijing. Structures within the complex include ceremonial halls, the emperor's palace, and buildings used for various governmental and state functions. Most of the buildings are rectangular and feature a similar framework structure to those in the Temple of Heaven, with overhanging roofs supported on a network of posts, beams, and brackets. The floors are of baked bricks, and the roofs covered with ceramic tiles, both of which are colored golden in the buildings used by the emperor. Like many Chinese buildings, some of the structures of the Forbidden City have been renewed and restored over time but retain their Ming layout and appearance.

▲ **Forbidden City**
The city contains a mixture of wooden buildings with tiled roofs and walkways and flights of white-marble steps.

King's College Chapel

1446–1515 ■ CHAPEL ■ CAMBRIDGE, UK

REGINALD ELY

King's College, which is part of the University of Cambridge, was founded in 1441 by Henry VI, and the jewel at its heart is the college chapel, one of the most striking late-Gothic buildings in Europe. The building is an excellent example of a kind of Gothic architecture unique to Britain, known as the Perpendicular style, which was developed by masons working at the royal court in London during the 14th century and spread rapidly across the country. Perpendicular Gothic buildings, as the name suggests, focus on vertical elements—slender columns, tall pinnacles and buttresses, windows with tall, thin panes of glass, and walls decorated with paneling that imitates in stonework the form of the windows. In high-status buildings the ceilings have spreading fan vaults with exquisite filigree patterns of stone ribs. King's College Chapel has most of these features, but two of them are particularly outstanding: the tall, beautifully proportioned windows and the delicacy of its spreading fan vaults. They dominate its light-filled interior, which consists of a single huge space, divided by a wooden screen set at a level that is low enough to give uninterrupted views of the rows of windows and stone fans of the vault above. This sense of a sweeping space that the eye can take in at one glance distinguishes Perpendicular Gothic buildings from earlier Gothic structures, which often featured inner spaces and arched recesses.

Reginald Ely was the royal master mason who designed the chapel and oversaw the start of the construction. His work was, however, interrupted by the Wars of the Roses and, in 1471, by the death of the king. In the early decades of the 16th century another remarkable mason, John Wastell, took charge, and the building was eventually finished. In spite of this lack of continuity the chapel is a complete and hugely satisfying structure in the Perpendicular Gothic style, but with interior decoration that straddles the fashions of the 15th and 16th centuries. The huge, stained-glass windows were installed late in the construction process, after the death of the king, and their design style anticipates the Renaissance. The woodwork—both the screen and the impressive set of stalls for the choir—is also a late addition. The screen boasts classical pilasters (slight protrusions) and heraldic designs, together with the initials of Henry VIII and his wife, Anne Boleyn. These contrasting elements—the Gothic stonework and later glass and woodwork—were, however, executed with such brilliance by master artisans that they blend together harmoniously in one of the most dazzling religious buildings in the world.

HENRY VI

1421–71

Henry VI became king of England in 1422, while still a baby, and for the first 15 years of his reign the country was governed on his behalf by regents. Years later, the king gained a reputation for being a lover of peace and piety, but his reign was dominated by the Wars of the Roses, a series of dynastic conflicts between the House of Lancaster (to which Henry belonged) and the rival House of York. Henry also became king of France during his infancy, but his claim to the French throne was disputed, and as a consequence his army fought in wars there, too. In 1453, when his troops were defeated by the French, he lost control of Bordeaux, which left Calais as the only remaining English territory in France.

Henry had a mental breakdown, and this, together with military successes by the House of York, led to his being deposed in 1461, when the Yorkist Edward IV became king. Henry's fortunes improved in 1470, when he returned to the throne, but when the Yorkists won a major victory at the Battle of Tewkesbury in 1471, Henry's son was killed. The king died, apparently of melancholy, soon afterward. The main legacy of Henry's troubled reign was his educational work—he was the founder of Eton College, which also has a wonderful chapel, and of King's College, Cambridge.

Visual tour

▶ **TURRETS** Among the most striking features of the exterior are the four turrets that rise from each corner of the chapel, framing the east and west fronts. The turrets add a vertical accent—provided by the tower in other churches and chapels—and combine with shorter pinnacles on top of the buttresses to give the building a memorable skyline. The turrets were the work of John Wastell and are highly ornate. Their octagonal bodies have intricate pierced decoration on each face and protruding upright sections that resemble miniature buttresses at each corner. The pointed tops are studded with ornaments called crockets, which give the turrets a distinctive, jagged outline.

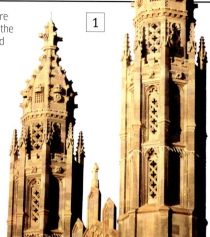

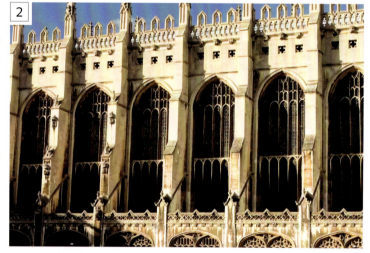

Substantial buttresses provide support for the vault and keep the structure stable

The series of tall windows is the focal point of the façade

▶ **BUTTRESSES AND WINDOWS** The two long walls of the chapel are made up almost entirely of tall, stained-glass windows, with buttresses to support the vaulted ceiling set between them. At the top of the wall is a delicate openwork parapet, which conceals the shallow-pitched roof behind. The resulting pattern of upright mullions (stone glazing bars) in the identical windows and the upward-pointing buttresses produces the pronounced vertical emphasis of the Perpendicular Gothic style.

▼ **CHAPEL INTERIOR** Inside, the building reads as one huge space consisting of a series of flattened arches that hold up the intricate fan-vaulted ceiling. The enormous windows and the large areas of pale color used in the stained glass make this a very light interior, in spite of the dark wood of the Renaissance stalls and screen that fill up the lower part of the space. The chapel's high ceiling and rectangular shape produced the excellent acoustics that have led to the formation of one of the world's most famous choirs.

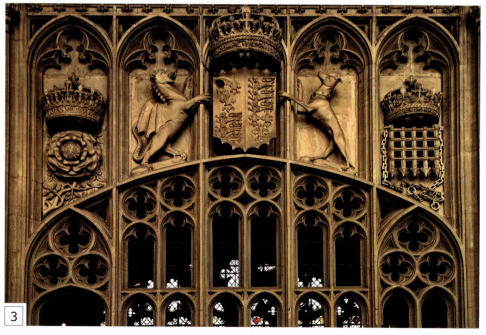

▲ **ROYAL SYMBOLS** In his original instructions for the building Henry VI told his masons to avoid elaborate moldings and carvings. The internal carving of the western part of the interior was, however, completed in 1515, during the reign of the more flamboyant Henry VIII, and this part of the chapel displays many carved royal symbols. At the center of this group is the royal coat of arms with the Welsh dragon as one of its supporters. On either side are the Tudor Rose and portcullis.

KING'S COLLEGE CHAPEL ■ UK   105

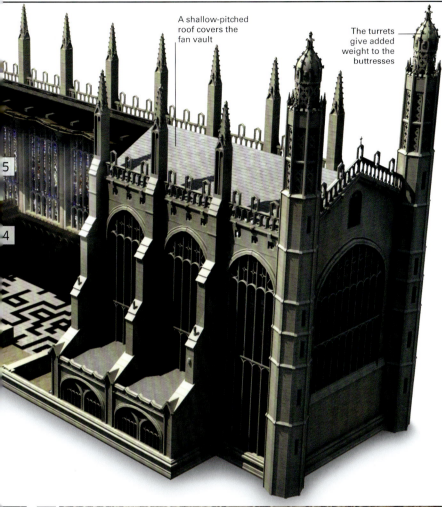

A shallow-pitched roof covers the fan vault

The turrets give added weight to the buttresses

ON DESIGN

Henry VIII brought the best artisans to Cambridge to complete the decoration of the chapel. Royal glaziers Barnard Flower and Galyon Hone (both from mainland Europe) oversaw work on the windows, which was carried out by a mixture of English and Netherlandish glass painters and designed by European artists, such as Dierick Vellert of Antwerp. At the same time another team was employed on the woodwork. The lead carver may have come from Spain, although local artists also worked on them. By bringing in European artisans to decorate the chapel, Henry VIII was introducing England to the artistic ideas of the Renaissance. The faces, poses, and colored Renaissance costumes of the realistic figures in the stained-glass windows, for example, bring to mind the portraits of other European artists attached to the court, such as Hans Holbein.

▲ **Stained glass**
The window shows the figure of the drunken Noah (right) in his vineyard.

▼ **FAN VAULT DETAIL** A close-up view of the vault reveals the intricacy of the carving. Many of the spaces between the ribs are filled with small carved crosses and tiny archlike forms similar to the tracery at the tops of the windows. At the center, where groups of four fans meet, are large projecting stones called bosses, which are carved in the shape of elaborate Tudor roses.

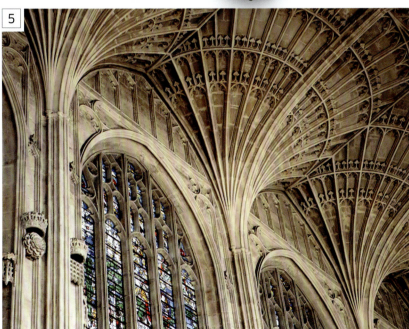

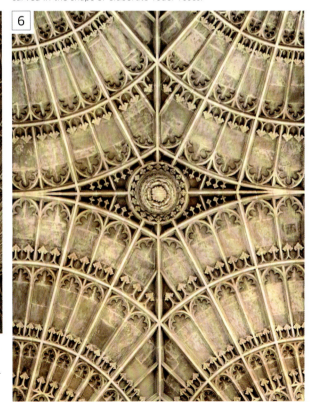

▲ **FAN VAULT** The vaulted ceiling is made up of a series of fan-shaped sections, each of which springs from a vertical pilaster running between two of the windows. The "fans" are divided up by a series of shallow ribs, which, unlike the ribs in earlier Gothic vaults, are not structural—their purpose is purely decorative. These beautifully carved and exquisitely patterned fans spread out and meet in the middle to form the largest fan-vaulted ceiling in existence.

Ducal Palace

1465-72 ▪ PALACE ▪ URBINO, ITALY

LUCIANO LAURANA

In its stunning hillside setting the Ducal Palace at Urbino is the perfect Renaissance house. It was built for Federico da Montefeltro, a war leader who employed architect Luciano Laurana to design the ultimate princely residence. Most of the famous Italian palaces of the Renaissance are symmetrical buildings with formal façades that front onto city streets or squares. Urbino is different, set on a rise, and with long, meandering walls that follow the lie of the land.

From the outside the palace looks big but plain. Reddish, clifflike walls built of locally made bricks rise high above the roofs of the surrounding town like the ramparts of a castle, except that the windows are too large for a defensible military structure. These rows of rectangular windows, some with dressed stone frames and some with plain brick surrounds, extend across the façade. Only a pair of slender round towers, topped with conical roofs, flanking stone classical arches containing balconies, signal that this building is something special as well as something huge.

Inside the gate things are quite different. At the heart of the palace is a typical feature of Renaissance design—a courtyard surrounded by a columned arcade. Here, perfectly proportioned round arches combine with sophisticated ornament to produce one of the most harmonious open-air spaces of the period.

The interiors display a similar mixture of qualities. Most rooms are plain, white-plastered, and adorned with exquisitely carved details. Others, such as the palace's two chapels (one a conventional Christian place of worship and the other a pagan "Temple of the Muses") and Federico's private *studiolo* (study), are intricately decorated. They are adorned with the best arts and crafts of the period—stunning wood inlay in the *studiolo* and marble and multi-colored stucco in the Christian chapel.

FEDERICO DA **MONTEFELTRO**

1422-82

Born the illegitimate son of Guidantonio da Montefeltro, Lord of Urbino, Federico da Montefeltro's birth was legitimized by Pope Martin V. As a young man Federico won fame as a military leader and, although involved in mercenary warfare, inspired loyalty from his men. In 1444 his half-brother Oddantonio was killed, and Federico became Duke of Urbino. He was suspected of playing a part in the murder, but this was never proved. As a war leader, Federico served the Dukes of Naples and Florence and several popes, although he had to step aside for a while after losing one eye in a tournament in 1450. From the 1460s onward he built his palace at Urbino, where he amassed an enormous library and patronized outstanding artists including Raphael. His political skill attracted the admiration of many, including the writer Niccolò Machiavelli, whose book *The Prince* is based partly on him.

Visual tour

▲ **COLONNADED COURTYARD** This arcaded inner courtyard, made in perfect Renaissance style, is in the middle of the building and provides access to a series of state rooms. Its architect, Luciano Laurana, was influenced by the work of Filippo Brunelleschi in Florence (see p.83). Laurana handled the classical elements—the semicircular arches, the pilasters (flat columns) on the walls above, and the friezes bearing inscriptions—with confidence and restraint.

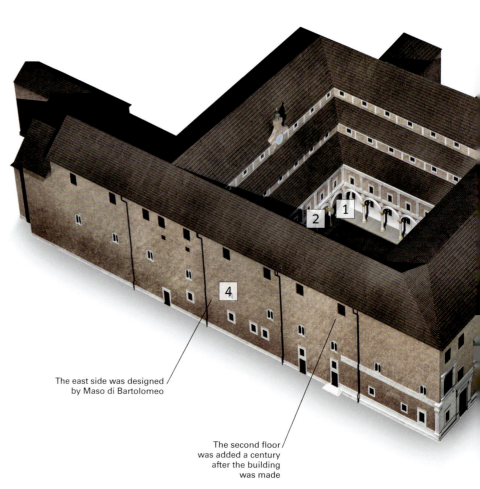

The east side was designed by Maso di Bartolomeo

The second floor was added a century after the building was made

▲ **CAPITAL** The courtyard columns are topped with ornate Corinthian capitals. Few Corinthian capitals have corner spirals that are so intricately carved. Combined with the short row of egg-and-dart molding, the effect is unusually rich. The design probably owes something to the way the Corinthian order is used on ancient Roman temples.

▲ **ARCHED BALCONIES** Between the two slender corner towers is a pair of balconies, each framed in a semicircular arch. These balconies look out over the roofs of the town and over Federico's domain, which included some 400 villages in the region.

▲ **WINDOW** On the first floor, the windows are flanked with carved stone pilasters to highlight their importance. Although classical, these window surrounds play variations on the standard motifs—only the upper two-thirds of the pilasters are fluted, for example.

DUCAL PALACE ■ ITALY

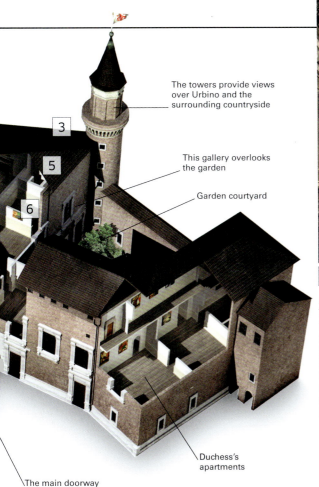

The towers provide views over Urbino and the surrounding countryside

This gallery overlooks the garden

Garden courtyard

Duchess's apartments

The main doorway leads to the entrance hall

▲ **CHAPEL OF REDEMPTION**
This high, narrow room is famous for its surface decoration. Up to cornice level, the walls are lined with panels of marble. The barrel-vaulted ceiling continues the decorative scheme in multi-colored stucco. The design is said to be the work of Venice's leading architect Pietro Lombardo.

▲ **DOORWAY** Most of the rooms in the palace have plain white walls, but many have outstanding carved fireplaces and doorways with sculpted surrounds. The best of these, alive with carved foliage, flowers, swags, and other designs, are the work of Italian sculptor Domenico Rosselli.

ON **DESIGN**

Intarsia is wooden or stone inlay used to make decorative patterns on furniture or on the walls or floors of buildings. The technique became popular in Italy in the Middle Ages, initially for abstract patterns. Around 1450 artists began to make pictorial designs, using different colored woods to create images of landscapes, still lifes, or architectural scenes. When Federico decided to decorate his most intimate room with intarsia, he employed a star artist, but no one knows who—the Florentines Baccio Pontelli and Benedetto di Maiano are the main candidates. The artist produced images of a range of subjects, from a portrait of the Duke to still lifes, animals, and a landscape.

◀ **STUDIOLO**
This small room is the most stunning space inside the palace. It served as a private study for the Duke and is lined with wooden paneling inlaid with a range of *trompe l'oeil* designs. The subjects indicate Federico's interests and include astronomical instruments, books, arms, and armor. Above the inlaid panels Federico hung a collection of portraits by the Flemish artist Joos van Wassenhove. The paintings show characters who interested or inspired the Duke—philosophers such as Plato and Aristotle, writers from Homer to Dante, and religious figures, including St. Augustine and St. Jerome.

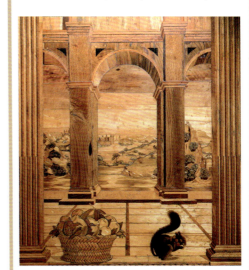

▲ **Intarsia panel in the *studiolo***
From the squirrel and basket of fruit to the landscape beyond, this panel is the work of a master.

- **BELÉM TOWER**
  Lisbon, Portugal

- **CHÂTEAU DE CHAMBORD**
  Loire Valley, France

- **ST. BASIL'S CATHEDRAL**
  Moscow, Russia

- **VILLA LA ROTONDA**
  Vicenza, Italy

- **HIMEJI CASTLE**
  Himeji, Japan

- **MASJID-I-SHAH**
  Isfahan, Iran

- **TAJ MAHAL**
  Agra, India

- **ROYAL PALACE**
  Amsterdam, Netherlands

- **PALACE OF VERSAILLES**
  Paris, France

1500–1700

Belém Tower

1515-21 ■ FORTRESS ■ LISBON, PORTUGAL

FRANCISCO DE ARRUDA

This fortified tower near the mouth of the Tagus River was a key part of Lisbon's defense system. Although the original idea came from King John II in the late-15th century, the fortress was only built in the reign of his successor, Manuel I. It is one of the best examples of the highly ornate Manueline style of architecture, which was a kind of late Gothic that was fashionable in Portugal in the early 16th century and named after the king.

The building consists of two main parts—a long, low bastion and the tower itself. The bastion houses a battery of guns in a vaulted chamber with a view over the river. The tower provides a lookout with platforms on two levels from which guards could shoot at invaders. Overhanging corner turrets known as bartizans add to the range of vantage points on both the tower and the bastion. Both parts of the building are lavishly decorated in typical Manueline style. This was designed to emphasize Portugal's success in nautical exploration. (Manuel was a notable sponsor of sea voyages.) The designs include armillary spheres and rope motifs. Heraldry is prominent too, especially the Portuguese royal coat of arms. There are also Moorish details—particularly the shapes of window openings and balconies—taken from Islamic North Africa, where the architect, Francisco de Arruda, had worked earlier in his career.

This mass of decoration, together with the elaborate architectural shape, shows that the tower was not merely a utilitarian fortress. It was also a ceremonial entrance to Lisbon harbor and a reminder to anyone approaching the port that they were entering the territory of the Portuguese king.

IN CONTEXT

King Manuel I was a prolific builder whose projects included a major royal palace, a hospital, fortifications, and several churches. During his reign at the very end of the Middle Ages Gothic architecture was becoming increasingly ornate in parts of Europe. Portugal was no exception. Among the most elaborate surviving buildings from Manuel's reign are churches, in which the rich development of the style is clear. Some have complex vaults with numerous ribs intersecting to make starlike patterns. Tall pillars, often octagonal in shape and intricately carved, support these vaults, giving the church interiors a delicate, filigree quality. A wide repertoire of decoration, including foliage and twisted-rope designs, makes the walls still more ornate and often also covers doorways and window surrounds. The Manueline style is transitional, leading away from the Gothic style and toward the new forms of the Renaissance. One example of change is the use of round-topped arches above windows and doorways, replacing the pointed forms used in earlier phases of Gothic.

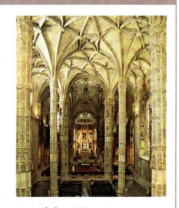

▲ **Jerónimos Monastery**
This church has one of the best examples of a Manueline interior.

Visual tour

1 ▼ BARTIZANS These turrets appear on each corner of the tower. Their purpose was to protect a watchman or archer, but they are also highly decorative. At the base of each one is a row of inverted V-shapes similar to the machicolations—holes on medieval castles—through which defenders dropped missiles on attackers. These V-shapes, however, have no holes and are purely ornamental. The stone-domed roofs with their pronounced ridges are unusual in European architecture of this period. The architect probably adapted designs he had seen on buildings in Islamic countries.

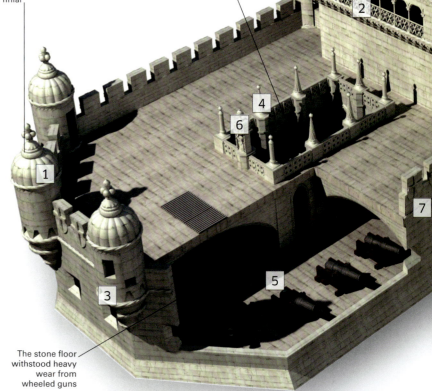

The armillary spheres symbolized Portugal's history of exploration

The cloisters connect the casemates with the upper level of the bastion

The bartizan is topped with an ornate finial

The stone floor withstood heavy wear from wheeled guns

2 ▲ LOGGIA This side of the tower, overlooking the bastion, shows the ceremonial and symbolic aspect of the building. The main feature is the arched loggia, from which dignitaries could look out over the river. Above this are carved heraldry and a pair of stone armillary spheres. The crenellations (the battlements on the next level up) bear the cross to indicate the king's allegiance to Christianity.

3 ▶ CORBELS AND MOLDINGS Carved rope moldings and corbels in the form of various animals look out from the corners. These creatures, sculpted from local limestone, have been eroded over time. One of the carvings depicts a rhinoceros, perhaps in honor of a live rhino that Manuel sent as a gift to the Pope in 1515.

BELÉM TOWER ■ PORTUGAL 115

5

CASEMATES This large vaulted room is inside the bastion. In contrast to the rest of the tower it is plain and functional. A series of casemates (arched openings) accommodates the guns, with plenty of free space behind each to allow for recoil. Smoke could escape through the adjacent cloisters or the vent hole in the ceiling.

▼ **STATUARY** During the 16th century, the Catholic church and the Portuguese crown were closely allied. As a result there are Christian symbols all over this secular building. The architect gave the place of pride to this statue of the Virgin and Child overlooking the bastion roof. Mary stands in a richly carved canopy, supported by shafts adorned with spirals and carved crosses.

The lower battlements provided an additional platform for the defending archers

▼ **FINIALS** In the center of the bastion roof, patrolling guards could look down from the balustrade on to the cloisters and gun positions below. This balustrade is adorned with a series of tall finials. From a distance they look plain, but a closer look reveals carving. The pointed finials have spiral ribs, while the round ones are topped with carved knobs in the form of armillary spheres.

ON DETAIL

Many of the motifs typical of Manueline sculpture are associated with the sea (for example, shells, coral, and seaweed) and seafaring (such as ropes, sails, and anchors). These subjects help recall Portugal's illustrious tradition of ocean voyaging and exploration. Another theme is plant forms— oak leaves, acorns, poppy seed pods, thistles, and laurel leaves are all used. Traditional decorations, such as coats of arms, were also popular. What was distinctive about Manueline decoration, however, was not only the subject matter, but also the lavish way in which it was applied to the buildings.

▲ **Coat of arms**
This carved coat of arms of King Manuel I is in a prominent position on the side of the tower.

6

7

▲ **KNOTTED ROPE** Since the early Middle Ages builders had used a form of flattened, stylized rope molding to decorate arches, but the Manueline architects used this motif more freely, boldly carving three-dimensional rope ornament. Here, a carving of a length of rope has been twisted into a knot on the side of the building to catch the sun and add interest to an otherwise plain stretch of wall.

4

Château de Chambord

c.1519–47 ■ CASTLE ■ LOIRE VALLEY, FRANCE

DOMENICO DA CORTONA

The most famous of the Loire châteaus, Chambord was commissioned by King François I as a base for hunting and entertaining. Its location was conveniently near the home of one of the king's last mistresses, the Comtesse de Thoury. Chambord took almost 30 years to build, and the structure that emerged defined a new French Renaissance style, influenced mainly by fashionable Italian architecture but also partly by the earlier French castles of the Middle Ages.

Although sources differ, the main architect of the castle seems to have been an Italian, Domenico da Cortona. Other architects may well have been involved, perhaps in modifying his design during the lengthy construction period. Cortona planned the building along the lines of a medieval castle, with a moat, an outer wall, an inner wall with corner towers, and a central block corresponding to a castle donjon (keep), but unlike a medieval castle, the château was not fortified. Instead of the narrow arrow

slits of a medieval castle, it has rows of large rectangular windows in the Renaissance style, making it look more like a palace than a fortress. The Italian Renaissance influence is also shown by other details, including the stone columns, pilasters (vertical protrusions), and moldings.

Many aspects of the building, however, are quite different. Where an Italian palace would have a flat-fronted façade, Chambord's elevation is broken up with towers. Instead of being hidden behind a parapet, the roof is visible, set with dormer windows and adorned with tall ornate chimneys and turrets topped with cupolas (domed roofs). Many of these details, especially the elaborate roofs, became hallmarks of grand French buildings for centuries. Others, such as the luxurious interiors, the high barrel-vaulted halls, and the inventive double-spiral stone staircase, are special features of Chambord that make it such a magnificent building and a fitting residence for a great Renaissance ruler.

DOMENICO DA **CORTONA**

c.1465–1549

Trained in his native Italy, Domenico da Cortona worked for the Florentine architect and sculptor Giuliano da Sangallo, who was also a military engineer. Domenico moved to France to work for King Charles VIII, who may have been attracted by his military engineering experience. Cortona continued in the royal service when François I came to the throne, working on military projects and designing settings for royal celebrations, such as those surrounding the birth of the heir to the throne in 1518. In France Domenico also worked on buildings in Paris, including the Hôtel de Ville (demolished in the 19th century) and the church of Saint-Eustache. In these he displayed his ability to mix Renaissance and Gothic styles—Saint-Eustache, for example, is built on the Gothic model, with high stone vaults and flying buttresses, but has Renaissance-style windows and other details. The architect skillfully blended old and new styles when planning the Château de Chambord, although his design may have been altered later.

Visual tour

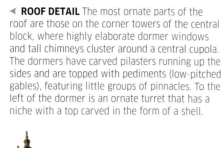

1 ◀ ROOF DETAIL The most ornate parts of the roof are those on the corner towers of the central block, where highly elaborate dormer windows and tall chimneys cluster around a central cupola. The dormers have carved pilasters running up the sides and are topped with pediments (low-pitched gables), featuring little groups of pinnacles. To the left of the dormer is an ornate turret that has a niche with a top carved in the form of a shell.

As in a medieval castle the central block houses the principal rooms

The outer range occupies the position of a castle's curtain wall

2 ▲ CAPITAL These carved column heads show variations on standard classical design. Ancient Roman capitals of the Composite order have acanthus leaves topped by spiral scrolls. In contrast the Chambord capitals have acanthus with openwork scrolls in the shape of inverted Cs, and tiny carved heads.

▶ EXTERIOR STAIRCASE A pair of spiral staircases set in polygonal, open-stone turrets links the floors of the building in the corners of the main courtyard. People ascending or descending can look out over the courtyard through arched openings between Renaissance columns. The stone balusters of the stairway cut diagonally across the openings, breaking the rigid symmetry.

CHÂTEAU DE CHAMBORD ■ FRANCE

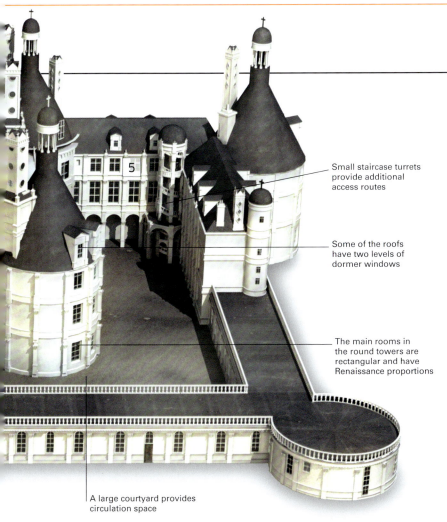

5 — Small staircase turrets provide additional access routes

Some of the roofs have two levels of dormer windows

The main rooms in the round towers are rectangular and have Renaissance proportions

A large courtyard provides circulation space

IN **CONTEXT**

The Château de Chambord was designed to reflect François I's personality and achievements. Its grandeur represented the king's power, and its contemporary design his sophistication. François liked to link himself with the ideas of the Italian Renaissance and even employed Leonardo da Vinci as court artist. Some believe that da Vinci had a hand in the design, but there is no hard evidence. What is clear is that Chambord bears the stamp of its extravagant owner, from the many uses of the king's initial (F) to the ubiquitous presence of his personal symbol, the salamander, which is said to make more than 700 appearances in the château. This creature was a powerful motif: cold-blooded salamanders were said to be able to withstand extreme heat and to extinguish fires. The creature was also associated with the practice of alchemy. Da Vinci wrote about the salamander's amazing abilities and may have influenced the king's choice of the animal as his personal motif.

▲ **Salamander**
This is one of the many carvings of salamanders at Chambord. The crown indicates that it is a royal emblem.

◀ **BEDROOM** Since its construction the château has been redecorated several times, and many of the rooms have lost their 16th- and 17th-century interiors. A few rooms, however, survive in the original style. One example is this bedroom, which has a painted ceiling, gilded cornices, and tapestries on the walls. It is furnished with a four-poster bed with rich hangings and carved woodwork in the Renaissance style.

◀ **DOUBLE STAIRCASE** The most inventive staircase in the château is in the central block, connecting grand rooms such as this spacious stone-vaulted hall. It is a double-spiral staircase, with two stairs in one, arranged so that the king and his family using one staircase would never see the servants, who took the other. The twin stairs are housed in an openwork shaft with classical details similar to, but more restrained than, the stairs in the courtyard.

▲ **CHAPEL** The chapel in the western wing of the château was completed after the death of François I by his son and heir Henri II, under whom construction work continued. This interior is in the same Renaissance style as the rest of the building, with a barrel-vaulted ceiling, classical pilasters, and attached columns that run up and down the walls. The main windows are at the east end, behind the altar, and bear the initial H, commemorating the king in whose reign the room was completed.

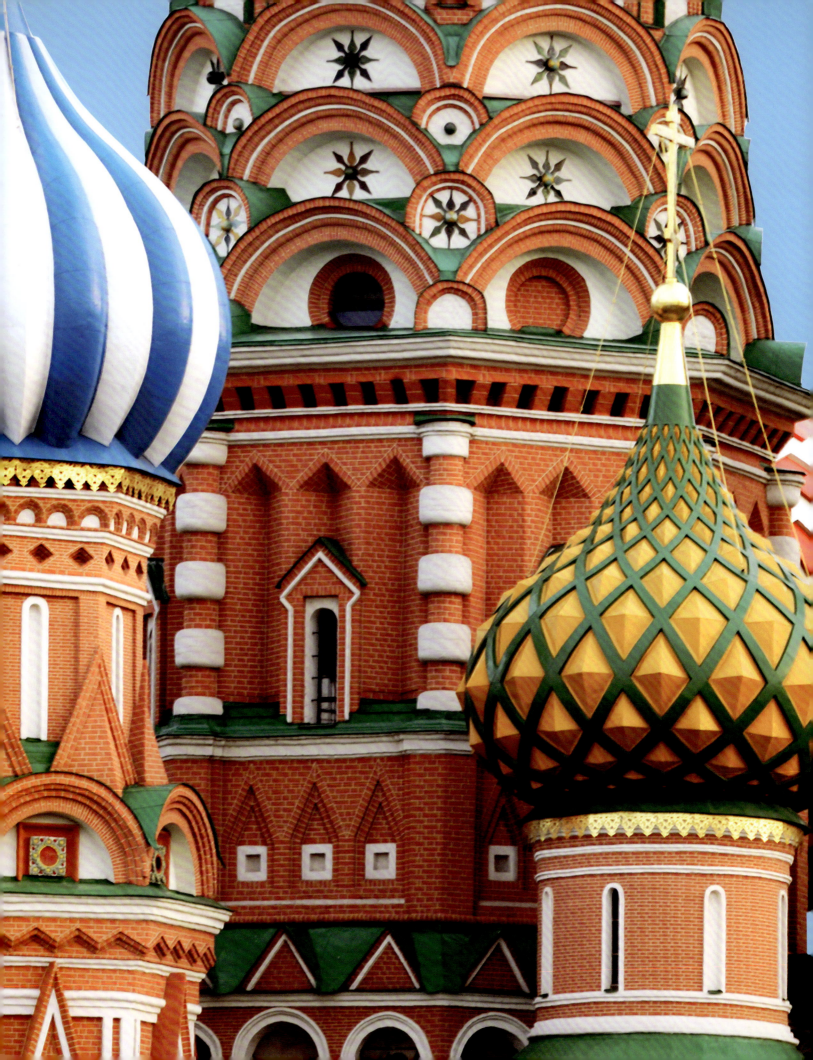

St. Basil's Cathedral

c.1561 ▪ CATHEDRAL ▪ MOSCOW, RUSSIA

POSTNIK YAKOVLEV

This unique building, usually known as St. Basil's Cathedral, but more correctly called the Cathedral of the Protection of Most Holy Theotokos on the Moat, is one of Russia's most distinctive sights. Built by Tsar Ivan IV (Ivan the Terrible) to commemorate his defeat of the Mongols at the Battle of Kazan in 1552, it stands just outside the Kremlin in Red Square, in the heart of Moscow. Its extraordinary onion-shaped domes, painted in bright colors, create a memorable skyline, making St. Basil's a symbol both of Moscow and of Russia as a whole.

Although the cathedral looks asymmetrical from the outside, with its domes rising apparently at random, the plan of the building is in fact highly structured. The main church stands at the center and eight chapels are arranged around it—four at the cardinal points of the compass, and a further four between them. Each of these side chapels has its own distinctive tower, capped by an onion dome, and is linked to the others by narrow, winding passages. This plan is based on an eight-pointed star—a potent Christian symbol because it is the shape of the New Jerusalem as described in the Book of Revelation. The Virgin Mary is also often shown in the paintings and icons of the Orthodox churches wearing a veil decorated with eight-pointed stars.

The planning and design of the building are unusual, and little is known about the architect said to be responsible for it. Some historians have found the building's architectural roots in the wooden churches built in northern Russia in the period before this cathedral was constructed. They were possibly also influenced by the domed churches of the Byzantine empire (see pp.32–37), while certain details, such as the brickwork in the vaults, suggest that some of the builders may have come from western or central Europe.

IVAN IV

c.1530–84

Known in the West as Ivan the Terrible, the Muscovite prince Ivan IV was the first person to be crowned Tsar of all Russia, a title he took in 1547. He began his reign with legal and governmental reforms, forming assemblies of the nobility and restructuring local government in the provinces. He also developed Russian trade and led successful military campaigns against the Khanates of Kazan, Siberia, and Astrakhan, hugely expanding his power and turning Russia into a vast empire. His later reign was, however, dogged by problems. After his first wife died and Ivan himself survived a serious illness, the Tsar suspected nobles of killing the Empress and trying to poison him. He cracked down on their power, launched costly wars, and massacred his enemies in Russia. His reign ended in terror, but he left a legacy of centralized power that influenced the way Russia was ruled for centuries.

Visual tour

▶ **BRICKWORK** It is easy to miss the fact that this polychrome building is a masterpiece of brickwork. Millions of bricks must have been used in the construction of St. Basil's, including some specially made to create the intricate details of the towers and façades. This section from one of the towers has a repeating motif of brick arches, some of which have circular brickwork openings inside. Smaller arches link the large ones.

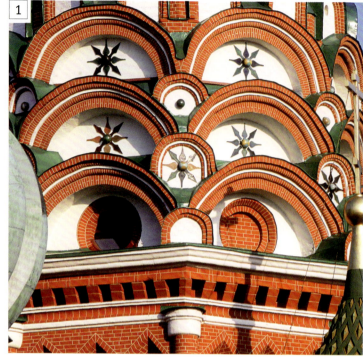

▲ **CENTRAL SPIRE** A tall brick spire crowns the central church at the heart of the cathedral. It is raised up on an octagonal brick tower and soars above the rest of the building. The architects based this shape on that of Russian churches, such as the church of the Ascension at Kolomenskoye, which was built in 1532 and also has a tall octagonal spire. St. Basil's spire, however, has an additional small onion dome, which enhances the skyline.

ON DESIGN

The cathedral has gone through several phases of decoration. Early in its history, parts of the building were plastered and covered with fresco decoration that imitated brickwork, while others were adorned with floral murals, many of which date from the 17th century. 19th-century restorers added a number of murals in oil-based paints. More recent conservationists have removed these and restored the original floral decorations, replacing them where necessary.

▲ **Flower motif**
This mural on the entrance wall dates from a recent restoration and reproduces 17th-century work.

▶ **DOME DETAIL** Each of the domes has its own dazzling form of decoration, ranging from prisms and spirals to chevrons and stripes, all emphasized with brilliant colors. The color is unusual—most Russian domes are either plain or gilded. Originally, the domes at St. Basil's had a gold finish with some blue and green ceramic decoration. The bright, painted colors were added at various times from the 17th to the 19th century.

ST. BASIL'S CATHEDRAL ▪ RUSSIA

A short spire marks the church dedicated to St. Basil

The octagonal "drum" of brick increases the height of the dome

This onion dome was originally tin-clad and is now covered in painted copper

This is the dome of one of the eight chapels arranged around the central church

Brickwork patterns adorn the walls

Cathedral entrance

The outer "galleries" were walled in during the 17th century

▲ **GALLERY** The cathedral's interior was extended in the 1680s, when builders walled in an open arcade that ran around the outside. This created a gallery, in which altars taken from 13 nearby wooden churches were placed. At the same time, artists adorned the passages within the cathedral with murals, mostly with curvaceous designs of flowering plants.

▼ **CENTRAL CHURCH** The cathedral's central church is dedicated to the Intercession of the Most Holy Theotokos ("God-bearer," a Greek title used for the Virgin Mary in Orthodox churches). It is larger inside than the surrounding chapels but is still compact. It is narrow and extremely tall—the ceiling is some 150ft (46m) above the floor.

▶ **WALL OF ICONS**
The iconostasis (a wall or screen of icons) stands between the nave and sanctuary in Orthodox churches. It separates the "public" space of the nave from the church's holiest part, which is mainly the domain of the priests. The icons depict Jesus Christ, the Virgin Mary, saints, and the Apostles. They are traditionally displayed in five tiers, and a set of rules dictates their exact arrangement.

Villa La Rotonda

1567–c.1592 ■ COUNTRY HOUSE ■ VICENZA, ITALY

ANDREA PALLADIO

Set on a hilltop in northern Italy, the supremely elegant Villa La Rotonda is the most famous of the country houses designed by the Renaissance architect Andrea Palladio for noble families from Venice and the surrounding area, the Veneto. In these houses, which served as rural retreats for sophisticated clients, details drawn from classical Roman architecture were combined with a very formal geometry in which, for example, rooms might be planned as perfect circles or squares. La Rotonda is in some ways the most perfect of these villas. It has inspired the admiration of architects and visitors alike for its classical design, rigorous symmetry, and outstanding setting.

Palladio designed the villa for Paolo Almerico, a high-ranking, retired clergyman. He laid out the house as a perfect square, with the main rooms located on the first floor above a low basement. Each of the four elevations is fronted by a columned portico at the top of a broad flight of exterior steps. Inside, a corridor leads from each portico

to the two rooms on either side, and ends in a stunning, circular hall topped by a shallow dome. Apart from slight variations, each of the four façades is identical and the rooms are exactly the same size and proportions, making the building perfectly symmetrical both inside and out—a symmetry that Palladio wanted to be immediately clear.

The house was not finished exactly as Palladio designed it, partly because he died before the dome and exterior stairs had been completed. The work was continued by his pupil and assistant, Vincenzo Scamozzi, who oversaw the building of a dome that was shallower than the one in Palladio's published drawing of the house. The interior is decorated with frescoes depicting mythological subjects, which were also completed after Palladio's death and may not follow his plans. Nonetheless, La Rotonda is an outstanding building, and its embodiment of classical grandeur on a domestic scale has inspired generations of architects.

ANDREA **PALLADIO**

1508-80

Often described as the first great professional architect, Andrea Palladio was born in Padua, Italy, and worked first as a stonemason. He studied architecture thanks to the patronage of Giangiorgio Trissino, a philosopher and amateur architect who encouraged Palladio to read the Roman architectural writer Vitruvius, and who accompanied him on visits to Rome. In 1549 Palladio won a competition to remodel an early Renaissance palace in Vicenza, and over the next 30 years he became very successful, designing many churches, palaces, and villas, especially in and around Vicenza and Venice. Palladio's buildings drew upon his study of the architecture of ancient Rome. The columns at the front of many of his villas and churches such as S. Giorgio Maggiore and Il Redentore in Venice, for example, were based upon those of Roman temples. His famous Teatro Olimpico, Vicenza, was also influenced by classical models. Palladio's reputation increased with the publication of his books, especially *I Quattro libri dell'architettura* (The Four Books of Architecture), which were widely translated and had a lasting influence on architects all over Europe.

Visual tour

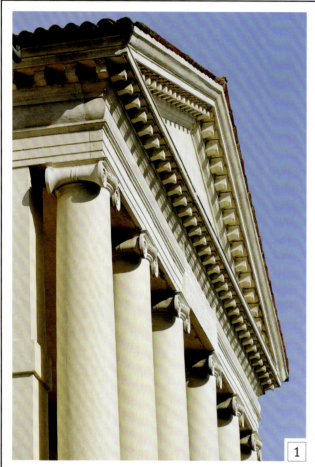

▶ **PORTICO STATUE** Adorning the pediments of the Villa La Rotonda are 12 large statues, carved by Giovanni Battista Albanese at the end of the 16th century. Although they were added after Palladio's death, he did include statues in his drawing of the house, and they suit the building well, adding interest to its skyline. The statues represent Roman gods and goddesses. This one is probably Diana, the goddess of the hunt.

◀ **PORTICO** Each of the villa's four entrance porticoes is designed in a similar way, with six Ionic columns topped by an entablature (a horizontal band of masonry) and a triangular pediment. The layout and proportions of the porticoes draw on Roman models such as the Pantheon (see pp.28-31), and the effect is quite austere. The columns are unfluted, the entablature has simple moldings, and the pediment a plain center, but its course of small square blocks creates a strong pattern of light and shadow.

A plain pediment conceals the pitched roof

The statues were added later but conform with Palladio's overall plans

▲ **DOME INTERIOR** The centerpiece of the villa, the dome, with its magnificent balustrade and central lantern, establishes the decorative scheme of the interior. When Palladio began work on the house, he planned to leave an open hole or oculus at the top of the dome, like that of the Pantheon in Rome. This would have increased the amount of light in the hall, but the idea must have proved impractical, and the design was altered. The frescoes, which depict allegorical subjects such as the virtues, were added during the 17th century when the villa was owned by the Capra family.

VILLA LA ROTONDA ▪ ITALY

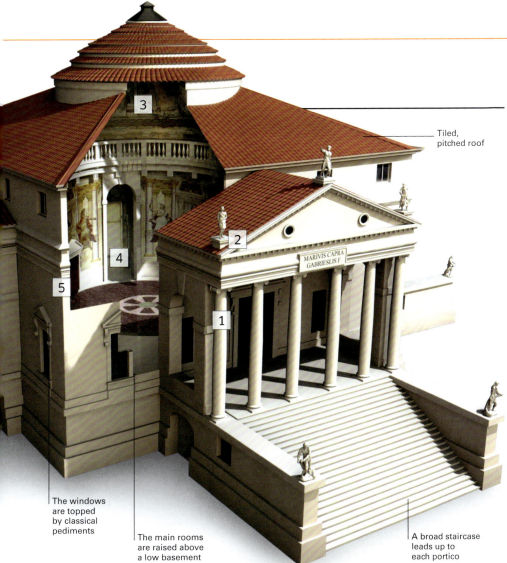

- Tiled, pitched roof
- The windows are topped by classical pediments
- The main rooms are raised above a low basement
- A broad staircase leads up to each portico

ON SITE

Most of Palladio's villas were located at the heart of country estates, and there were usually farm buildings close to the house. La Rotonda is different. Palladio wanted this perfect building, set in a hilly region southeast of Vicenza, to be seen in isolation. There were no adjacent farm buildings, and the house originally stood on its own, although auxiliary buildings were added later. The building's setting on a hill meant that it could be seen and admired from a distance, but more important were the wonderful views from the villa itself. With large windows and porticoes on all four sides the occupants could look out across the surrounding landscape in four different directions. As Palladio wrote, "The loveliest hills are arranged all around it, and afford a view into an immense theater."

▲ **Aerial view**
The surrounding fields still come up very close to the paths around La Rotonda, bringing the villa and the countryside together.

◀ **CENTRAL HALL** The circular hall lies at the center of the building, where the four entrance corridors meet, and is lavishly decorated. The floor is made from precious Venetian *battuto*, a type of stucco made by mixing lime with fragments of colored marble, and the walls are covered with frescoes depicting mythological figures and scenes, some of which were painted as late as the 18th century. The artist has skillfully used the *trompe l'oeil* technique to integrate his paintings of columns with the real, three-dimensional architecture of the grandiose door frames, which are surmounted by sculptures.

▲ **CEILING PAINTINGS** The paintings on the ceilings of the smaller rooms at each corner of the villa, which correspond to the four points of the compass, were created at the same time as those in the central dome. They are all thought to be the work of the mannerist artist Alessandro Maganza, who was born in Vicenza and worked in Venice. The paintings are arranged as a series of small rectangular and circular inset images. They are set off by a pale background that continues down the coved cornice, which is richly decorated with plasterwork by the renowned stucco artist Agostino Rubini.

IN CONTEXT

Palladio's book, *I Quattro libri dell'architettura*, proved very popular among both architects and clients. People liked it because the text explained classical architecture clearly, provided easy-to-follow rules for construction, and included plans and drawings of real buildings, including La Rotonda. Architects were strongly influenced by it—in England alone there were Palladian movements in the 17th and 18th centuries, and the style even spread to the US, inspiring houses such as Monticello (see pp.168–71). Both Chiswick House in London and Mereworth Castle, also in the UK, were closely modeled on La Rotonda.

▲ **Chiswick House**
This London house, built for Lord Burlington, is very similar to La Rotonda, except that it has only two porticoes and the dome is higher.

1500–1700

Himeji Castle

1601–18 ■ CASTLE ■ HIMEJI, JAPAN

ARCHITECT UNKNOWN

Impressive and beautiful, Himeji is one of the greatest of the Japanese castles built by the country's feudal *daimyo* (warlords) during the 16th and 17th centuries. Himeji consists of a cluster of structures, built mainly between 1601 and 1618 on the site of an earlier castle. It is centered on a tall tower linked to four smaller towers by corridors and surrounded by walls and gates. Like most castles of the period, it was designed not only as a fortress but also as a luxurious, high-status residence for the powerful warlord and his family who occupied it.

The outer walls have massive stone bases and upper sections made of dried mud, sometimes with embedded metal plates—construction materials that made the castle not only fire-resistant but also virtually impossible to knock down. To get inside Himeji, invaders had to pass through a series of gates, each approached by a narrow walkway, making the central part of the castle almost impregnable.

At the heart of the building are several towers that contain storerooms, living accommodation, arsenals, and firing platforms for both marksmen and archers. In construction these towers have wooden frameworks that could be prefabricated by carpenters while masons built their solid, stone bases. The wooden surfaces are also coated in white plaster—a further precaution against the risk of fire. Defenders could shoot out through purpose-built slatted openings, and special chutes or "stone-dropping windows" enabled them to drop missiles on attackers who attempted to scale the castle walls.

Himeji's substantial yet elegant structure is enhanced by stunning details, including multiple pointed and curved gables, carved bargeboards, overhanging roofs, and ornate finials. The interiors combine exposed natural wooden beams with magnificent, large-scale painted panels, often depicting scenes from nature, which was revered in Japanese culture.

IKEDA TERUMASA

1565–1613

A *daimyo* of the Japanese early Edo period, Ikeda Terumasa was a noted samurai warrior who was involved in extended military campaigns in western Japan in the late-16th century. In 1600 he fought in the Battle of Sekigahara, a conflict between clans over the right to become the Shogun – the official who was second-in-command to the emperor and virtual ruler of Japan. Ikeda and his contingent of 4,560 warriors fought for Tokugawa Ieyasu, his father-in-law. Tokugawa won the battle and subsequently became Shogun. As a reward Tokugawa gave Ikeda the castle of Himeji together with its extensive dependent lands, which brought in a huge income. Ikeda rebuilt the stronghold to create one of the largest castles in Japan, increasing his power, wealth, and influence to such an extent that by the time he died he was sometimes referred to as the "Shogun of Western Japan."

Visual tour

1 ▲ **ACCESS WAY** The castle is carefully planned so that entrance routes and access ways to the various courtyards and towers are narrow and winding. Any enemy who had managed to break into the castle would find their progress severely impeded, and only two people at most would be able to walk abreast. The main access way rises, bends, and in some places, doubles back on itself, confusing attackers. It also passes through numerous gates and occasionally takes the form of a dark passage. At each stage the route runs past numerous defensive walls, some with shooting holes for defenders to take aim and fire.

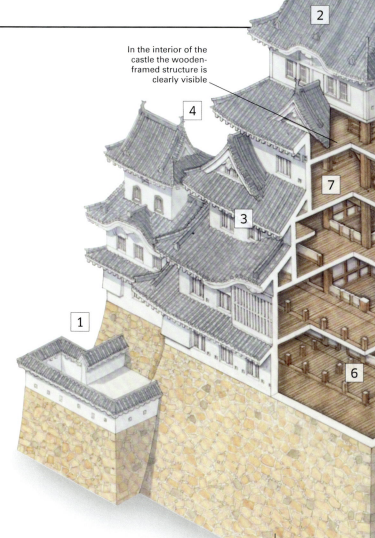

In the interior of the castle the wooden-framed structure is clearly visible

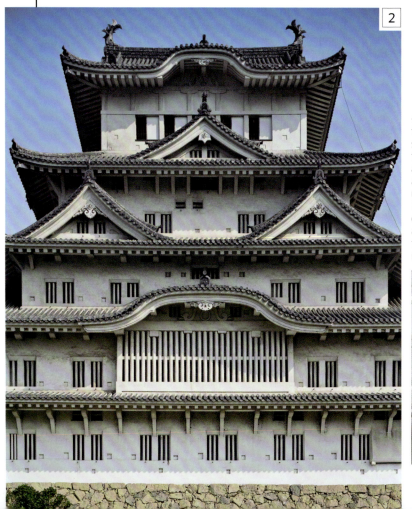

2 ◀ **TOWER** From their solid stone bases, the castle's towers rise to multiple stories. The lowest level of the main tower, enclosed in the stone base, was a storage area for essential supplies, such as rice and salt, and also had a well. The upper levels contained a mixture of living accommodation and places where defenders could keep watch and fire on attackers. Archers aimed their arrows through the slender openings in the rows of slatted windows.

The supporting walls are constructed of massive stones, strengthened with even larger blocks at the corners

3 ◀ **ROOF DETAIL** Straight and curved ceramic tiles cover the castle's overhanging, upturned roofs. These tiles provided better protection from attack by fire than other traditional roof coverings, such as thatch. The roofs are also decorative— the rounded ends of the tiles could be stamped with the *mon*, or heraldic symbol, of the warlord who occupied the castle.

HIMEJI CASTLE ■ JAPAN   131

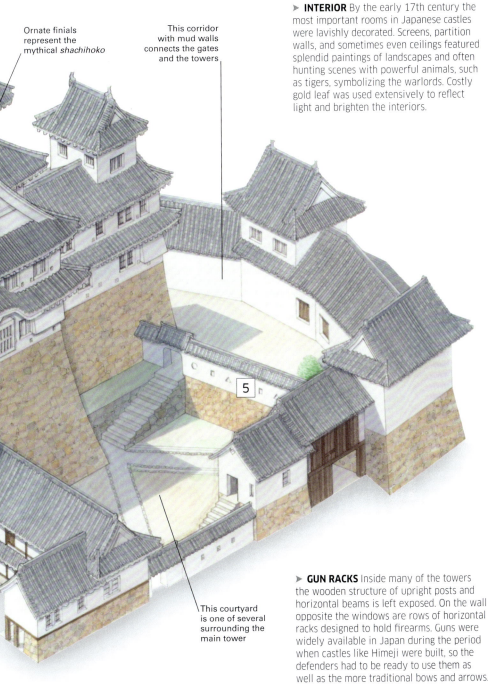

Ornate finials represent the mythical *shachihoko*

This corridor with mud walls connects the gates and the towers

This courtyard is one of several surrounding the main tower

▶ **INTERIOR** By the early 17th century the most important rooms in Japanese castles were lavishly decorated. Screens, partition walls, and sometimes even ceilings featured splendid paintings of landscapes and often hunting scenes with powerful animals, such as tigers, symbolizing the warlords. Costly gold leaf was used extensively to reflect light and brighten the interiors.

▶ **GUN RACKS** Inside many of the towers the wooden structure of upright posts and horizontal beams is left exposed. On the wall opposite the windows are rows of horizontal racks designed to hold firearms. Guns were widely available in Japan during the period when castles like Himeji were built, so the defenders had to be ready to use them as well as the more traditional bows and arrows.

◀ **GUARDIAN BEAST** The roofs of Himeji feature 11 carved mythical creatures, called *shachihoko*, with the body of a tiger and the tail of a fish. They are depicted with their tails in the air, which suggests they are creating waves. On a symbolic level the falling water would protect the building from fire. These mythical creatures are common on Japanese castles and are usually arranged in male and female pairs, one on either end of the roof ridge.

◀ **WALLS AND LOOPHOLES** The lower walls are built of local stone that was left uncut and laid randomly. Some of these structures are ramparts built against an earth bank, while others are thick walls with outer "skins" of stones and a filling of earth and rubble. Both form a solid base, above which are smoother earth walls, covered in bright, white plaster. Along the earth walls are a number of holes—round, rectangular, and triangular—designed for firing guns.

1500–1700

Masjid-i-Shah

c.1611–30 ■ MOSQUE ■ ISFAHAN, IRAN

OSTAD SHAYKH BAHAI

The soaring turquoise dome of its prayer hall and the intricate design of the tiled decoration are just two of the elements that make the Masjid-i-Shah one of the most beautiful buildings in the Islamic world. It was constructed during the reign of the powerful Safavid dynasty, whose huge empire centered on Persia (modern Iran). Their great ruler, Shah Abbas I, moved the Safavid capital to Isfahan and began a major rebuilding program with the Masjid-i-Shah as the city's principal mosque, with a grand entrance on the south side of the new central square.

The Masjid-i-Shah is an outstanding example of Safavid architecture. Like most of the great mosques of the time, its prayer hall is roofed with a dome that covers a single huge space, in contrast to the prayer halls of the earliest mosques, which had a forest of pillars supporting the roof. As well as providing excellent acoustics, this spatial arrangement was practical, since it meant that the mosque could accommodate a large congregation, and it became popular in places where the resources were available to build a large dome. Masjid-i-Shah's curving dome is also astonishingly decorative, with its covering of brightly colored tiles bearing stunning Islamic patterns.

The building has another key feature of a major Persian mosque—a large courtyard with several elaborate *iwans* (gateways). This courtyard plan was popular for large mosques, partly because it provided a place where members of the congregation could perform their ablutions before entering the prayer hall. The courtyard also provided scope for buildings leading off it, such as the religious school and winter prayer hall at Masjid-i-Shah. Throughout the complex the design of the details—especially in prominent parts of the building, such as the tops of the minarets and the *iwans*—is meticulous and reveals innovations in ceramic technology, such as the use of deep shades of brilliant color.

ON SITE

Shah Abbas I ruled Persia from 1587 to 1629. The most successful of the Safavid rulers, he reorganized the Persian government, creating a centralized administration in his new capital city, Isfahan. To make this a fitting center, Shah Abbas undertook an extensive building program with his architect and planner, Ostad Shaykh Bahai. The city was redeveloped around a vast central avenue and a large open space, Naqsh-e Jahan Square. The square was the site of the Masjid-i-Shah, the Ali Qapu Palace (the royal residence from which Shah Abbas governed and where he entertained visiting dignitaries), and the imperial bazaar, one of the biggest in the Islamic world. The mosque's prayer hall faces Mecca. By arranging these key buildings around a square, Shah Abbas drew together his kingdom's powerful institutions—the monarchy, the merchants, and the clergy—so that he could exercise control from a central point.

▲ **Setting** The mosque is set at a 45-degree angle to the square.

Visual tour

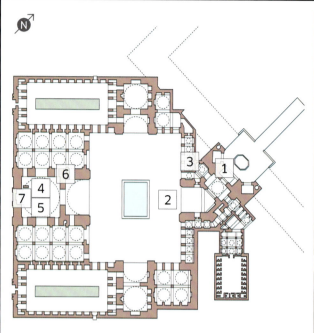

▼ **IWAN** The four tall entrance gateways, or *iwans*, are among the most striking features of the courtyard. Each consists of a large pointed archway surrounded by walls that rise to form a rectangle and, in the case of the two *iwans* that lead to the prayer hall, are topped with slender minarets. Inside each opening is a vaulted space with intricate, stalactite decoration that contains the doorway.

▲ **COURTYARD** On each side of the mosque courtyard an *iwan* is framed by rows of arches in a two-story arcade. This arrangement creates a satisfying symmetry that is reinforced by the patterns of the decorative tiles and the reflections in the central pool. The Safavids did not use minarets for the call to prayer. Instead, they built a *goldast*—a small rectangular structure with a pyramidal roof—on top of one of the *iwans*, and from here the muezzin would call the faithful.

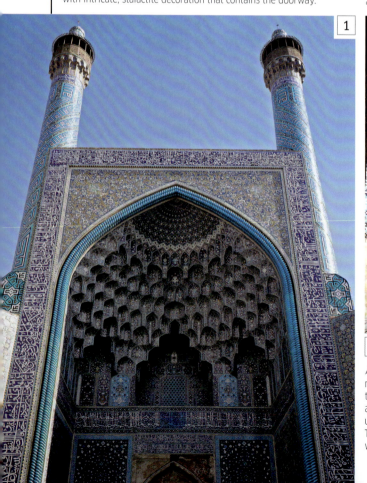

▲ **ARCADE INTERIOR** The arcades that run around the mosque courtyard are supported by the flattened arches that were popular in Islamic architecture. Their ceilings are vaulted in a star pattern, and both the ceilings and upper parts of the walls are covered in ceramic tiles. These sophisticated spaces were appreciated by worshipers—they offered shade from the hot sun.

MASJID-I-SHAH ■ IRAN

ON DESIGN

Colored ceramic tiles were widely used to cover walls and floors in western Asia even in pre-Islamic times. By the 13th century they were popular in Persia and the surrounding area, and Persian artists developed the use of tiled mosaics, cutting small cubes (tesserae) of tile and arranging them to make intricate patterns. By the 16th century, however, tiles painted in more than one color were popular, not only on account of the visual effects they created but also because applying colored glazes to a single tile before firing was faster than assembling patterns out of thousands of tiny tesserae. The Masjid-i-Shah's tiles display an impressive color palette, with dark and light blues dominating, in combination with small areas of yellow, black, white, green, and beige.

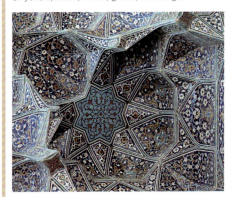

▲ **Tiling detail**
The patterns in this piece of vaulting show a skillful use of blue, white, and yellow in a flowerlike pattern that yields more and more detail when viewed closely.

▲ **DOME INTERIOR** The deep blues and golds of the dome's glazed tiling give out a rich glow. The architects made the transition from octagonal spaces to circular dome by building a series of triangles called squinches above the arches. These triangles are divided into a series of three-sided and diamond-shaped facets, and this treatment, together with the tile patterns, makes the structure appear much less massive. The builders found that such a space had excellent acoustics.

◀ **DOME EXTERIOR** Persian architects were notable builders of domes and had used them to roof mosques since at least the 12th century. Masjid-i-Shah's is one of the biggest and most decorative. It has a double-skin structure, the outer layer rising some 174ft (53m) and the inner dome about 46ft (14m) lower. This method of construction allowed the builders to create the tallest dome in the city, while keeping the interior ceiling at a lower, more aesthetically pleasing level. On the outside the masonry drum on which the dome sets forms a horizontal band that is covered with ceramics bearing inscriptions from the *Qur'an*. The dome's decoration consists of artistic, curling arabesque forms.

▶ **MINARET** Although not fulfilling the usual function of minarets, those at Masjid-i-Shah are prominent architectural features. Arranged on either side of the two principal *iwans*, they act as signposts to show worshipers the main route to the prayer hall and are covered in intricately patterned tiles. At the top each minaret broadens to accommodate a balcony, and this is supported by corbels treated in the multi-faceted stalactite form much favored by Safavid architects. The balustrade of the balcony, with its openwork pattern, is beautifully carved and finished.

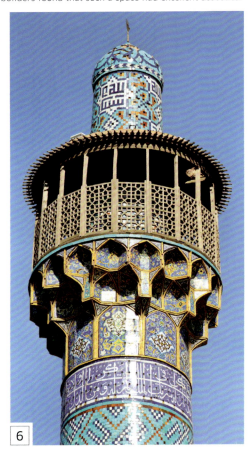

▲ **MIHRAB** A niche in one interior wall of the prayer hall (here the southwest wall), the mihrab indicates the direction of Mecca and therefore the way the congregation should face during prayers. As in most major mosques the mihrab at Masjid-i-Shah, with its multifaceted vaulting and rich blue-and-gold tiling, has been designed and decorated with great visual flair. Some of the tiles bear inscriptions, and sacred calligraphy runs vertically up and down the sides.

Taj Mahal

C.1648CE ▪ MUGHAL MAUSOLEUM ▪ AGRA, INDIA

ARCHITECT UNKNOWN

A vision of shimmering white marble, the Taj Mahal was built by the Mughal emperor, Shah Jahan, as a mausoleum for his favorite wife, Mumtaz Mahal, who died shortly after giving birth to her fourteenth child in 1631. Work began the following year, and the structure was finally completed in 1648, while the landscaping of the gardens and the construction of the surrounding buildings continued for several more years. At the end of his life, Shah Jahan was also entombed in the Taj Mahal alongside his wife.

From the mid-16th century onward, the Mughal rulers began to create a distinctive style of architecture and built a number of notable tombs for members of the royal family. The simplest of these were cube-shaped stone or brick structures, surmounted with a dome. Other, more elaborate tombs included the mausoleum of the emperor Humayun in Delhi. Built according to a complex plan and featuring a central octagonal hall, Humayun's tomb shares many features with the Taj Mahal and had a strong influence on its design. The identity of the architect of Mumtaz Mahal's mausoleum has not been established, but it may have been Ustad Ahmad, who designed other buildings for Shah Jahan, including Delhi's grand Red Fort.

Although influenced by earlier buildings, the proportions of the Taj Mahal—the symmetry of the large and small arches, the relationship between the central onion-shaped dome and the smaller domes of the minarets, and the way the building is set on its raised terrace—combine to place the building in a category of its own. Its graceful quality is further enhanced by the canal of still water in front of it, which creates a mirror image of the building, and by the carvings on the white marble façades, inlaid with colored stone. Supremely intricate and of great beauty, they add exquisite pattern and texture.

SHAH **JAHAN**

c.1592–1666CE

The fifth emperor of the Mughal dynasty and grandson of the great emperor Akbar, Shah Jahan became the ruler of India in 1627. An able, vigorous ruler, he improved and centralized the Mughal administration while at the same time spending many years on military campaigns in order to expand and consolidate his empire. Shah Jahan was a notable patron of the arts, from painting to poetry, but he is remembered above all for his architectural achievements. An enthusiastic commissioner of buildings, he constructed the magnificent Red Fort and the Jama Masjid mosque in Delhi, parts of the fort at Lahore, and a mausoleum for his father, Jahangir. While still a teenager, Shah Jahan married Arjumand Banu Begam, who became known as Mumtaz Mahal (jewel of the palace) and, despite taking other wives, he was devastated by her death and remained devoted to her. Shah Jahan's reign ended when he became ill in 1658. After a dispute, the throne passed to his son Aurangzeb.

Visual tour: exterior

1 ◀ **THE DOME** Raised on a "drum" of masonry to give it extra height, the central dome rises to some 200ft (61m). The white marble masonry bulges to give the dome its onion-shaped exterior, but the inner ceiling has straight sides.

The dome has thick walls, to give extra height from outside while avoiding excessive height within

Chhatri

The minarets are said to lean outward slightly to create the illusion that they are straight when seen from the garden

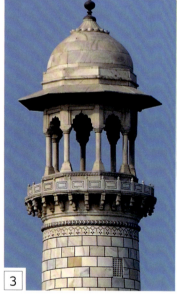

A long water channel reflects the building

2 ▲ **FINIAL** The main dome's gilded finial incorporates both Islamic motifs, such as the crescent moon, and Hindu elements, including the bulbous water vessel.

3 ▲ **MINARETS** On a mosque the minarets are towers from which the call to prayer is given. The minarets of the Taj Mahal are just ornamental and frame the main building.

4 ◀ **PINNACLES** Slender, octagonal marble pinnacles with chevron-patterned, inlaid shafts topped with lotus-petal motifs stand at each corner of the building. They add sculptural interest to the Taj Mahal's silhouette against the sky.

5 ▶ **CHHATRIS** Small pavilions that have a domed roof standing on slender pillars are called *chhatris* (umbrellas). Those on the roof of the Taj Mahal have ornate, multifoil (multi-lobed) arches between the pillars, which match those on the minarets.

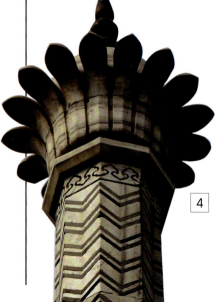

TAJ MAHAL ■ INDIA

Pinnacle

▼ **ARCHED PORTAL** The centerpiece of each façade is a large arched opening containing a doorway, a window, and an array of carved and inlaid decoration. Around this opening is an inscription from the 36th Sura of the Qur'an, which speaks of God's gifts to humanity on Earth and the promise of eternal life to the faithful.

The terrace raises the building above garden level

ON SITE

Shah Jahan selected the site of the Taj Mahal with great care, choosing a position by the River Yamuna so that the building would be reflected in its water, and elevating the mausoleum on a raised terrace between the river and its garden. Following a geometric plan, the garden is divided into four sections, each separated by channels of water that meet at a central pool. The fourfold gardens of Islam represent the unity that underlies the teachings of the Qur'an, and the watercourses symbolize the four rivers of life, flowing with water, milk, honey, and wine.

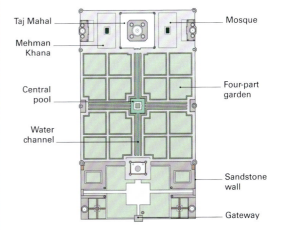

▲ **Plan of the tomb and garden**
The visitor goes through a gateway and past other tombs before entering the garden in front of the Taj Mahal. The Taj is flanked by a mosque and a matching building called the Mehman Khana.

IN CONTEXT

The Mughal dynasty ruled India from the early 16th to the early 18th century. During this time a style of architecture evolved that drew on the buildings of their ancestors in central Asia as well as on those of their Muslim predecessors in India, the Delhi sultans of the 13th and 14th centuries. Including elements such as onion domes, straight-sided pointed arches, and multifoil arches that were seen in both Persian and Delhi architecture, the Mughals favored more restrained color schemes than many central Asian buildings, which often boasted brightly colored tiles. Although the Mughals were skilled military architects—the emperor Akbar built a notable city at Fatehpur Sikri near Agra—their most outstanding buildings were tombs. The Mughal tombs were more elaborate than those of the earlier Delhi sultans, incorporating complex plans and intricate decoration, and the Taj Mahal is the most elaborate of all.

▲ **Tomb of Humayun, Delhi**
Humayun's Tomb, which was built in the 1560s, was a predecessor of the Taj Mahal. It has a large dome, *chhatris*, an octagonal central hall, and a raised terrace—all features later incorporated in the Taj Mahal.

▲ **QUR'ANIC INSCRIPTIONS AND INLAID DECORATION**
The flowing script of the Qur'anic verses, seen on the upper section of this detail, was carved by calligrapher Amanat Khan, who signed his work. He is, however, the only one among the many artists and craftworkers employed on the mausoleum whose identity is known for certain. Below the verses and immediately above the arch, the colorful inlaid decoration features stylized leaves, stems, and flowers.

▲ **RELIEF CARVING**
Symmetrically arranged plants and flowers carved in shallow relief are also found on the exterior. The strong sunlight catches the raised stems and blooms, giving form and texture to the façade.

Visual tour: interior

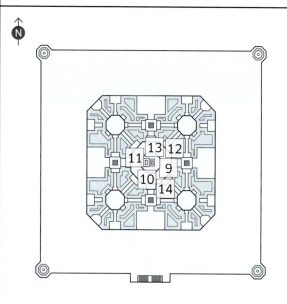

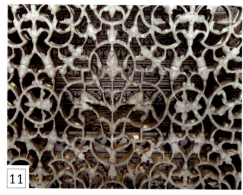

▲ **JALI** An eight-sided lattice-work screen called a *jali* surrounds the two cenotaphs. The original *jali* was made of gold but Shah Jahan replaced it with this marble one, in an intricate tracery pattern, because he feared that the gold screen might be stolen.

▲ **GEOMETRIC FLOOR PATTERN** The marble floors are tiled in a typical Islamic pattern made up of stars and crosslike shapes. Islamic artists used their understanding of geometry to develop many similarly ornate interlocking patterns.

▶ **CENOTAPH** Muslim custom favors simple tombs, and both Mumtaz Mahal and Shah Jahan were laid to rest in plain sarcophagi on the Taj Mahal's lower floor. On the main level are elaborately decorated cenotaphs (empty tombs) commemorating the emperor and his wife. The cenotaph of Mumtaz, who died before her husband, was placed in the center of the building.

▲ **EPITAPH** At the foot end of the empty tomb of Mumtaz Mahal is an inscription identifying the queen. The sides are inscribed with quotations from the Qur'an, which were intended to comfort the soul of the deceased.

TAJ MAHAL ■ INDIA   141

▲ **APEX OF THE DOME** Even at the very highest point in the interior, at the limits of human eyesight, the meticulous patterning continues. On closer inspection the network of interlocking triangles and a sunlike design at the center is apparent.

▲ **SCREEN SUPPORTS** At each corner of the *jali* are supporting posts that are faced with inlaid white marble. Their decoration reflects the patterns around the bases of the cenotaphs and in the spandrels (triangular areas between the arches and above the windows).

ON DESIGN

Many of the wall surfaces are decorated with inlaid patterns using a range of semi-precious stones including cornelian, coral, jade, jasper, lapis lazuli, onyx, and turquoise. The style probably shows the influence of the Italian technique called *pietra dura* (meaning "hard stone"), and western scholars once thought that European craft workers came to Agra to work on the building. This is very unlikely. There were examples of Italian inlaid furniture at the Mughal court, and there may also have been books in the libraries that included these designs. The artisans working at the Taj Mahal adapted these, but used their own color schemes and patterns.

Islam prohibited representational art, and the ban was especially strict when it came to portraying "higher" forms of life, such as people or animals. Designs based on plant forms were far more acceptable, and the decorators of the Taj Mahal used them extensively in their inlays, to stunning effect.

▲ **Elaborate inlays**
Flowers, leaves, and vines in a variety of greens, reds, and yellows enliven the white marble inside the Taj Mahal.

ON DETAIL

The mix of plant designs and abstract motifs found in the Taj Mahal's *pietra dura* decoration is also used in another form of adornment—carvings in low relief—found widely in the interior of the building. In this work, however, the designs are in stone of a single color, usually the white marble that is used as a facing material. This stone came from quarries at Makrana in Rajasthan, and a number of letters from the emperor survive, ordering supplies of the stone. These letters also demand that masons come from Rajasthan to Agra to carve the material, disproving older theories about European involvement in the work. The Rajasthani carvers were highly skilled, producing beautiful and accurate representations of the forms of flowers and leaves.

▲ **Exquisite carvings**
Details from the reliefs show the carvers' skill at producing both geometric designs and decorations based on plant motifs.

Royal Palace

1648-55 ■ PALACE ■ AMSTERDAM, NETHERLANDS

JACOB VAN CAMPEN

In a commanding location on Dam Square, Amsterdam's Royal Palace was originally built as the city's Town Hall in the mid-17th century. During this period, known as the Dutch Golden Age, the Netherlands was growing wealthy from trade, and the Dutch arts and sciences flourished. Jacob van Campen, the architect, designed a building that was appropriate in both size and grandeur for this most powerful of Dutch cities. He drew upon Roman sources for the palace's classical details to reflect the global ambitions of the Dutch, who saw themselves as the successors to the rulers of imperial Rome.

The building he created, however, goes beyond any Roman precedent, and the massive palace with its tall octagonal tower, dominates the low-rise city center of Amsterdam. The splendid interior, in which grand architectural and sculptural decoration form an integral part of marble-clad rooms, is similarly monumental.

The proportions of the building are based on classical ideals. A central section juts slightly forward from the rest of the façade and is topped by a triangular pediment. The side bays also project to balance the central section, and there is a simple ground floor with entrance arches.

The whole façade is on a grand scale. There are five stories altogether, and they are arranged as if a pair of palaces have been placed one on top of the other—the ground, first, and second floors forming one unit, with the third and fourth floors separated from them by a cornice. These floors have no fewer than 23 windows each at the front. Both the first and third floors have taller windows, and this variation in size gives the exterior sandstone walls visual variety.

This massive building, which became Louis Napoleon's palace in 1808, stands on more than 13,000 wooden foundation piles and places a great weight on the city's damp soil.

JACOB VAN CAMPEN
1596-1657

The son of rich parents, Jacob van Campen studied painting before traveling in Europe. He was impressed by the architecture of Palladio and his followers, and he also read the Roman writer Vitruvius, on whose ideas the Palladians based much of their work. On returning to the Netherlands van Campen began to design houses, including one for the poet and diplomat Constantijn Huygens, for which he created his own version of the Palladian style. Van Campen's social connections and talent brought him numerous commissions for both buildings and decorative designs. As well as the Town Hall he designed the Mauritshuis (now an art museum) and the Paleis Noordeinde, both in The Hague. Van Campen initially collaborated with other designers and artists, but he later worked independently, and his style influenced architecture in the Netherlands as well as other parts of northern Europe.

Visual tour

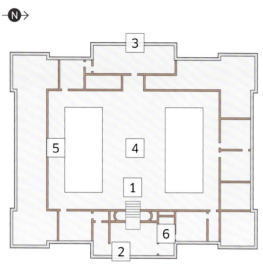

▶ **TOWER AND CUPOLA** Palladian buildings are sometimes topped with a cupola, a dome set on a small tower that is often supported by classical arches. At the Royal Palace the cupola is large enough to alter the skyline of the building without seeming out of proportion to the huge façade. Although enormous, it has many meticulous details—the carved swags (loops of sculpted fruit and vegetation) above the arches, the openwork balustrade, and the Corinthian capitals atop the columns. Most remarkably, at the top of the dome there is a second, miniature cupola, surmounted by a metal finial, adding height and another level of decoration.

▲ **FAÇADE** Although the façades of the building look like plain, monolithic masses of masonry from a distance, a closer inspection reveals rich decoration. The windows are separated vertically by pilasters (protruding strips of masonry) with Corinthian capitals, and beneath many of the windows there are swags similar to those on the cupola. The long cornice between the second and third floors has strong moldings and a row of dentils (rectangular protruding blocks).

▶ **PEDIMENT SCULPTURE** Overseen by Antwerp sculptor, Artus Quellien, the decorative carvings on the exterior walls glorify the city of Amsterdam. The marble pediment sculptures on the eastern façade, for example, show figures representing the oceans of the world paying tribute to the city. Above the pediment a bronze figure of Atlas, bearing the globe on his shoulders, looks down on Dam Square.

[4] ◀ CITIZENS' HALL This assembly room is the most impressive space in the palace. Its walls are lined with marble, built to imitate classical columns and cornices and featuring carvings representing the four elements. On the floor maps of the world and of the heavens, made of inlaid stone and copper, symbolize Dutch global power. Above the doorway at the far end of the room a sculpture of a figure personifying Amsterdam holds olive and palm branches (symbolizing peace and rewards for loyalty) and is flanked by others representing power and wisdom. When the building became the Royal Palace, this hall was used for grand receptions.

▶ GALLERIES These long circulation spaces join the Citizens' Hall at each corner—the photograph (right) shows a view of the southwest gallery from the Citizens' Hall. The galleries have similar architectural decoration to the hall itself, with relief sculptures and spaces for large paintings depicting the conflict between the Romans and the Batavians (Dutch). The windows look out on to one of the building's inner courtyards, and doors lead off to ancillary rooms, stairs, and passages. After the Town Hall had been converted to a palace, the gallery spaces became rooms for the pages, officers, and officials who attended the royal family.

[5]

[6]

▲ TRIBUNAL When the building served as the Town Hall, magistrates gathered in this solemnly decorated room to pronounce the death sentence after serious crimes had been tried. Behind the magistrates, who sat on a bench running along one side, were relief carvings depicting episodes from classical and biblical writings, in which justice was dispensed with wisdom, mercy, and fairness. King Solomon, who represented wisdom, is shown judging the rival claims of two women in a maternity dispute. In another scene the Roman consul Brutus, who had his sons executed for treason, represents a sterner form of justice.

IN CONTEXT

When trade and conquest brought new riches to the Netherlands in the 17th century, there was a building boom in cities such as Amsterdam and The Hague. At first Dutch builders and architects used a traditional style, in which Gothic features were mixed with some Renaissance details. From the mid-century onward, however, architects such as Jacob van Campen, Pieter Post, and Hendrick de Keyser introduced more classical elements, drawing on the architecture of ancient Rome and Renaissance France. They also began to build with stone rather than the traditional brick. The result was a style in which classical proportions were combined with features such as central pediments, prominent doorways, balconies, and traditional pitched roofs. Carved reliefs, sculpted figures, and grander classical details, such as pilasters, were also incorporated into large houses and palaces. This style was widely copied, especially in England.

▲ Mauritshuis, The Hague, Netherlands
Built for John Maurice, Prince of Nassau-Siegen, this elegant house in the Golden Age classical style was designed by Jacob van Campen and Pieter Post.

Palace of Versailles

c.1660–1710 ■ PALACE ■ PARIS, FRANCE

LOUIS LE VAU & JULES HARDOUIN-MANSART

One of the world's largest and most magnificent palaces, Versailles was built for Louis XIV by two of the country's most prominent architects, Louis Le Vau and Jules Hardouin-Mansart. Built around Louis XIII's hunting lodge, the palace expanded over several decades, taking the form of a grand central block and two flanking wings set around a central courtyard. The design and initial building was done by Le Vau, and Hardouin-Mansart extended the palace after 1678, when the royal court took up residence and Versailles became the seat of government. He added the huge north and south wings and incorporated large state rooms such as the Hall of Mirrors. Both architects worked in the baroque style, best typified by grand exteriors and rooms decorated in the most lavish manner, with integral paintings, gilded ceilings and cornices, specially commissioned wall-coverings, large mirrors, and other ornate fittings. Most of these interior details were the work of celebrated painter and designer Charles Le Brun.

Many of the rooms were grouped into suites or apartments allocated to specific members of the royal family, with those for the king and queen situated at the heart of the palace. These central suites were intended as ceremonial or state rooms, in which the ruler or his consort would receive guests according to an elaborate system of ceremony and etiquette. The rich decoration included sun motifs, symbolic of the absolute power of Louis XIV, the "Sun King," and mirrors and gilding designed to reflect his glory.

After the French Revolution of 1789 the all-powerful monarchy was removed, but many later rulers also lived at Versailles and modified the palace to suit their needs. The overall layout of the palace—the great masterpiece of Le Vau and Hardouin-Mansart—has survived, however, and many of the rooms are still decorated in the grandiose 18th-century style, with original details from Louis XIV's reign, such as paintings, gilding, and door surrounds.

JULES **HARDOUIN-MANSART**

1646-1708

Born Jules Hardouin, Hardouin-Mansart trained under his great-uncle, the famous French architect François Mansart. He not only adopted his great-uncle's name, but also inherited his great collection of plans. Quick to learn, Hardouin-Mansart rose to become royal architect and worked on a number of projects for the king. As well as taking over Versailles, extending the building, and bringing it to completion, he designed the nearby Grand Trianon and another royal palace, the Château de Marly. In Paris he was responsible for several major projects, including the Pont Royal and the church of Saint Roche, as well as notable public spaces such as the Place des Victoires and Place Vendôme.

Hardouin-Mansart's buildings are typical of the later phase of French baroque, in which rows of windows, classical pilasters, and mansard roofs are given generous proportions and are treated with heavy decoration. For his rich, ornate interiors, he worked with prestigious artist-decorators such as Le Brun. His style became very popular and was imitated all over the world.

Visual tour: exterior

▶ **GILDED GATE** A place of protocol and etiquette, the palace of Versailles had different zones allocated to different users. This dazzling gateway separates the outer or Ministers' Courtyard from the inner, Royal Courtyard and forms an important boundary between the zones. The lavish gilding indicates that only the most privileged are permitted to enter this part of the palace. The canopy over the gate is topped by an enormous crown and adorned with other royal symbols. The central roundel resembles the sun, Louis XIV's personal motif, and there are also three fleurs-de-lis, heraldic emblems of the French monarchs.

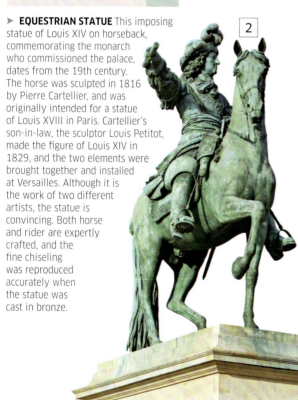

▶ **EQUESTRIAN STATUE** This imposing statue of Louis XIV on horseback, commemorating the monarch who commissioned the palace, dates from the 19th century. The horse was sculpted in 1816 by Pierre Cartellier, and was originally intended for a statue of Louis XVIII in Paris. Cartellier's son-in-law, the sculptor Louis Petitot, made the figure of Louis XIV in 1829, and the two elements were brought together and installed at Versailles. Although it is the work of two different artists, the statue is convincing. Both horse and rider are expertly crafted, and the fine chiseling was reproduced accurately when the statue was cast in bronze.

▶ **MARBLE COURTYARD** The courtyard is paved with marble slabs, and its two-tone masonry walls are dotted with busts that flank large windows. The mansard (double-sloped) roof has round attic windows with ornate, gilded surrounds. The royal apartments are immediately below, and the king's bedchamber opens onto the central balcony, supported by twin columns of red marble. This portion of the façade is flanked by tall pilasters and topped with elaborate sculpture. When Louis died in 1715, the clock was stopped at the time of his death.

PALACE OF VERSAILLES ■ FRANCE

► ROYAL CHAPEL

With its curved end and high roof the two-story chapel, in the north wing of the palace, breaks up the symmetry of the building. It was the last part of the palace to be completed under Louis XIV, and its design was the work of Hardouin-Mansart and Robert de Cotte. This large stone structure with an apsidal (curved) end interrupts the pattern of straight lines in the rest of the building. The treatment is grandiose, with giant pilasters topped by Corinthian capitals and big classical cornices. Tall stone statues are a notable feature of the upper section.

▼ GRAND TRIANON

A smaller palace within the vast grounds of Versailles, the Grand Trianon was designed by Hardouin-Mansart and features a pair of single-story wings on either side of a columned walkway. The most spectacular feature of the exterior are the rows of pilasters in pinkish Languedoc marble. Inside are suites of rooms—grand, but not on the vast scale of the main palace—where the king could enjoy a degree of privacy (and see his mistress) away from his courtiers and officials. Although much altered and extended under later rulers, the Grand Trianon still retains much of its original exterior.

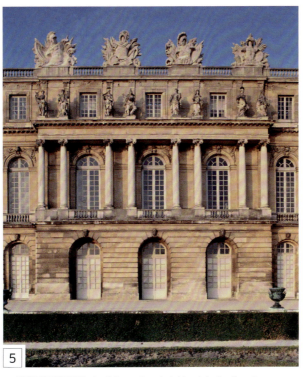

▲ SOUTH WING

Much of the palace is laid out in the Renaissance manner, with the main rooms on the first floor, which was known in Italian as the *piano nobile* (noble level). Here, the windows are tall, and there are pairs of widely spaced columns between them, supporting a cornice with statues—an elaborate treatment that conveys the importance of this part of the building. The low-status rooms of the top story have smaller windows, while the ground floor has slightly smaller French windows and the masonry is treated with banded rustication (exaggerated bands), a convention common since Palladio's time to indicate less important rooms on a lower floor.

ON **DESIGN**

The palace was not designed in isolation. Louis XIV wanted Versailles to be seen in the context of its surroundings, and he employed the great French landscape gardener, André le Nôtre, to design the extensive grounds. Close to the palace Le Nôtre placed parterres—formal, open arrangements of plants, flowers, and pools designed to be seen from above. These were edged with low hedges and flanked by rows of topiary trees and shrubs. Straight paths and avenues radiated out to shady groves, artificial lakes, fountains, a grand canal for boating, and a grotto. The entire plan was designed so that it could be appreciated best from the royal bedchamber.

▲ Parterre
A beautiful and precise scroll pattern is surrounded by orderly rows of orange trees and topiary in pots.

Visual tour: interior

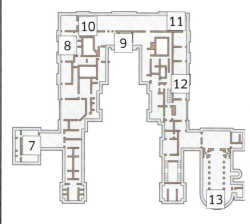

▼ **QUEEN'S BEDROOM** This lavishly ornate room was redecorated during the 18th century. Paintings and sculpted decorations were installed for Marie Leszinska, wife of Louis XV, in the 1730s, and among the work by renowned 18th-century artists is a set of medallions, painted by François Boucher. The room was later modified for Marie-Antoinette, and the silk wall coverings are exact copies of those that adorned the walls in 1786. These summer fabrics would have been replaced in winter by heavier brocades or velvet.

▼ **HALL OF BATTLES** This vast, double-height gallery, which is 394ft (120m) long and faces the gardens, occupies virtually the entire length of the south wing. This part of the palace was originally known as the Princes' wing and contained the rooms where the royal children lived. The hall was redecorated in the reign of Louis-Philippe (1830–48), who installed a collection of paintings depicting famous victories in French history. The sequence extends from Clovis I's success at Tolbiac in 496 to the decisive battle of Wagram, in which Napoleon defeated Austrian forces.

▶ **KING'S BEDROOM** Originally a drawing room, this chamber at the center of the north side of the Marble Courtyard later became the royal bedroom. Here, surrounded by courtiers, the king would dress and prepare for the day in a ceremony known as the *Lever* (the rising). Much of the rich decoration, including the gilded pilasters and cornices, as well as paintings by great artists such as Van Dyck, has survived.

PALACE OF VERSAILLES ■ FRANCE   151

◄ **HALL OF MIRRORS** This large and elaborately decorated room has a row of 17 tall windows. Opposite each one is an arch filled with mirrors—a great luxury in the 17th century—that reaches almost from the floor to the ceiling, giving the hall its name. On either side of the arches are marble pilasters crowned with gilded capitals, and between them are niches containing ancient classical statues from the collection of Louis XIV. The ceiling, painted by Le Brun, depicts Louis XIV's reign, including episodes from his military campaigns: the painting at its center, "The King Governs Alone," alludes to his absolute power. This vast, theatrical room was the scene of official receptions, balls, and other large-scale events during the reign of Louis XIV and other monarchs. It is still used for state occasions today.

◄ **SALON D'APOLLON** Taking its name from the ceiling painting of the Greek god Apollo, this was one of the most luxurious royal suites, first a bedchamber, then the throne room. When it became a drawing room, many of the original furnishings were removed, but the walls are covered in red damask, as they were in the 17th century, so the space retains some of its original appearance. The furnishings include many tall, floor-standing candelabra, their gilded bases held aloft by putti and other figures. Originally made for the Hall of Mirrors, these opulent furnishings give an idea of just how luxurious the royal chambers and rooms of state were.

◄ **ROYAL CHAPEL** The chapel is dedicated to St. Louis, patron saint of the Bourbon monarchs of France. It has two levels: an upper story with a gallery for the king, a lower level with accommodation for courtiers, and side chapels dedicated to the royal family's other patron saints. The most striking feature of the chapel is the painted ceiling. The enormous painting above the nave, the work of baroque artist Antoine Coypel, depicts "God the Father in His Glory Bringing the Promise of Redemption to the World." The painted half-dome, by Charles de la Fosse, shows the Resurrection of Christ.

▲ **SALON DE LA GUERRE** This room was originally the king's private chamber, but it was redesigned to commemorate Louis XIV's military victories, especially those over Holland and its allies. The huge, carved medallion shows the victorious king on horseback, crossing the Rhine River. Beneath it two gilded figures are bound in chains.

- **MELK ABBEY**
  Melk, Austria

- **BLENHEIM PALACE**
  Woodstock, UK

- **AMALIENBURG PAVILION**
  Nymphenburg, Germany

- **MONTICELLO**
  Charlottesville, VA

- **HOUSES OF PARLIAMENT**
  London, UK

- **NEUSCHWANSTEIN CASTLE**
  Bavaria, Germany

- **SAGRADA FAMILIA**
  Barcelona, Spain

- **HÔTEL TASSEL**
  Brussels, Belgium

- **GRAND PALAIS**
  Paris, France

1700–1900

Melk Abbey

c.1702-14 ■ MONASTERY ■ MELK, AUSTRIA

JAKOB PRANDTAUER

From its elevated position on a rocky outcrop the great Benedictine abbey of Melk towers over the Danube in Lower Austria. Founded in the 11th century, it became renowned as a center of faith and learning, but by 1700 its buildings were no longer fit for the purpose, and the dynamic abbot, Berthold Dietmayr, commissioned the architect Jakob Prandtauer to redesign it. Prandtauer specialized in the baroque style, and he created a new church, accommodation, library, and other structures that transformed Melk into one of the largest and most elaborate baroque buildings in the world.

Baroque architecture developed in Italy in the late 16th century, and by 1700 it had spread across Catholic Europe. The style is characterized by a dramatic use of light and space, curving walls, ornate domes, decoration using painting, sculpture, and stucco (plaster rendering), and a fondness for illusionistic, *trompe l'oeil* effects. In Catholic countries the Baroque, with its scope for large-scale religious imagery, came to be synonymous with the renewal of the Church after the Reformation and explains why monasteries such as Melk embraced it so enthusiastically.

The abbey church at Melk stands at the heart of the complex, its large dome and towers topped with cupolas that dominate the skyline. The surrounding buildings are lower, yet palatial in style, with the living quarters, state apartments, large library, and school arranged around several courtyards. Their impressive scale and decoration are reminders that the abbey's inhabitants expected a high standard of comfort and convenience. Even from a distance, many features establish the abbey as baroque—the intricately shaped cupolas, curving gables, and the use of colored stucco all combine to make this one of the world's most impressive religious buildings.

JAKOB **PRANDTAUER**

c.1660-1726

Born at Stanz in the Tirol, Jakob Prandtauer began his working life as a stonemason, learning the craft from his father. He also worked as a sculptor before becoming a master builder, which gave him the responsibility for the design as well the construction of his buildings. He worked at first in Sankt Pölten, near Vienna, before becoming involved with the reconstruction of several important Austrian monasteries and churches. These included the monasteries of St. Florian, near Linz, the abbey at Garsten, near Steyr, and the pilgrimage church on the Sonntagberg. He acted both as architect and builder, supervising the construction and overseeing the work of painters, decorators, and sculptors. He became well-versed in the baroque style and was ideally suited to take on the rebuilding of the monastery at Melk, a project that occupied him from 1702. Much of his work remained unfinished at his death, but his cousin and assistant Josef Mungenast completed his projects.

Visual tour

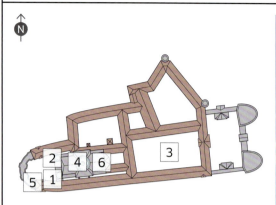

◄ **WEST FRONT** Laid out in the style of a medieval cathedral, the west front of the church features twin towers above a central doorway. The details, however, are quite different. There are cupolas instead of spires on the tops of the towers, and the front is broken up with classical pilasters (vertical protrusions) and cornices. There are fewer statues than on most medieval church fronts, but they are much larger and include a group on the skyline, which is a typical baroque touch.

▼ **CHURCH INTERIOR** This is the most stunning interior in the whole monastery, with natural light falling from high windows to illuminate a wealth of gilded details on everything from the pulpit canopy to the statues behind the high altar. In the nave the side walls curve gently, dipping in and out past arches leading to side chapels. The line of the curving cornice (the darkest detail in this bright interior) leads the eye toward the dome and the vaulted sanctuary beyond.

▲ **FAÇADE DETAIL** The clock towers show Prandtauer's handling of baroque motifs, which feature very few right-angles or straight lines. The moldings and cornices curve one way and another to create a sense of movement. Their flowing lines are echoed in the outlines of the scrolls on each corner and in the curvaceous molding around the clock face. The urns are another baroque touch, adding an extra layer of decoration and also breaking up the skyline. Prandtauer emphasized these effects with his use of color, picking out the moldings in terra-cotta against the white of the walls.

► **COURTYARD** The courtyards are lined with rectangular windows topped with curving moldings, picked out with darker stucco than the surrounding walls. The pattern of windows creates an impression similar to the grandiose palace courtyards in many Central European cities. In the center of the paved quadrangle a baroque fountain is supported on sculpted figures. The replacement seen here was brought from a monastery at Waldhausen, Upper Austria, when Berthold Dietmayr gave the original to the town of Melk.

MELK ABBEY ■ AUSTRIA

▶ **MARBLE HALL** The Rule of St. Benedict, by which monks of the order lived, instructed them to receive guests "as if they were Christ" and accord them due honor. This magnificent room was intended as a dining hall fit for guests of the highest social rank, including members of the ruling Hapsburg dynasty, who often visited Melk. The main door surrounds are made of marble, but the walls are decorated with stucco painted to look like marble. In the center of the floor is an iron grating, beneath which a heater brings warm air into the room, making it as comfortable as it is grand. The ceiling has a huge painting showing scenes from classical mythology, including one of the hero Hercules killing the "hound of hell" with his club. Hercules was seen as a virtuous figure and was a favorite of the Hapsburgs.

5

6

▲ **DOME INTERIOR** The dome forms the church's spatial center, and light from its windows helps illuminate the rich decoration. The painting is a *trompe l'oeil* depiction of the heavens and, like the others in the church, it was probably designed by Italian-Austrian artist Antonio Beduzzi and painted by Austrian baroque master Johann Michael Rottmayr. God the Father, Jesus Christ, and, in the lantern, the dove representing the Holy Spirit are all depicted.

ON **DETAIL**

Baroque artists aimed to dissolve the rigid lines and rectangular interiors of previous architecture by means of curving walls and hidden windows. Decorative ceilings, which often featured religious or mythological figures, reinforced this effect. Painted in the *trompe l'oeil* style, the ceilings created the illusion that the room was open to the skies, and that the figures in the painting were looking down at the world below them. Painters such as Rottmayr, who created the ceiling frescoes in the church at Melk, became adept at perspective, foreshortening the figures so that they seemed to float in mid-air. The artist sometimes added architectural details around the edge so that the walls of the building seemed to extend upward, and employed specialists, such as Gaetano Fanti from Italy, to paint these elements.

▲ **Ceiling figures**
The ceiling artists who worked at Melk adjusted the perspective of their paintings carefully, enlarging feet and limbs that were closer to the viewer.

ON **DESIGN**

Baroque churches can seem rather crowded with decorative details. Window surrounds, cornices, niches, and other architectural features are adorned with ornamental scrolls or shells, or populated with statues of saints or small angels (cherubim and seraphim) often portrayed as winged children. Important fixtures and fittings, such as the reredos (the screen behind the altar), the pulpit, and the organ are singled out for special attention, with statues of saints or reliefs showing biblical scenes.

▲ **Organ**
Gilded statues of cherubim sit above the organ pipes at the west end of the nave in the church at Melk.

Blenheim Palace

1724 ■ PALACE ■ WOODSTOCK, UK

JOHN VANBRUGH

John, 1st Duke of Marlborough, was a British military hero who won a major victory at the Battle of Blenheim in Bavaria in 1704 during the War of the Spanish Succession. As a reward Queen Anne, the British monarch, offered to build a vast country house for him and his wife Sarah. Sir John Vanbrugh was chosen as architect and rose to the challenge by designing one of the grandest houses in Europe, a building on a staggering scale designed to rival Louis XIV's palace at Versailles (see pp.146–51). Blenheim soon became known as a palace itself. Like Versailles it is set around a huge courtyard with the residential apartments in the center. Flanking this section are two additional buildings—a stable block and a kitchen wing—each laid out around its own courtyard and each larger than many country houses.

The style used by Vanbrugh for this enormous house was his own personal version of Baroque. In mainland Europe, Baroque buildings are often typified by a blend of intricately curving walls and highly ornate decoration that creates a feeling of lightness. Vanbrugh's style, which he developed with his assistant, Nicholas Hawksmoor, is far more ponderous. Blenheim combines classical features, such as a large central portico, with heavy, elaborate details that are more Baroque in style—monumental arches, heavily banded masonry, and an abundance

of statues. The massive scale and symmetrical layout of Blenheim create an overwhelming impression of grandeur, accentuated by the dramatic silhouette produced by the gigantic chimneys and exaggerated finials.

The symmetry of the palace's exterior is replicated inside. Vanbrugh designed the interior in a formal manner, as was customary at the time. In the middle of the central block are two lofty double-height rooms, the Great Hall and the Saloon, a state dining room. On either side of the Saloon, along the south front, are two matching suites of large staterooms for important guests, such as the monarch and consort. In each suite the largest, most public chamber adjoins the central Saloon, and the smaller, more private rooms stretch out on either side. On the east front there is a similar but smaller pair of suites, also symmetrical in layout, for the Duke and Duchess. More modest rooms, corridors, and staircases run behind them. Because the 18th-century custom of using suites went out of fashion, many of these rooms are now furnished differently, but their magnificent proportions and some of their lavish decorative schemes have been preserved.

JOHN **VANBRUGH**

1664-1726

Born in London, John Vanbrugh had both English and Dutch ancestors. In his 20s he was an army officer and participated in the political maneuvers that led to the accession of a Dutch king, William III, to the English throne in 1689. In the 1690s he became a dramatist, writing many comedies, of which *The Relapse* and *The Provoked Wife* are the most famous. At the end of the decade, apparently without any training, he began to design buildings, becoming especially successful as an architect of country houses. Some, including Castle Howard, Seaton Delaval Hall, and Blenheim, were on a vast scale. Although Vanbrugh undoubtedly learned from theatrical design, it is unlikely that he would have been able to achieve these grand and complex buildings without professional help. He was fortunate to work with Nicholas Hawksmoor, an architect who had learned his art with Sir Christopher Wren and designed many churches and houses in the Baroque style. No one knows for sure how the two men worked together—Vanbrugh may have drawn up the plans and left the details to Hawksmoor, but Vanbrugh is credited with the grandiose conception of these palatial country houses, and of smaller buildings that display the same dramatic Baroque style.

Visual tour: exterior

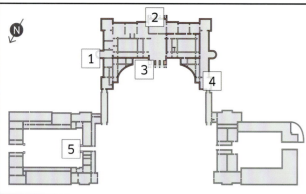

▶ **EAST FAÇADE** Vanbrugh created the most dramatic impression using standard architectural features—windows, cornices, walls, and chimneys. The main windows are tall and round-topped, which gives them a grandeur that rectangular windows lack. The walls of the corner towers have banded masonry and look monumental. The real drama, however, is at the tops of the towers. Above the projecting cornice is a cluster of turrets and chimneys, linked by small arches. Bulbous finials at the top of the four corner turrets create a bizarre skyline.

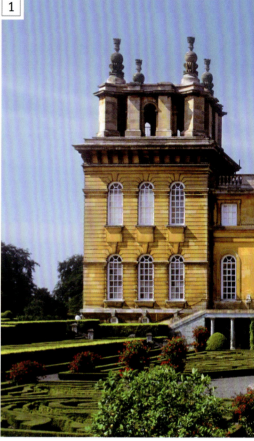

▲ **SOUTH FRONT** Two corner towers balance the ends of the south front, but the architecture draws your eye toward the center of the building. Here, a row of tall columns—known as a giant order—rises the full height of the two main stories. This marks the central portion of the building as the most important. Behind the doorway is the Saloon and beyond it the Great Hall, which, like the giant order, is two stories high. The façade is perfectly symmetrical, and on either side of the saloon is a series of equally symmetrical rooms, mirroring the poise and balance of the façade.

▶ **COLUMN DETAIL** Although Vanbrugh always strove for large-scale effects, the small details were carefully worked out too. This view of the top of one of the Corinthian columns that supports the pediment on the north front is an example. The carving of the capital, with its curling acanthus leaves, is rich and deep. The pediment above it is also copiously carved. Each of the dentils, the small repeating blocks along the base of the pediment, has a tiny rosette, and even the spaces between the dentils are decorated, as are many of the moldings.

▼ **HERMS** Female statues line the upper level of one of the semicircular bays that protrude from the palace façades. These statues are herms, a form from ancient Greek sculpture in which a human head or torso is mounted on a plain base. Ancient herms were usually male, but at Blenheim the herms are female, giving the sculptor the chance to carve the rich drapery of their costumes in flowing Baroque knots and folds.

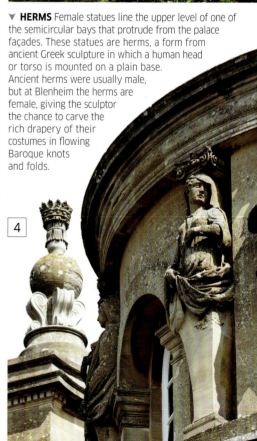

BLENHEIM PALACE ■ UK

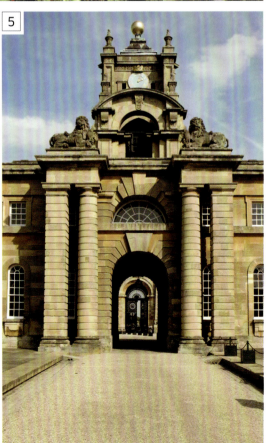

▶ **ENTRANCE ARCH** The clock tower rises above an entrance arch to one of Blenheim's courtyards. Vanbrugh's treatment of the masonry and details adds to the sense of grandeur. One example is the choice of keystone, the wedge-shaped stone at the top of the arch. This is normally sizable, but here it is three or four times the size of the stones on either side of it, giving a sense of enormous weight.

The design of the semicircular window varies this approach. There is another large keystone, this time flanked by two pairs of blocks that are almost as big. The columns on either side of the arch work in a similar way. Their banded masonry makes them look as if they are composed of huge stone blocks. This is an illusion, because each band consists of two or three blocks, discreetly joined. The architect and builders worked closely together to produce these theatrical effects.

IN CONTEXT

Blenheim is set in a large park, and work on laying this out began at the same time as the building. Marlborough's gardener, Henry Wise, designed formal gardens close to the house, with symmetrical flower beds making intricate patterns separated by low hedges. Farther from the house Vanbrugh created a bridge to form part of an approach route across the marshy valley of the River Glyme. Later in the 18th century fashions changed, and the duke of the time brought in the great landscape gardener Lancelot "Capability" Brown to redesign the park in a less formal style. Brown created a natural-looking landscape, with clumps of trees, vistas, and a lake in the valley making two great curves on either side of Vanbrugh's bridge. Today the gardens are a creative compromise between these two styles. Formal gardens near the house have been restored, with flower beds, statuary, and fountains installed in the 1920s, but Brown's natural-looking park, with its trees and lake, remains as a fitting landscape setting.

▲ **Grand Bridge**
Vanbrugh's bridge originally crossed a river but is now partially submerged in Capability Brown's lake.

ON DESIGN

From the very first stage of design it was clear that Blenheim Palace was intended to be a house fit for a hero, a man who, in the words of Marlborough's descendant Sir Winston Churchill, had, through his military victories, "changed the axis of the world." The palace is heroic in scale, as it is in the symbolism of many of its details. At several points on the building there are sculptures representing weapons, flags, drums, and other spoils of war. Military symbols were an ancient theme in sculpture and were especially popular in the Renaissance to indicate that the person who owned or commissioned the sculpture was a war hero or had been successful in battle.

▲ **Triumphal sculpture**
This carved collection of arms, armor, and flags is at the top of the building so it stands out defiantly on the skyline.

Visual tour: interior

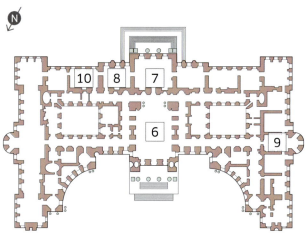

▼ **SALOON** This large room is furnished as a state dining room. Vanbrugh wanted Sir James Thornhill to paint the walls and ceiling, but Marlborough's wife Sarah contended that the artist had overcharged for the ceiling in the Great Hall. A French painter, Louis Laguerre, did the job instead. Laguerre depicts the nations of the world around the walls and the Duke of Marlborough in a victory procession on the ceiling.

▼ **GREAT HALL** This is the largest room in the Palace and is some 67ft (20m) high. It combines the roles of entrance hall and reception room and gives access to the long corridors that lead to the other principal rooms. The Great Hall is lined with stone arches, and their sculpture, including the Corinthian capitals and the coat of arms of Queen Anne in the center of the large arch, are by Grinling Gibbons, the greatest carver of the period. The enormous arch at the end of the room is a typical Vanbrugh touch and was probably meant to remind visitors of Roman triumphal arches.

▶ **GREEN WRITING ROOM** This room, which has a ceiling with rich gilded decoration, pale paneling on the walls, and paneled doors, is most notable for its furnishings. Chief among these is the tapestry, which was specially commissioned for the palace and spans one corner of the room. It shows the Duke of Marlborough on horseback, accepting the surrender of the French leader Marshall Tallard after the Battle of Blenheim. The details, which include burning buildings in the distance and French troops fleeing toward the Danube River, are realistic and probably based on the Duke's memories of the event.

▲ **RED DRAWING ROOM** Taking its name from its red damask wall covering, the Red Drawing Room is typical of the reception rooms on the south front of the Palace. It owes its appearance to more than one period. The shape of the room, with its high, coved ceiling, is original, and the ceiling design probably stems from Vanbrugh's assistant, Nicholas Hawksmoor, but the room was altered later in the 18th century, when the architect Sir William Chambers was brought in to redecorate parts of the building. Chambers designed the fireplace in the elegant neoclassical style of the 1760s.

◀ **LONG LIBRARY** This huge, double-height room runs along the entire west front of the building and is 183ft (56m) long. Vanbrugh and Hawksmoor originally planned it as what they called a "room of parade." The occupants of the house would be able to walk up and down and admire the collection of pictures on the walls, as they did in similar "long galleries" in Tudor country houses. The architects broke up the space by dividing it with arches and treating the ceiling as a sequence of rectangles and circles, which look like shallow domes. Thornhill was originally going to paint the ceiling, but because Sarah objected to the artist's fees, it was left blank. In 1744 the room became a library, and its shelves hold around 10,000 volumes.

Amalienburg Pavilion

1734–39 ▪ HUNTING LODGE ▪ MUNICH, GERMANY

FRANÇOIS CUVILLIÉS

One of the gems of the European rococo style, the Amalienburg Pavilion was built by the ruler of Bavaria, Elector Karl Albrecht, as a hunting lodge for his wife, Maria Amalia. Designed by François Cuvilliés, the small, richly decorated building is set in the grounds of the vast Nymphenburg Palace, the Elector's summer residence in Munich, and is surrounded by extensive wooded parkland.

The Pavilion was intended as a base for hunting parties, an ornamental feature of the park, and a refuge from the formality of palace life. Cuvilliés designed it like a palace in miniature: although a single story building, it contains a beautiful reception hall, bedroom, dressing room, and hunting room, all meticulously decorated, as well as a kitchen, and even a room for the Elector's hunting dogs.

The rococo decoration of the Amalienburg Pavilion was overseen by Cuvilliés but carried out by an impressive team of decorators including court woodcarver Johann Joachim Dietrich and German painter and stucco artist Johann Baptist Zimmermann. The overall effect is one of filigree delicacy. Carvings of plants in low relief run up the interior walls, and the foliage theme is continued in stucco around the cornices. The predominant colors are pale—as is typical of rococo—and the Bavarian national colors of blue and silver are extensively used in tactful allusion to the power of the Elector. The handling of light is masterful. Both main façades of the building have full-height windows, the central hall is partly lined with mirrors to maximize natural light, and large chandeliers illuminate the rooms at night. The result is a glittering jewel-box of an interior.

FRANÇOIS **CUVILLIÉS**

1695–1768

Born in Belgium, Cuvilliés was very short and became court dwarf to Maximilian Emanuel, Elector of Bavaria, who was living in exile in France. Maximilian recognized Cuvilliés' talent and paid for his education, setting him to work with court architect Joseph Effner when the Bavarian rulers returned to Munich. In 1726, when Karl Albrecht became Elector, Cuvilliés was made court architect. He did part of his training in Paris, where rococo was fashionable, and is usually credited with bringing the style to Germany. His work for the Elector included a chapel at Brühl, a hunting lodge (Falkenlust), and the decoration of rooms in the Munich Residenz. An accomplished decorative designer, he was well known for furniture designs, staircases, mirrors, and fireplaces, all adorned with the delicate, fanciful ornament that is seen at its best in the Amalienburg Pavilion.

1700-1900

Visual tour

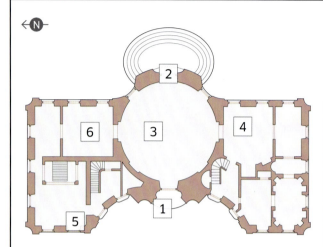

▼ **FAÇADES** The front and back of the Pavilion are unified by the repeated French windows with their small panes of glass and by the horizontal bands of pale pink and white stucco, (known as banded rustication) running across the front. These linear details are set within a variety of curves—the grand, sweeping concave curve of the façade, the convex curve of the cornice above the central doorway, and the segmental (less than semicircular) arch. The use of contrasting concave and convex curves is typical of baroque and rococo architecture, and gives the exterior a fluid quality that is matched by the flowing decoration inside the Pavilion.

▲ **EXTERIOR DETAIL** The decorative language of the exterior is classical, but this is classicism with a fanciful twist typical of the rococo style. The pilasters (vertical protrusions) are topped with Ionic capitals but have trails of ornamentation dangling from the scrolls. The decorative reliefs portray classical scenes and hunting trophies, and the central figure of a hunting goddess breaks out of her frame, with one leg dangling below and one arm raised so that she almost touches the arch above.

▶ **HALL OF MIRRORS** This circular room is the largest in the building. Set in the center of the Pavilion, it is both the entrance hall and a reception room. The doors, windows, and mirrors are arranged around its curved walls, filling the room with light and creating multiple reflections. Light from the windows and mirrors also catches the stucco work. It highlights the silver and gold of the exquisite foliage that curls and climbs toward the shallow domed ceiling, which looks like a pale blue sky arching above scrambling plants.

AMALIENBURG PAVILION ■ GERMANY

◄ **BEDROOM** Leading directly off the Hall of Mirrors, this is one of the Pavilion's principal rooms. The pale yellow walls are covered with silver-painted, wooden carvings by master craftsman Johann Joachim Dietrich, who contributed significantly to the decoration of the Bavarian palaces. The bed is tucked away in a niche and on either side of it are the portraits of Elector Karl Albrecht and his wife Maria Amalia, both of whom are dressed for the hunt.

◄ **HUNTING ROOM** Although planned on a much smaller scale, the Amalienburg Pavilion boasts a picture gallery, like any great house. On the walls of this small room hang paintings of hunting, including some that depict the Elector's court in the field. The décor of the room was designed around these paintings, which fill most of the available wall space and are displayed close to one another in 18th-century fashion. The picture frames are rococo in style, as is the ornate carved decoration on the small areas of wall between the paintings.

▲ **KITCHEN** Even the small kitchen is elaborately decorated. Its walls are covered with specially made Dutch tiles, and the ceiling is painted in blue and white. The decorative theme in this room reflects the strong interest of 18th-century architects and designers in Chinese art. The ceiling features scenes in a Chinese style, and the tiles are decorated with images of flowers and landscapes. Both the style and color palette (mainly blues and yellows on a pale ground) imitate the decoration seen on Chinese porcelain.

ON **DETAIL**

The decorative details of the Pavilion, which swirl across the walls and ceilings, twine around chair legs and the arms of chandeliers, and cluster around the mirrors and picture frames, are typically rococo. This exuberant style originated in France as a reaction against the heavy, monumental style of buildings such as Versailles. Plant forms—flowers, foliage, and swags of vegetation—dominate, but there are also motifs, such as putti (cherubs) and urns. Although the architecture of the Pavilion is symmetrical, the decorative elements often are not, and this asymmetry, together with the restless curves of the cornices and moldings, gives the whole decorative scheme a sense of fluidity. The other striking feature of the decoration is its sparkling lightness—a reaction against the dark colors used by earlier decorators.

▲ Rococo carving and stucco work in the Hall of Mirrors

Monticello

1769–1809 ■ PRIVATE HOUSE ■ CHARLOTTESVILLE, USA

THOMAS JEFFERSON

In 1769, when Thomas Jefferson, an American statesman, began to design his own house, the style he chose was neoclassicism. This style was, to some extent, based on the classical architecture of ancient Rome, as interpreted by architects and writers of the Renaissance, especially Andrea Palladio. From these sources Jefferson took the overall symmetry of his design, which was similar to that of Palladio's celebrated villas in northern Italy (see pp.124–27). Details such as the columned porticoes also echo Roman and Renaissance architecture.

When Jefferson spent time in France during the 1780s, he found another rich source of neoclassicism in the grand houses of many European cities, and the subtlety of their design seemed to reflect the sophisticated thinking of the Enlightenment, a movement that interested Jefferson. Influenced by the architectural styles prevalent in France, Jefferson then modified his design, adding the octagonal dome and creating a hybrid neoclassicism made up of a mix of ancient and modern elements. Finally, he incorporated features of his own, such as skylights. The resulting house, Monticello ("little mountain"), is both innovative and classically restrained, and its design influenced builders and architects in 19th-century North America.

THOMAS JEFFERSON

1743–1826

Thomas Jefferson was born into a family of Virginia plantation owners and enslavers. He had a successful career as a lawyer. In the 1770s he became a member of the group that worked for US independence and was the principal author of the Declaration of Independence. During the 1780s, Jefferson argued for the emancipation of enslaved people, despite being an enslaver himself; his support for emancipation waned during the 1790s. He became US Minister to France in 1785, the first Secretary of State in 1790, and President for the first of two terms in 1800. His successes included the purchase of the Louisiana Territory from France.

Visual tour

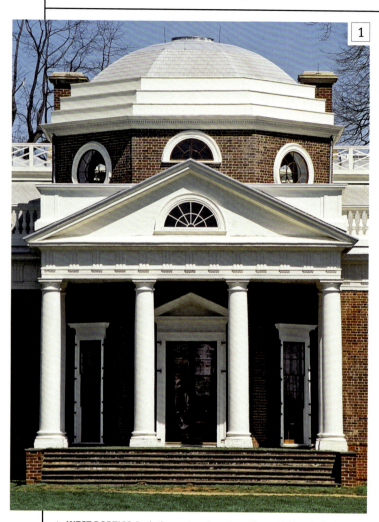

▲ **WEST PORTICO** Both the east and west porticoes at Monticello have a triangular pediment supported by a row of white columns in a version of the Doric order. Unlike ancient Greek Doric columns (see p.23) they lack flutes, but have bases. The columns on the east portico, which was built first, are made of stone, but skilled stone workers were in short supply, so Jefferson chose to build the west portico columns using specially manufactured curved bricks.

▲ **CLASSICAL DETAILS** The neoclassical architects of the 18th and 19th centuries based their designs on certain elements, such as columns and pediments, drawn from the buildings of ancient Greece and Rome. They also added elements of their own, such as this parapet, which goes all the way around the building, concealing the roof. While some architects preferred a solid parapet, Jefferson chose one with rows of baluster shafts. This added visual interest and made the structure look lighter.

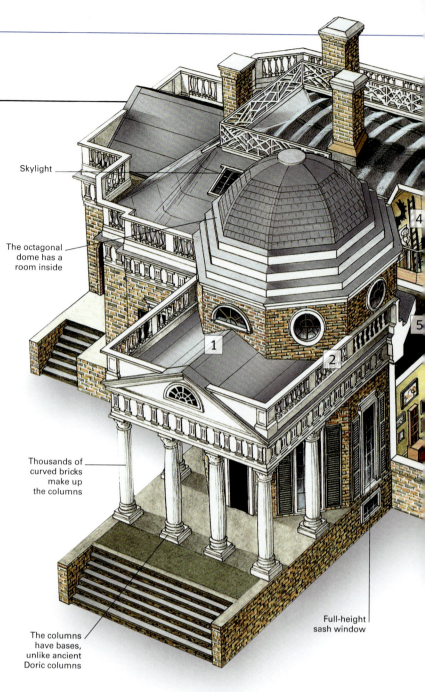

ON DESIGN

With its porticoes, dome, and sash windows, Monticello looks like a straightforward neoclassical building, but its sober exterior conceals a number of unusual gadgets and devices that Jefferson, with great ingenuity, incorporated into the fabric of the house. Near the stairs leading to the kitchen in the dining room, he installed a revolving serving door with shelves, together with a dumb waiter to bring wine up from the cellar. The house had indoor bathrooms, which were unusual at the time. Some of the windows had two sets of sashes for insulation, an early form of double glazing, while the parlor had a set of doors that opened automatically. Other innovations, such as the closet concealed above Jefferson's bed and accessed by a ladder, involved clever use of space.

▲ **Compass rose** Linked to a rooftop weather vane, this feature was positioned so that Jefferson could read the wind direction without going outside.

MONTICELLO ■ USA

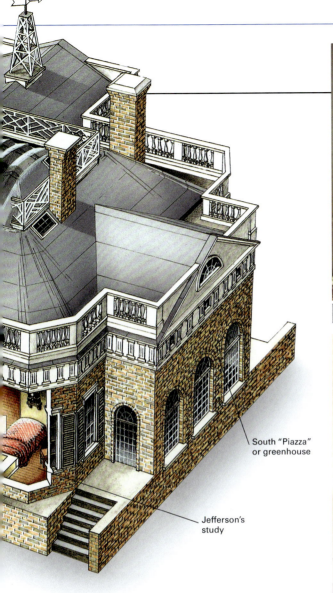

South "Piazza" or greenhouse

Jefferson's study

▼ **JEFFERSON'S BEDROOM** The space-saving properties of alcove beds, which he saw in France, appealed to Jefferson. He liked the way in which the bed was tucked away, giving plenty of uncluttered floor space in the bedroom. Jefferson placed his own bed in an alcove between his bedroom and his study, which is visible beyond the bed in the photograph. It created a visual and functional link between the two rooms.

◀ **TRIPLE-SASH WINDOWS** Many of the rooms, including the parlor, have windows made up of three sliding sashes rather than the pair of sashes more often used in windows of this period. With a triple-sash window that extends to the floor, the two sashes at the bottom can be raised so that the window becomes a door, making it easy to step in and out on warm summer days. Alternatively, lifting the bottom sash and lowering the top sash creates a flow of air for ventilation.

▲ **ENTRANCE HALL** In this reception area Jefferson displayed his most prized possessions such as maps, images showing the early history of the US, and busts of heroes such as the French writer, Voltaire. The ceiling decoration features an eagle and a group of stars (probably representing the number of states in the Union in 1812 when the ceiling was installed). Hanging from the center of the room, a brass oil lamp can be raised and lowered on pulleys.

Houses of Parliament

c.1840–70 ■ GOVERNMENT BUILDING ■ LONDON, UK

CHARLES BARRY AND AUGUSTUS WELBY NORTHMORE PUGIN

Work on Britain's Houses of Parliament, also known as the Palace of Westminster, began after the previous building had been almost totally destroyed in a devastating fire. The winner of the competition to design the prestigious new building was the experienced architect Charles Barry, whose victory was due in part to an impressive set of drawings by A. W. N. Pugin, his younger colleague. Pugin made a huge contribution to the design of both the exterior and interior, which continued to evolve over the 30-year construction period. The competition brief specified a building in the Elizabethan or Gothic style.

Barry's and Pugin's design is a version of Gothic influenced by the English churches of the 15th century and the domestic architecture of the Tudor period. It combines a long, horizontal river façade of repeating windows with a forest of vertical pinnacles and turrets and two graceful towers—the huge Victoria Tower and the soaring Clock Tower (largely Pugin's work), which soon became the most famous landmark in London.

This vast building contains hundreds of rooms, which the architects planned with great care. Running down the center is a "spine" of large rooms—the Lords and Commons

debating chambers and their lobbies, arranged on either side of the spacious Central Lobby. At one end of them, next to the House of Lords, is the Royal Gallery, a large state reception room. Corridors off the spine lead to offices for the Members of Parliament, committee rooms, and service rooms. The architects used the latest technology, and the building has a ventilation system way ahead of its time—many of the apparently ornamental turrets are air vents.

Pugin, the foremost Gothic Revival designer of the era, was responsible for the decorative details that make this building so special—from moldings to wallpapers, furniture, door handles, and ink stands. The interiors that best exemplify his flair are the most ornate in the building—the Robing Room and the House of Lords—in which rich gilded woodwork and deep-red upholstery combine to luxurious effect. These lavish interiors are a reminder that, although Barry won the competition and produced the overall plan, Pugin made the plan work and turned the building into a national symbol.

CHARLES **BARRY** AND A.W.N. **PUGIN**

1795-1860; 1812-52

Charles Barry was one of the most prolific architects of the 19th century. As a young man he traveled widely, visiting not only France and Italy, but also Jerusalem and Damascus. He was drawn to the classical and Renaissance styles but also designed some Gothic-style churches at the beginning of his career. He is, however, most famous for a series of secular buildings—London clubs, civic buildings, and large country houses. These projects prepared him for the large-scale planning needed for the Houses of Parliament.

Pugin was totally committed to the Gothic style. A Catholic convert, he was fascinated by the Middle Ages and was convinced that this period represented the best in European life and architecture. He is especially known for his Catholic churches, but he also designed a number of schools, houses, and other buildings. His love of traditional craft skills and the emphasis he placed on unpretentious design was to have a powerful influence on the architects of the late 19th-century Arts and Crafts movement.

▲ **Charles Barry**

▲ **A. W. N. Pugin**

Visual tour

1 ◀ ELIZABETH TOWER Designed by Pugin, this tower is a refined version of the one he had designed for Scarisbrick Hall, a country house in Lancashire, and contains the famous bell known as Big Ben. Pugin placed the tower at one end of the building, with no surrounding structures, so that the vertical focus of the stonework, buttresses, and windows is visible all the way up, emphasizing its height. At the top the pyramidal roof, broken into two parts, elongates the tower further. The finials (roof ornaments) and other details add a whimsical touch.

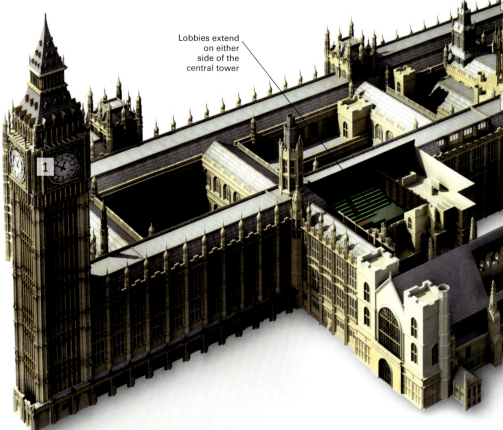

The central tower was originally designed as a chimney and air vent

Lobbies extend on either side of the central tower

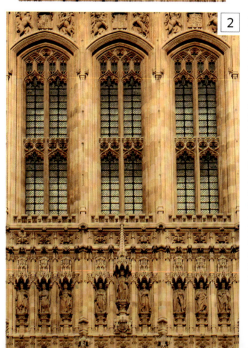

2 ◀ VICTORIA TOWER The large tower at the southwestern end of the building housed the ceremonial royal entrance and had space for the parliamentary archives above. The massive structure and the weighty contents of the archive are supported by an iron framework, concealed beneath the beautifully decorated stone façade. As well as the intricately detailed tall windows—in the late-medieval Perpendicular Gothic style—are numerous statues, standing in niches under ornate stone canopies.

3 ◀ TOWERS AND TURRETS Dozens of pinnacles, finials, and turrets enliven the skyline of the Houses of Parliament. Pugin designed all of these to be highly decorative, with ogees (double curves), carved crockets (curved, leaflike decorations running up the edges of spires and roofs), and other features. These forms of ornament appear all over the building, both on the towers and along the main façades, giving it interest and variety reminiscent of one of the great medieval cathedrals.

HOUSES OF PARLIAMENT ■ UK 175

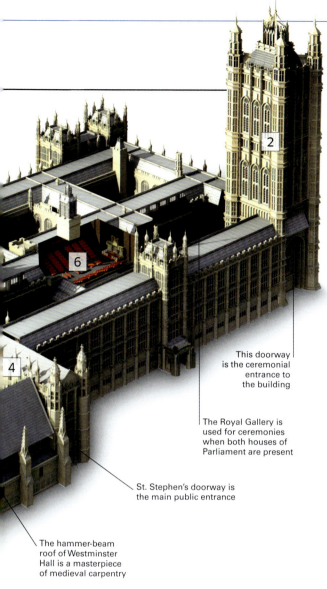

This doorway is the ceremonial entrance to the building

The Royal Gallery is used for ceremonies when both houses of Parliament are present

St. Stephen's doorway is the main public entrance

The hammer-beam roof of Westminster Hall is a masterpiece of medieval carpentry

▼ **ST. STEPHEN'S HALL** The public entrance to the Houses of Parliament opens into this vast Gothic hall, which leads to the Central Lobby. Built on the site of St. Stephen's Chapel, this large meeting space formed part of the medieval Palace of Westminster. It is roofed with a lierne vault—a type of late medieval stone vault with a very complex pattern of ribs—and is lit with rows of stained-glass windows.

▲ **CENTRAL LOBBY** The Central Lobby is a large octagonal room in the heart of the building, at the midpoint of the central "spine," with the two debating chambers and their lobbies on either side. It is a tall space, rising through several stories of the building and topped with a stone vault. The vault's starlike pattern is similar to that seen on the ceilings of the chapter houses of medieval cathedrals.

◀ **HOUSE OF LORDS** The Lords' debating chamber is a high, spacious room, richly furnished with red leather seats and decorated with gilding. Unlike the Commons chamber, which suffered bomb damage during World War II, the Lords retains most of its original features. The focal point is the huge canopy and throne on which the monarch sits to address Parliament.

IN CONTEXT

The Houses of Parliament are built on the site of the medieval Palace of Westminster, a former royal residence that became the meeting place of Parliament when democratic government evolved in England. When most of this building was burned down in 1834, only one substantial part escaped the flames—the room now known as Westminster Hall. This vast chamber, some 240ft (73m) in length, was the heart of the old palace and the scene of royal banquets and state occasions. It was originally built in 1097 but owes its present appearance to the magnificent hammer-beam roof, begun in 1393 under Richard II. The work of mason Henry Yevele and carpenter Hugh Herland, the roof is a combination of broad wooden arches and protruding hammer beams, supported by stone buttresses built by Yevele. This form of construction enabled Herland to span the room's 60ft (20.7m) width without using posts or columns—an amazing achievement at the time. The hall sits on the southern side of the present building.

▲ Westminster Hall

Neuschwanstein Castle

c.1869-81 ▪ CASTLE ▪ BAVARIA, GERMANY

EDUARD RIEDEL

High on a crag near the village of Hohenschwangau in southwest Bavaria lies the fairy-tale castle of Neuschwanstein. It was built in the late 19th century for King Ludwig II of Bavaria, who had been inspired by visits to two ancient castles—the Wartburg in Germany and Pierrefonds in France—both reconstructed in the medieval style with massive walls, tall towers, and battlements, but furnished with palatial interiors. Ludwig was obsessed by medieval history and the operas of Richard Wagner—dramatic sagas of gods, heroes, and knights—and wanted a mock-medieval castle with interiors that reflected a bygone age of chivalry. The king's architect, Eduard Riedel, may have based his work on that of stage designer Christian Jank to create the ultimate romantic castle.

The Romanesque-revival style chosen by Riedel was popular in Germany, where many architects considered its round-topped arches, barrel vaults, and sturdy walls to be essentially Germanic in character, in contrast to the more delicate Gothic Revival style with pointed arches, which they associated with the French. The version of Romanesque used by Riedel is fanciful: there are none of the fortifications of a true castle, but every feature of the building—towers, turrets, and the way the structure seems to rise organically out of the hill—is designed to recreate the image of an "ideal" castle. The towers and turrets, for example, were included solely for dramatic effect.

Ludwig worked closely with Riedel and influenced the design of the exterior as well as that of the interior, with its wall paintings of mythical scenes and the precise positions of decorative details. Although the fruit of one man's very personal vision, the building encapsulates many people's idea of the ultimate fairy-tale castle.

LUDWIG II

c.1845-86

Ludwig II became king of Bavaria in 1864, when he was 18. He was unprepared for rule and suffered a major blow when Prussia conquered Bavaria in 1866, bringing Ludwig under the control of his uncle, Wilhelm I of Prussia. As a result Ludwig had little real power, and he put his energy into creating a fantasy world, building elaborate residences including Herreninsel and Neuschwanstein. Here he could imitate the life of the kings and knights of the Holy Grail legends, becoming more of a recluse in the process. His building projects were also hugely expensive, and Ludwig spent his vast private fortune before taking on loans from foreign banks. When he refused to pay them back, the banks threatened to seize his assets. The Bavarian government declared him insane and imprisoned him. He drowned under mysterious circumstances in Lake Starnberg, near Castle Berg, where he was held.

Visual tour

1 ◀ GATEHOUSE In a medieval castle the main purpose of the gatehouse was to provide an entrance that could be securely barred against enemies. The purpose of the gatehouse at Neuschwanstein was to look impressive and provide a ceremonial gateway for visitors, a fitting prelude to the courtyard and the lavish apartments inside. Riedel therefore added features such as the royal coat of arms, the bartizans (small projecting corner turrets), plus a stepped gable to give extra height. These features evoke the military history of real castles, while also creating an interesting and impressive skyline that looms above visitors as they pass through the gate.

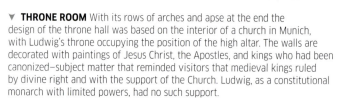

The buttresses provide extra support where the castle walls rise above the crag

2 ▶ TOWER This is a good example of how the architect added features to the castle purely to enhance the visual effect. Medieval castles often feature overhanging battlements with machicolations—holes in the overhang for dropping missiles on attackers. The towers at Neuschwanstein have these overhangs and battlements with beautifully carved masonry but not the defensive features.

▼ THRONE ROOM With its rows of arches and apse at the end the design of the throne hall was based on the interior of a church in Munich, with Ludwig's throne occupying the position of the high altar. The walls are decorated with paintings of Jesus Christ, the Apostles, and kings who had been canonized—subject matter that reminded visitors that medieval kings ruled by divine right and with the support of the Church. Ludwig, as a constitutional monarch with limited powers, had no such support.

3 ▶ PALAS Rising tall at one end of the courtyard, the residential block (*Palas* in German) contains the royal apartments and state rooms on the upper floors and servants' rooms below. The shape of the turrets on this building was influenced by those at the Château de Pierrefonds in France. The lower building to the right is called the Knights' House. The name alluded to the age of chivalry, but in reality Neuschwanstein's offices and service rooms were located here.

NEUSCHWANSTEIN CASTLE ■ GERMANY

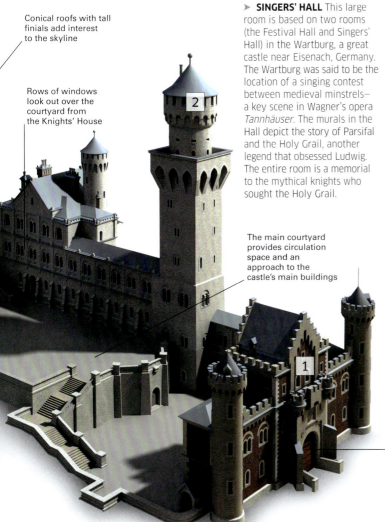

Conical roofs with tall finials add interest to the skyline

Rows of windows look out over the courtyard from the Knights' House

▶ **SINGERS' HALL** This large room is based on two rooms (the Festival Hall and Singers' Hall) in the Wartburg, a great castle near Eisenach, Germany. The Wartburg was said to be the location of a singing contest between medieval minstrels—a key scene in Wagner's opera *Tannhäuser*. The murals in the Hall depict the story of Parsifal and the Holy Grail, another legend that obsessed Ludwig. The entire room is a memorial to the mythical knights who sought the Holy Grail.

The main courtyard provides circulation space and an approach to the castle's main buildings

The gatehouse is the only part of the castle not totally clad in white stone

◀ **ROYAL BEDROOM** This room is covered in wooden paneling, and the bed has a Gothic-style wooden canopy and coverings embroidered with symbols that were personal to Ludwig, including swans, lilies, and the Bavarian coat of arms. The furnishings include elaborately carved chairs and a washstand that incorporates a fountain in the shape of a silver-plated swan. Above the wall paneling is a sequence of paintings depicting the story of Tristan and Isolde, the doomed lovers of medieval legend and the protagonists of *Tristan and Isolde*, one of Wagner's greatest operas.

ON DESIGN

Richard Wagner, the composer who inspired Ludwig to build his castle, wanted his operas to be "total works of art" in which music, words, costumes, sets, and other elements came together to produce an overwhelming experience. Ludwig aimed for a similar effect architecturally, bringing together his architect and painters, carvers, metalworkers, and other artists to create his own version of a medieval castle, where he could withdraw from the problems of everyday life. Numerous characters from Wagner's operas appear in the works of art in the castle, but it was Parsifal's son Lohengrin, a knight and protector of those in need, with whom Ludwig identified closely. Lohengrin traveled in a boat drawn by a swan, and this inspired the many images of swans in the castle.

▲ *Lohengrin* mural cycle
The murals related to *Lohengrin* can be found in Neuschwanstein's Singer's Hall, a room designed for musical performances.

Sagrada Familia

1883- ■ CHURCH ■ BARCELONA, SPAIN

ANTONI GAUDÍ

The Expiatory Church of the Holy Family, Barcelona, usually known as the Sagrada Familia (Holy Family), is the masterwork of Antoni Gaudí, the great Catalan architect. Gaudí spent the last 40 years of his life on the project, designing the church in a very personal blend of Gothic and the Art Nouveau style that was fashionable in the late 19th century. When he died, however, only a small part of the enormous church had been completed. Since then, building work has continued, largely based on Gaudí's design, but with major interruptions at various stages, notably during the Spanish Civil War, which lasted from 1936 to 1939. Some parts of the church, however, had to be planned from scratch, because Gaudí did not leave detailed plans of every feature. Although it has still not been finished, the resulting building is a staggering achievement—a cluster of strange, elongated spires topped with colored finials, an idiosyncratic assortment of pointed gables and roofs above Gothic-style windows, and a mass of sculpture. It is a church on a vast scale, in a style unlike any other, with a totally original handling of space, form, structure, and decoration.

Like many churches, the Sagrada Familia is based on a cruciform plan with an apse (curved end) housing the high altar, but Gaudí modified the layout by incorporating numerous treelike columns as well as vaults and walls that curve and divide in an unusual manner. Churches have often been likened to forests, but never has this comparison been so apt as at the Sagrada Familia. Other imaginative details—from pinnacles that resemble seed pods and honeycomb patterns on the walls to the organic twists and turns of the carvings—are based on plant designs.

The church's slender spires, emphasized by the pattern of openings and carvings that extend from top to bottom, create a striking profile as they rise majestically above the center of Barcelona. Eighteen spires are planned in total—twelve representing the Apostles, four the Evangelists, and one each for Jesus and Mary. The church's sculpted façades are also outstanding. They look Gothic at first, but the sloping columns, bizarre canopies, and carved figures make them seem to distort and change before your eyes.

Decoratively, the building is typical of its creator. Gaudí loved bright colors, and although much of the church is finished in natural stone, the tops of the spires are covered with the mosaics made from ceramic tiles that Gaudí used so widely on his secular buildings. Inside the church, color is provided not just by stained glass, but also by colored light fittings that twinkle from the high vaults. Some critics have found this decorative exuberance lacking in taste, but many of the details have symbolic significance. Crowning the Nativity façade, for example, is a large sculpted cypress, an evergreen tree that represents everlasting life. Its leaves are green, and its branches are festooned with white alabaster doves that represent the souls of the faithful entering Heaven. This Tree of Life is topped with symbols of the Holy Trinity. Gaudí's inspired use of decoration and his architecture as a whole reflect an artist single-mindedly committed to a very personal vision—a vision that Gaudí's successors in the 20th and 21st centuries have done their best to realize.

ANTONI **GAUDÍ**

1852-1926

The son of a coppersmith, Antoni Gaudí i Cornet was born at Reus, Tarragona, Spain, and began an apprenticeship at a mill before studying architecture in Barcelona. Although interested initially in revival movements and the works of art critics such as John Ruskin, Gaudí grew up at a time when artists in Catalonia were seeking a way to express their nationalism, and he became an exponent of Catalan modernism, in which ideas from the past (including the Moorish and Gothic styles) were fused with more recent influences, such as Art Nouveau, to forge a distinctive style.

Most of Gaudí's buildings are in Barcelona. The Casa Milá and Casa Batlló are city apartment blocks with curving walls, and he designed lavish private houses, such as the Palacio Güell (for his patron Don Basilio Güell), where he developed his signature forms—parabolic arches and eccentric roofscapes. In these buildings Gaudí translated the decorative curves of Art Nouveau into architecture. He also designed the Park Güell, a remarkable landscape on a hill above Barcelona, its structures studded with his trademark mosaics. After 1882 Gaudí spent most of his time on the Sagrada Familia, a building that gave him unique scope to be inventive, and the one with which his name will always be most closely associated.

Visual tour: exterior

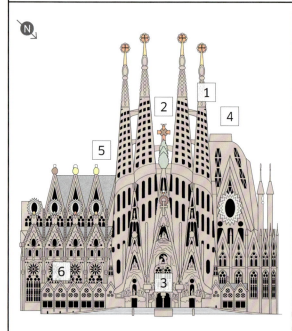

▲ **FINIALS** Natural stone is often left exposed on church exteriors. At the Sagrada Familia, however, the spires terminate in a riot of applied color that picks out carved symbols, such as the cross and the bishop's ring, and words of prayer and praise, such as *excelsis*. The spires' twisted, multifaceted forms catch the sun as it moves across the sky, picking out splashes of red, gold, white, and green. The finials are covered with mosaics made from broken tiles—favored by Gaudí because the color of the ceramics was tough and permanent, fading less with the passing of time than paint.

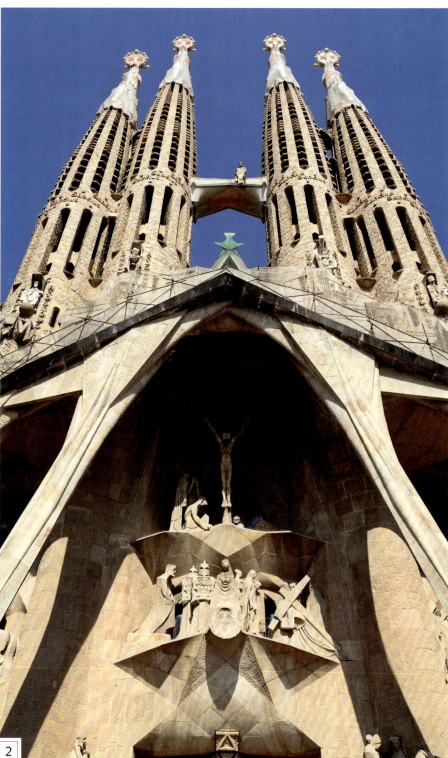

▲ **PASSION FAÇADE** The north entrance of the church is through a portal in the Passion façade, a vast wall topped by four spires and adorned with sculptures depicting the Passion of Christ, from the Last Supper to his Crucifixion and entombment. This part of the church was built in the late 20th century, but the overall layout is based on Gaudí's design. An enormous sloping canopy protects the entrance, its overhanging roof supported on a series of bizarrely angled columns whose form resembles that of giant bones or branches. To support the carvings, Gaudí designed a series of stone platforms that seem to emerge organically from the walls. In 1989 the Catalan sculptor Josep Maria Subirachs began work on the figures that adorn the platforms.

SAGRADA FAMILIA ■ SPAIN   183

▲ **PASSION SCULPTURES** Working more than 100 years after Gaudí began the building, Josep Maria Subirachs sculpts in a bold, dramatic style. His figures, such as that of Nicodemus seen here anointing Christ's body, are almost cubist in form, often with angular heads and multifaceted limbs. The sculptures are very different from those Gaudí envisioned and have provoked controversy, but many visitors find them powerful.

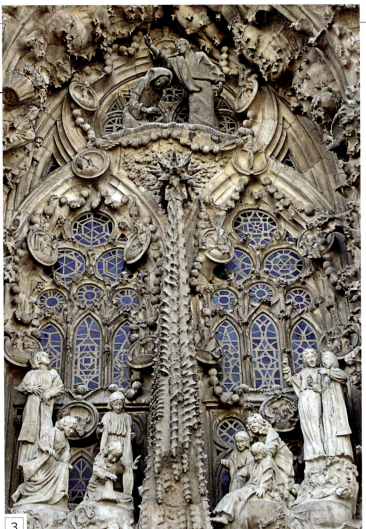

◀ **NAVE** When working with traditional Gothic forms, such as this rose window, Gaudí simplified them to emphasize their sculptural qualities. All intricate medieval tracery has been eliminated from this nave window to leave 12 plain, glazed openings and a central roundel. This simplicity provides the backdrop for a more complex treatment of the stonework.

▲ **NATIVITY FAÇADE** Located on the south side of the church, this was the first façade to be completed. Although not painted in bright colors as the architect originally intended, it is built according to Gaudí's wishes, with swirls of sculpture rising above a trio of portals. The carvings show the birth and early life of Jesus and include groups of singing and trumpeting angels. A wealth of incidental detail covers the surface of the complex façade, including crosses, rosaries, plants, birds, animals, and even the carpentry tools of Joseph's workshop.

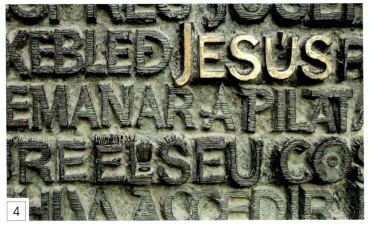

ON **CONSTRUCTION**

Work is still continuing on the Sagrada Familia. In Gaudí's lifetime many thought that the complex church would take centuries to build, but a completion date of the late 2020s is now expected. The drawing on the right shows what the final church will look like. To complete the building's 18 spires and the Glory façade, where the entrance to the nave will be, the architects and builders have had to rely on diverse sources. Some of Gaudí's original plans have not survived, so architects have had to work out the missing details, using computers to help model Gaudí's unusual shapes and forms. Fortunately, some of the models made in Gaudí's time still exist, and these have enabled builders to construct the roofs and other incomplete parts of the church.

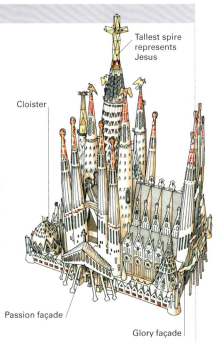

Tallest spire represents Jesus

Cloister

Passion façade

Glory façade

▲ **LETTERING** There are sacred writings and words on many of the walls of the Sagrada Familia, acknowledging the importance to Christians of the word of God and the text of the Bible. Some of these inscriptions are in a flowing, organic Art Nouveau style evolved by Gaudí, while others are more recent. The inscriptions on the bronze portals of the Passion façade—twin doors that open like a book—are among the latter. These are the work of the sculptor Subirachs, and contain texts from the Gospels in capital letters wedged closely together. Most of the words on the doors are finished quite roughly, their surfaces broken up by numerous horizontal striations. Important words or phrases, such as the name of Jesus (above), are beautifully polished to make them stand out from the others.

Visual tour: interior

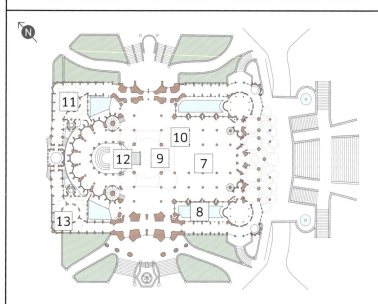

▼ **NAVE COLUMNS** Gaudí's columns are unique in the history of architecture because they change shape as they ascend—they are fluted at the base and smooth-sided higher up, and the polygonal cross section becomes circular. The columns branch out like trees toward the top to form clusters of slender branches that support different parts of the vault. In the nave, where the columns are most numerous, they form a spectacular forest of uprights and diagonals, with strange multifaceted capitals and swellings or "knots" where the uprights divide.

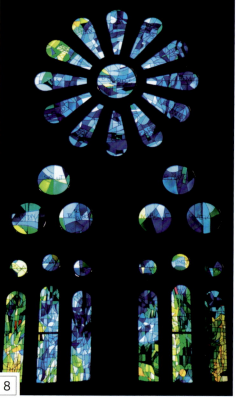

▲ **CROSSING** At the heart of the building is the crossing. Here, the nave and sanctuary, which form the main north-south axis of the church, meet the transepts, which extend from east to west. The nave, to the right, is longer and wider than the other arms, with two pairs of side aisles, while the sanctuary and transepts have one aisle on each side. All these spaces are vaulted, and the upward-sweeping lines of the columns draw your eye toward the patterns of light in the stone vaults. The church interior is vast and held around 6,500 people during the consecration ceremony of the church in 2010.

▲ **STAINED-GLASS WINDOW** The artist Joan Vila-Grau has been working on the stained-glass windows for the Sagrada Familia since 1999, following the general plan outlined by Gaudí. Using abstract patterns of saturated color, Vila-Grau creates the vivid light that suffuses the interior. The glass is made in the workshop of Josep Maria Bonet, whose work for the church dates back to the time when the crypt windows were glazed.

SAGRADA FAMILIA ■ SPAIN

◄ **VAULT DETAIL** The columns divide at the top to support a series of concave compartments in the vaults, each of which has a circle in the center containing a light fitting. Although influenced in part by the stone vaults of medieval cathedrals, the design of these compartments, is unusual. Unlike the linear ribs of medieval vaulting, there are jagged edges where each compartment adjoins the others, creating the effect of a series of starbursts. The curves of the vaults reflect the light from above, illuminating the interior of the church. These vaults are also reminiscent of the leafy crowns of trees—a reference to the natural world that was such a great source of inspiration to Gaudí.

▲ **GALLERIES** High galleries, sometimes used to accommodate choirs, line the church's interior and are reached via spiral staircases that run up the walls. These narrow galleries have undulating stonework, and the undersides are carved in a scalloped form to harmonize with the leaflike vaults above them.

▲ **APSE** The east end (in the liturgical sense) of the church is the part of the building most similar to a medieval church. The space is curved in shape, like the apse of a Gothic cathedral. The radiating series of high windows and the semicircle of seven small chapels are also Gothic features. There are two main reasons for the strong Gothic influence here. Firstly, Gaudí had to follow the lines of the crypt, which had been built in the Gothic revival style before he joined the project. Secondly, the apse was the first part of the church to be built above ground, and Gaudí had not yet developed his later idiosyncratic style.

▲ **TOWERS** The tapering towers of Gaudí's masterpiece are just as striking within as from outside. Long vertical protrusions in the stonework—similar to pilasters in conventional buildings—run all the way up the inner walls of the towers, drawing your eye upward and emphasizing their immense height.

Hôtel Tassel

c.1893–94 ▪ TOWN HOUSE ▪ BRUSSELS, BELGIUM

VICTOR HORTA

The end of the 19th century saw the birth of a new design movement that rejected the revival of past styles, such as Gothic, and was characterized by expressive decoration. Known as Art Nouveau, its first great architectural exponent was the Belgian architect, Victor Horta. The Hôtel Tassel, the Brussels town house he designed for a wealthy client, not only epitomizes the new style but also shows the architect's imaginative handling of interior space.

The most striking feature of the house is the lavish decoration: balustrades and columns are sinuous in form, and plantlike designs adorn the walls and floors. This beauty is, however, more than skin-deep. Horta was daring in his use of materials, such as iron, and in the confident way he planned the Hôtel Tassel around the stunning top-lit, central stairwell.

VICTOR **HORTA**

1861–1947

On completing his studies in Brussels, Victor Horta went to work for Alphonse Balat, architect to King Leopold II, and worked on the design of the royal greenhouses. In the 1880s he set up his own practice and gained a reputation for designing shops and town houses in characteristic Art Nouveau style. The deep economic depression after World War I, however, made the lavish ornament of Art Nouveau unaffordable, and Horta simplified his style, designing modern, logically planned buildings such as the Central Station in Brussels.

HÔTEL TASSEL ■ BELGIUM 187

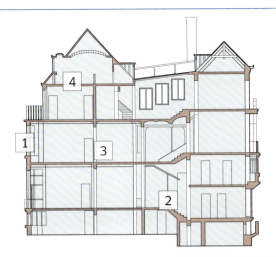

▶ **EXTERIOR IRONWORK**
The street façade of the house has a huge bow window which, with its narrow uprights and floor-to-ceiling expanses of glass, floods the interior with light. The iron railings that front the window are typically Art Nouveau in form, curving back and forth to make lines based on the stems and tendrils of plants.

◀ **DOOR HANDLES** When working for wealthy and design-conscious clients, such as Emile Tassel, Horta preferred to design all the fixtures and fittings in his buildings and, if possible, the furniture as well. Even small items like these door handles had his imprint. The swirling, organic form of the handle seems to have been designed both to complement the decorative scheme and to fit the hand comfortably.

◀ **STAIRCASE** The staircase runs up the center of the house, creating a stunning public space between the front and rear. Every surface is decorated with complex curves—the ornate tops of the metal columns are particularly expressive. The spatial handling is innovative too, with few straight lines and a series of odd-shaped spaces leading the eye past windows, columns, and railings toward the stairs.

ON **DESIGN**

Horta's town houses often occupy narrow sites that extend a long way back from the street frontage. Such sites were challenging because rooms in the middle of the house lacked exterior windows. At the Hôtel Tassel, Horta solved this problem by designing the house in three sections. Most of the rooms are in the front and rear sections, and natural light enters via windows looking either onto the street or out of the back of the building. These two parts of the house are linked by a central portion, which is lit by a glass roof. This central section contains the stairs, so the daylight from the dome can reach all three main floors. The Hôtel van Eetvelde, another of Horta's town houses, has a similar light well.

▲ **STAINED GLASS** These exquisite panels show Horta's flair with abstract decoration. The strong shapes of the design are based on the whiplash curve—a linear form typical of Art Nouveau in which a line curves one way, and then bends sharply back in the opposite direction, like the cord of a whip.

▲ **Hôtel van Eetvelde**
Here the stairs are lit by a glazed dome held up on slender columns and edged with curvilinear decoration.

Grand Palais

1897–1900 ■ GALLERY AND MUSEUM ■ PARIS, FRANCE

CHARLES GIRAULT

With a floor area of some 775,000 sq ft (72,000 sq m) and perimeter walls around 0.6 miles (1km) in length, the Grand Palais is the largest surviving 19th-century exhibition building from the era of world fairs. It was built in just three years for the Universal Exhibition of 1900 and combines a main structure of iron and glass with monumental stone façades in the grand, neoclassical Beaux Arts style that was promoted by the academic École des Beaux-Arts in Paris. Another style, Art Nouveau, is also evident both in the exterior decoration and the sinuous interior ironwork of the building. Its juxtaposition with the strong neoclassical stone elements was bold and innovative.

Four architects collaborated on the building of the Grand Palais. Charles Girault had the coordinating role, while Henri Deglane worked on the nave, Albert Thomas on the west wing, and Albert Louvet on the connecting section between the wings. The metal and glass structure they designed was light in weight, but the scale of building was so vast, and its stone façades so heavy, that construction posed a challenge. The soil on the site proved unstable, and the builders had to drive 3,400 oak piles into the ground to support the foundations. Once these were established, a long, symmetrical superstructure was erected, in which the main space was the huge nave, 656 ft (200m) long. It was roofed by a steel and glass barrel vault and featured a stunning glass dome 148ft (45m) high.

The nave formed the main exhibition area, but the additional space created by the transepts resulted in a truly cavernous interior. The building was intended primarily for displaying works of art, but it could also house larger exhibits, such as motor cars and early flying machines. Its elegant metal structure, imposing façades, and array of sculpture in stone and bronze still make it a show-stopping landmark.

CHARLES **GIRAULT**

1851–1932

Born at Cosne sur Loire, Charles Girault studied at the prestigious École des Beaux-Arts in Paris, where he was taught the fashionable style of neoclassicism that the establishment favored. In 1880 he won the Premier Prix de Rome, a competition held for young artists, architects, and musicians, which entitled him to travel to Rome, live at the city's Villa Medici, and study Roman architecture. Back in Paris, he worked on many projects: the tomb of Louis Pasteur, the Hôtel de Choudens (built for a French music publisher), and the grandstands at Longchamps racecourse. He had a key supervisory role at the Grand Palais and was the sole architect of the neighboring Petit Palais. Leopold II, the Belgian king, was particularly impressed by the Grand Palais and commissioned Girault to design the Cinquantenaire Arch in Brussels and the Congo Palace (now the Royal Museum for Central Africa) outside the city.

Visual tour

◀ **GLASS DOME** Forming the centerpiece of the building, the dome bridges the junction between the nave and transepts, like the crossing of a cathedral. Compared with a conventional masonry dome, it is lightweight, so the concentric rings of panes of glass stay in place with little in the way of heavy beams or trusses. At the center of the dome is a finial, some 148ft (45m) from the ground, that terminates in a flagpole. Although dwarfed by the size of the building, the finial forms a visible focus for the vast roof when the building's huge flag is flying.

▼ **WALKWAY** There are walkways and access stairs all over the roof so that maintenance workers can climb over the vast expanse of metal and glass to clean it and carry out essential repairs. One gangway runs around the edges of the nave roof at the bottom of the glass barrel vault. Along these edges much of the roof is covered in zinc rather than glass.

The zinc-covered area provides easy access to the glass roof

▲ **PORTICO** Enormous classical columns rise from large bases almost to the top of the outer walls of the building. This grandiose façade, with its bold cornice and huge statues, was mainly the work of the architect Henri Deglane, who was true to the spirit of the Beaux Arts style. The sculptures depict allegorical figures such as Peace, Inspiration, and Minerva, protecting the arts.

▶ **NAVE INTERIOR** Evenly spaced metal arches, linked to twin lateral beams, support the nave ceiling and made it possible to use the maximum amount of clear glass. Natural light pours through this roof, providing the best conditions in which to view the items on display. When the Grand Palais was opened, electric light was still a novelty, and exhibition buildings were naturally lit.

GRAND PALAIS ■ FRANCE

The nave is the main exhibition area

The columned stone façade dominates the surrounding streets

IN **CONTEXT**

The fashion for large exhibitions, and vast glazed buildings to house them, began with the 1851 Great Exhibition in London. The Crystal Palace, the building that housed this event, was the brainchild of the engineer Joseph Paxton, a former gardener and designer of greenhouses who was supremely confident in his handling of glass and metalwork. Glazed building were popular for exhibitions because they let in plenty of natural light and were very quick to build. The components could be prefabricated in workshops and then transported to the site for assembly.

▲ **The Crystal Palace, London**
This 1851 exhibition hall was so successful that it was taken apart and re-erected at another location.

▶ **METALWORK DETAIL**
By the time the Grand Palais was built, the Art Nouveau movement was at its height in Paris, and the swirling curves that run across the metalwork above these arches are typical of the style. Some of the patterns are made by metal strips on the surface, so that they stand out in low relief. Others are cut straight into the metalwork.

◀ **DOME INTERIOR** Large iron supports, held together with thousands of rivets, soar from the floor up to the cornice level, where they split in two. Their branches then continue upward to form the dome's structural ribs. These metal components, which carry the weight of the glass, are enormous, and even have balconies. For much of their height, however, they are of openwork construction, which conveys an overall impression of surprising lightness.

▲ **GRAND STAIRCASE** Sweeping staircases were a prominent feature of Beaux Arts buildings and were intended to be a focal point. As well as providing access to upper levels, they were equipped with landings from which fashionable people could admire the building and be seen by their friends. The ornate Art Nouveau banisters and supports of this grand staircase were designed as a flattering setting for the elegant clothes of the affluent visitors.

- **CHRYSLER BUILDING**
  New York City, NY

- **VILLA SAVOYE**
  Poissy, France

- **FALLINGWATER**
  Mill Run, PA

- **SYDNEY OPERA HOUSE**
  Sydney, Australia

- **BRASÍLIA CATHEDRAL**
  Brasília, Brazil

- **POMPIDOU CENTRE**
  Paris, France

- **NATIONAL GALLERY OF CANADA**
  Ottawa, Canada

- **GUGGENHEIM MUSEUM, BILBAO**
  Bilbao, Spain

- **JEAN-MARIE TJIBAOU CULTURAL CENTRE**
  Nouméa, New Caledonia

- **JIN MAO TOWER**
  Shanghai, China

- **SEATTLE CENTRAL LIBRARY**
  Seattle, WA

- **PALACE OF THE ARTS**
  Valencia, Spain

- **MAXXI**
  Rome, Italy

- **YUSUHARA WOODEN BRIDGE MUSEUM**
  Kōchi, Japan

1900 to present

Chrysler Building

1928-30 ■ OFFICE BLOCK ■ NEW YORK CITY, USA

WILLIAM VAN ALEN

The world's tallest tower at the time it was built, the Chrysler Building—commissioned by Chrysler to be their headquarters—is one of the most strikingly theatrical skyscrapers ever constructed. The 1,047-ft (319-m), 77-story structure is planned on a grand scale, rising from a broad, substantial base and becoming progressively narrower through the slender main tower to the unique spire that tapers to a point. The detailing is even bolder than the overall design—a series of flourishes, culminating in the famous spire, that mark out the architect, William Van Alen, as a great showman who was determined to make a building that would be instantly memorable and recognizable the world over.

Art Deco styling

The Chrysler Building is Art Deco in style. Art Deco took its name from the 1925 Paris Exposition Internationale des Arts Décoratifs et Industriels Modernes, and it quickly caught on in both Europe and North America as a way of designing both buildings and items for the home. Art Deco was characterized by bright colors; bold, geometrical decorations; modern surface materials (from dazzling new metal alloys to colorful plastics); and motifs borrowed from ancient Egyptian art. All these elements appealed to architects, and Art Deco became particularly popular for showy, eye-catching buildings, such as cinemas, grand hotels, and skyscrapers.

Van Alen made extensive use of Art Deco details in the Chrysler Building. For the exterior he took motifs such as hubcaps and hood ornaments from cars built by Chrysler and adapted them to suit the architecture of the building. Inside, rich wood inlays and metal decorations make the lobbies and elevators some of the most memorable in Manhattan. Van Alen originally intended to increase his already lavish use of glass by topping the tower with a dome, but he soon changed his plans. While the tower was under construction, New York's Bank of Manhattan building was completed at 927ft (282.5m)—about a yard taller than the Chrysler's planned height—so Van Alen decided to replace the dome with a spire. The spire was prefabricated in four sections, which were hoisted into position on October 23, 1929, adding 121ft (37m) to the building's height. The spire proved to be a masterstroke, a tapering structure made of a series of curves, each smaller than the one below. Clad in metal and with unusual triangular windows that shine like beacons at night, the spire resembles a series of sunbursts—another popular Art Deco motif.

By adding a spire to the Chrysler Building, Van Alen had designed not only the tallest tower in the world, but also the first human-made structure to top 1,000ft (305m). On a clear day visitors to the double-height observatory on the 71st floor could enjoy views of over 100 miles (161km). The Chrysler's height alone was enough to make the building famous, but it was also a world leader in terms of modernity and efficiency. The 10,000 people who worked in the building were served by 32 high-speed elevators, and there was a state-of-the art vacuum cleaning system. The communal rooms were decorated with mirror-clad columns and had Art Deco aluminium furniture. Both inside and out, the Chrysler was the ultimate Art Deco building.

WILLIAM VAN ALEN

1883-1954

William Van Alen was born in Brooklyn, New York, and took night classes at the nearby Pratt Institute. He worked for several New York City architects on buildings in the city before winning a scholarship in 1908 to go to Paris, which enabled him to study at the École des Beaux-Arts. When he returned to the US, he set up in partnership with H Craig Severance, and the pair worked on a number of tall commercial buildings before they quarreled and parted company. When Van Alen, now working independently, began constructing the Chrysler Building, he found himself in a race with Severance to build the tallest skyscraper—a race he eventually won. When the project was completed, however, Van Alen entered into dispute with his client, Walter Chrysler. The architect had no contract with Chrysler, and when he claimed his fee of six percent of the construction budget, the money was withheld. Van Alen sued Chrysler and won the case, but after such a high-profile conflict with an influential client, he found it difficult to obtain further work, especially during the Great Depression. Most of Van Alen's estate was left to the independent architectural organization that now bears his name.

Visual tour

▼ **SETBACKS** A visitor looking up at the tower from the main entrance is greeted by a symmetrical pattern of windows and a carefully arranged series of blocks. A few stories up in the center, the first setback (recession) gives a dramatic view of the tower, rising toward the sky. On either side the building tapers with further setbacks, so that sunlight can reach down to the frontages on 42nd Street and Lexington Avenue.

▲ **ORNAMENTATION** The building's unique decorative details include the stylized wing motif shown here, which is taken from Chrysler radiator caps. Another key element is a series of circles, based on Chrysler hubcaps, that run around the walls. These decorations not only made the building a successful advertisement for Chrysler automobiles, they also helped to set it apart from the white-walled austerity of modernism as well as the serious classicism of older buildings.

◄ **MAIN ENTRANCE** Many Art Deco buildings use glass creatively, and the Chrysler Building is no exception. High windows above the main entrance light the lobby, and the glazing is arranged in relatively small panes, which create a pattern of rectangles and diagonals. On each side triangular panels in a zigzag design add to the effect, and the bright metal finish of the glazing bars harmonizes with the steel-edged entrance doors below. This entrance is designed to be equally impressive at night, when the number of the building stands out against a glowing background.

CHRYSLER BUILDING ■ USA

◄ **SPIRE DETAIL** A late modification to increase the height of the tower, this glittering spire quickly became the most famous part of the building. Its distinctive tiers of shining crescents are clad in Nirosta stainless steel, which contains a percentage of nickel and chromium, making it weather-resistant, strong, and bright. Van Alen liked its low-maintenance properties, which ensured that the top of the building would shine brightly for many decades.

▼ **GARGOYLE** Taking the form of giant eagle heads and clad in Nirosta stainless steel like the spire, a number of striking gargoyles jut out from the corners of the building. Streamlined in design, they are the Art Deco equivalent of the gargoyles on Gothic cathedrals (see p.75). Van Alen based the birds on the hood ornaments of the 1929 Plymouth automobiles manufactured by Chrysler. The gargoyles' necks hold floodlights that illuminate the building at night.

▲ **ELEVATOR DOOR** The lobbies are among the most luxurious areas of the building and have walls of red Moroccan marble designed to impress anyone entering the main door. The elevator doors are inlaid with rare woods, including Japanese ash and Asian walnut. The inlay creates curling scroll patterns, with a fanlike design at the top that was probably influenced by Egyptian lotus-flower motifs. Some elevators took just a minute to reach the top of the building.

IN **CONTEXT**

Skyscrapers—tall buildings supported by a steel frame—were first constructed in Chicago in the 1880s. By the beginning of the 20th century they had spread to other American cities, especially New York, where owners and developers saw two advantages to building tall: they could cram in more offices on expensive city-center sites and could use a tall building for publicity. Landmark New York skyscrapers included the Gothic-style Woolworth Building (1913, 791ft/241m) and the Empire State Building (1931, 1,453ft/443m).

▲ **Empire State Building, New York**
For decades following its construction, this famous skyscraper remained the world's tallest building.

Villa Savoye

1929-31 ■ HOUSE ■ POISSY, FRANCE

LE CORBUSIER

With its white walls, generous windows, and open-plan living areas, the Villa Savoye is perhaps the most iconic house by the great architect, Le Corbusier. When he was commissioned to design this country retreat on the outskirts of Paris, Le Corbusier was already a pioneer of modernist architecture—an innovative style based upon the idea that the form of a building was determined by its function. In modernist buildings materials such as concrete and glass were used in striking new ways.

In his book of 1932, *Vers Une Architecture* (Toward An Architecture), Le Corbusier listed five principles that modern buildings should follow: they should use pilotis (narrow columns) to raise the building above the ground; have a "free façade," in which design was not dictated by structure; an open floorplan; strip windows to make the interior light; and a roof garden to compensate for the lack of ground space. At the Villa Savoye, the slender, white pilotis support the weight of the building, leaving open

space beneath it. Freed from structural constraints, the façades of the Villa Savoye have clean, uncluttered lines. The living accommodation is on the first floor above the pilotis, while the central block on the ground floor contains the entrance to the villa and the service rooms.

Le Corbusier was able to dispense with load-bearing walls inside the building too, and created a series of airy spaces that flow smoothly into each other. The long strip windows not only flood the house with natural light, but also provide it with views in all directions, and the roof garden replaces the green area on which the house stands. The ramps, screen walls, and extensive windows of this elegant house make it seem as if the interior and the roof garden merge seamlessly, creating an elegant, minimalist structure with beautiful, light-filled internal spaces. Widely admired, the Villa Savoye is considered one of the finest examples of modernist architecture.

LE CORBUSIER
1887–1965

Charles-Édouard Jeanneret, who practiced architecture under the name of Le Corbusier, was born in La Chaux-de-Fonds, Switzerland, where he attended the local art school. He also studied in Vienna, and as a young man worked for two great architects—French concrete pioneer Auguste Perret and German modernist Peter Behrens. After World War I Le Corbuisier set up in practice with his cousin, Pierre Jeanneret, and became famous for designing immaculate modernist houses that combined functionalism with a unique elegance. "A house is a machine for living in," he wrote. In the 1930s Le Corbusier worked on ideas for city planning, publishing *La Ville Radieuse* (The Radiant City) in 1935, and after World War II he built a number of large urban blocks called *Unités d'Habitation* (Living Units), which contained apartments, shops, and other facilities. During the same time he also worked on plans for the city of Chandigarh, India, and designed smaller-scale, sculptural buildings in concrete, such as the pilgrimage chapel at Ronchamp in France. Le Corbusier's innovative buildings and numerous writings have made him one of the most influential of all 20th-century architects.

Visual tour

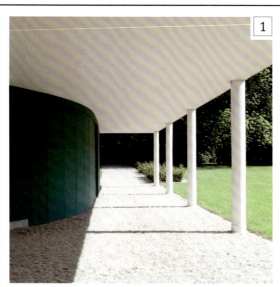

PILOTIS The owner's accommodation on the first floor and the terrace above it are raised up on plain, unadorned pilotis. This frees up the ground floor for a central block containing the entrance hall, stairs, and ramp, rooms for the chauffeur and maid, and the garage. The paved area beneath the main house was exactly the right width for the owner's car—a 1927 Citroën admired by Le Corbusier—to drive around.

FAÇADE Large strip windows run all around the façade, providing fine, uninterrupted views in all directions from the main rooms of the house. The walls above the windows appear to have no visible means of support. Le Corbusier was only able to build in this way because most of the building's weight is borne by the pilotis. As the walls were lightweight, rather than load-bearing, he had more freedom to concentrate on their appearance.

Plain white walls

LIVING AREA The main living room is uncluttered, and the walls, floors, and ceilings are all white, or pale in color. This interior connects seamlessly with part of the roof garden by means of a full-height glass wall and a sliding screen of glass. This layout is a perfect example of Le Corbusier's idea of the open floor plan. Because the walls do not have to support the weight of the house, they can be made of a non-load-bearing material such as glass and can be positioned wherever they are needed from an aesthetic point of view.

RAMP TO ROOF The main levels of the house are linked by stairs, but they can also be accessed by gently sloping ramps, such as this one that leads up toward the roof garden and sun terrace at the top of the building. The ramps cut through the house and open up interesting views. Le Corbusier wanted the ascent to end with one of the most important spaces in the house—the roof garden, where people could enjoy the warmth and beneficial effects of the sun.

VILLA SAVOYE ■ FRANCE

The evenly spaced pilotis support the weight of the house

Central block

> **STAIRS** The internal stairs set up a rhythm of curves that counterpoint the straight lines and rectangles that define most of the interior. The white curves are thrown into relief by black rails and uprights, reflecting a theme that runs throughout the villa, in which dark doors and window frames form a contrast to the white walls. This interplay of curves and straight lines, and black and white, gives the interior a sculptural quality that is emphasized by the natural light from the windows, which changes throughout the day.

▲ **BATHROOM** Next to the master bedroom is this bathroom. A curtain may be pulled across the end of it for privacy, or left open, as above. The bathroom has a blue-tiled bath with a built-in, raised, reclining seat running across one end rather like a wall. This unusual design was perhaps influenced by the Turkish baths that Le Corbusier had visited as a young man, when he traveled around the Mediterranean looking at local styles of architecture.

ON CONSTRUCTION

Le Corbusier was fascinated by the structural possibilities of reinforced concrete. From 1914 to 1915 he worked with the French architect Auguste Perret, a pioneer of modern concrete construction, on a design for a house he called the Dom-ino (a name in which *domus*, the Latin word for house, is merged with dominos, the game). The floors of the Dom-ino were to be made of concrete slabs and to have supporting concrete posts, thereby eliminating the need for horizontal beams. Setting the posts slightly inside the edges of the floor slabs made it possible to fit lightweight, non-load-bearing walls around them. Le Corbusier hoped that the Dom-ino would provide a cheap form of mass housing after World War I. The project was never realized, but it gave Le Corbuisier an insight into how to build houses such as the Villa Savoye.

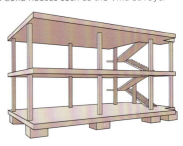

▲ **Design for the Dom-ino house**
The frame of the house consisted of flat slabs of concrete and pilotis, like those of the Villa Savoye.

IN CONTEXT

Le Corbusier is known as one of the leaders of European modernism. This style of architecture developed in the early decades of the 20th century and can also be seen in the work of German architects such as Ludwig Mies van der Rohe and Walter Gropius.

The modernists embraced the idea that "form follows function" and used industrial materials such as steel, glass, and concrete. They displayed structural elements that had previously been considered ugly and minimized applied ornament. They liked light, uncluttered interiors and preferred flat roofs to traditional pitched ones. Although these features sometimes made the buildings seem stark, good modernist architecture has a beauty of form and fitness for purpose that have ensured the style is still influential today.

▲ **Barcelona Pavilion**
Mies van der Rohe's German Pavilion for the Barcelona International Exposition of 1929 is an elegant composition of stone slabs and walls of glass.

Fallingwater

1936-39 ■ HOUSE ■ PENNSYLVANIA, USA

FRANK LLOYD WRIGHT

The American architect Frank Lloyd Wright created some of the most memorable and striking houses of the 20th century and Fallingwater, which he designed for Edgar Kaufmann, a wealthy department-store owner, is the most famous of them all. Built on a rock ledge right above a waterfall in the wooded countryside southeast of Pittsburgh, Pennsylvania, Fallingwater features dramatic, jutting balconies and big expanses of glass. The way in which its stone walls and concrete balconies emerge from the woodland setting and appear to float above the mountain stream creates a unique marriage of architecture and site.

Neither Kaufmann nor his building contractor were confident that the structure of the house would be stable, and the construction was plagued with disputes between Wright, his client, and the builders. The cantilevered (jutting) balconies were the most challenging element of the design, and the builders had to strengthen them with additional steelwork, but this made them heavier than Wright had originally intended them to be and probably contributed to a slight sagging.

The resulting house was, however, spectacular. A huge, stone-floored living room offered plenty of space for sitting and eating. On one side of this room Wright built a stone hearth around an existing boulder–at the very spot at the edge of the waterfall where the Kaufmann family used to picnic. The broad windows of the living room and bedrooms look out onto stunning views of the trees surrounding the house, and the generous balconies–two connected to the living room, two more to the bedrooms, and a fifth to the gallery at the top of the house–invite family and guests to step outside. This skillful linking of the interior and exterior, together with the way in which the house itself seems to form part of the waterfall and woodland, is perhaps the ultimate example of what Wright called "organic architecture."

FRANK **LLOYD WRIGHT**

1867-1959

Initially trained as an engineer, Wisconsin-born Frank Lloyd Wright worked for various architects, including Louis Sullivan, the great designer of early skyscrapers, before setting up his own practice. Based in Chicago, Wright made his name designing large, low-slung houses for wealthy clients, as well as his own homes, Taliesin in Wisconsin and Taliesin West in Arizona. He went on to design larger buildings, such as Tokyo's Imperial Hotel and the 1936 corporate headquarters for Johnson Wax in Racine, Wisconsin, known for its innovative interior columns. A series of less-costly houses in the 1930s brought Wright's design ideas to a wider clientele, and after World War II he continued to experiment, designing New York's Guggenheim Museum, with its unique spiral ramp. Such spectacular buildings made Wright one of the most influential architects of the 20th century.

1900 TO PRESENT

Visual tour: exterior

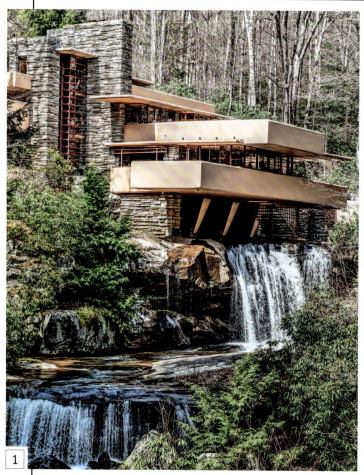

The gallery at the top provides the best viewpoint

The main bedrooms are on this floor

The living room windows look out onto the trees

Steps lead down from the house to the stream

The waterfall is on Bear Run, a mountain stream

▲ **TRAYLIKE BALCONIES** Appearing to float above the falls, these solid concrete balconies are cantilevered (project outward from their visible means of support). They are in fact balanced on reinforced concrete beams and steelwork that is anchored firmly to the bedrock beneath the house. Fallingwater's main balconies appear particularly large because they jut out so far from the core structure.

▶ **EXTERIOR STAIRS** Steps made from various materials, including natural stone, run up the sides of the house, linking the building both to the nearby guesthouse and the stream. The stone for the house came from the small quarry near the building site, which had been reopened by Wright. As a result there is perfect harmony between the rocks on which the house stands, the masonry that rises up from them to form the core of the building, and other stone features.

◀ **GLASS AND STEEL** Few of the rooms in the house have conventional window frames. The panes of glass are held between horizontal red metal glazing bars and run right up to the walls and into a caulked (waterproofed) gap between the stones. Wright liked the way in which a fragile material such as glass could butt up against rough, rugged stone, creating an unusual contrast in texture. By using window frames without edges, he could also maximize the amount of natural light coming into the house.

FALLINGWATER ■ USA

The walls are made from local stone

ON DESIGN

A famous story tells how Kaufmann called Wright to say he was on his way to the architect's office later that day. Wright, who had still not done any drawings for Fallingwater, his client's new house, duly produced drawings in a couple of hours. Although the initial drawings may have been produced quickly, the actual design of the house evolved over a lengthy period of time, with various stages of preliminary and more final drawings. Toward the end of this process, Wright, who loved to make elegant perspective drawings of his buildings, often influenced by the Japanese graphics he liked, created his most famous image of the house (below). This shows Fallingwater from a low viewpoint, its balconies stretching out above a sheer curtain of water.

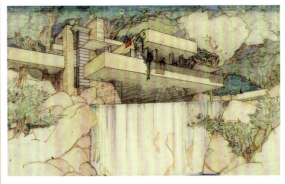

▲ **Fallingwater**
The perspective in Wright's drawing, made from below the falls, exaggerates the size and cantilevering of the balconies.

IN CONTEXT

In the early years of the 20th century Wright designed a series of houses for rich clients in the Midwest. Inspired by the wide open, flat landscape of the prairies, these buildings, known as Prairie houses, were large and ground-hugging, often with generously overhanging roofs and long, horizontal strips of windows. They tended to be on a cross-shaped plan, focused on a central hearth, and featured innovative details such as built-in furniture. Natural materials, especially plain wood, dominated, and the big reception rooms had porches or terraces, blurring the boundary between the interior and exterior. The Prairie houses established Wright as one of the leading architects of his time and redefined American domestic architecture.

▲ **The Robie House**
Completed in 1910, this Chicago home, built by Wright in the Prairie style, is a striking forerunner of Modernist architecture.

◄ **GUEST HOUSE** Linked to the main house by a curving path are a guest house, where the Kaufmanns' servants lived, and a car port. Built two years after Fallingwater, these were constructed to the same specifications and with similar materials. Wright made sure that water—such an important presence in the main house—was also a feature of the guest house by incorporating a swimming pool, fed by a spring, which overflowed into the river.

Visual tour: interior

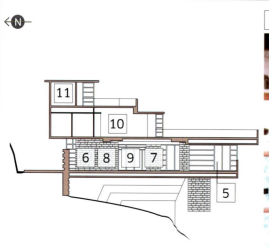

▶ **LIVING ROOM** The huge living room shimmers with light from the wide row of windows running along its southern side. When opened, these let in the sound of the waterfall below. The natural stone-flagged floor and exposed stone walls harmonize with the rocks outside, while the plain ceiling is a neutral off-white in color. The living room is large enough to contain several groups of seats—one by the windows, another near the hearth (to the right in the photograph), and a seating area in a "music alcove."

▼ **DINING AREA** Above the dining table, which is set at one end of the large living room, rises a stone pillar punctuated by a series of red wooden shelves, their curved ends reminiscent of the Art Deco style popular during the 1930s. The tone of the interior is set mainly by the abundant use of natural materials, particularly the rugged stone of both the wall and the stairs that lead up to the next floor.

◀ **HEARTH AND KETTLE** For Wright the hearth was the vital, living center of any house, providing physical warmth and light as well as emotional sustenance. The hearth at Fallingwater is set on a natural stone. Above it hangs a large spherical kettle for making warm drinks. It could be swung over to one side when not in use so the Kaufmanns could feel the full heat of the log fire.

▶ **STONEWORK DETAIL** Although the interior stone is quite rough in terms of its finish, the builders shaped the blocks with care. Many of these are long and thin and have been skillfully laid in neat patterns. The horizontal lines of the stonework echo, on a smaller scale, the whole layout of the house—the rooms spread generously and are fairly low. Wright's houses are often variations on a horizontal theme.

GLAZING This detail shows the glazed "hatch," where steps descend to the stream beneath the house. The striking red glazing bars of the window continue the strong horizontal theme that runs throughout the house. At the corner the two glass surfaces have been joined together without any frame at all, providing an uninterrupted view of the surrounding woods and "dissolving" the corner of the building.

▶ **EDGAR KAUFMANN'S BEDROOM** This view through the bedroom window to the trees shows Wright's mastery of spatial and textural effects in one of the smaller rooms. There is a strong sense of continuity between the exterior and interior, especially clear where the glazing meets the stone wall, and the external masonry seems to merge with the internal stonework. The glazing bars cast a striking pattern of light and shade on the stone floor.

EDGAR KAUFMANN'S DESK This desk is one of many built-in pieces of furniture that were specially designed by Wright for the house. The architect also created bookshelves that are fitted directly into the masonry above the desk. At one end Wright cut out a quarter-circle of wood from the desktop so that the adjacent casement window could open into the room.

Sydney Opera House

1957–73 ■ OPERA HOUSE ■ SYDNEY, AUSTRALIA

JØRN UTZON

In 1956 the government of New South Wales, Australia, announced an international competition to design a new opera house for Sydney. The site was Benelong Point, a promontory with views to the sea and the famous Harbour Bridge. Many architects submitted proposals, and the winner was Jørn Utzon, a Danish architect little known outside his home country.

Utzon's design incorporated a series of sculptural white roofs that swept up from near the ground, like the billowing sails of the yachts on the water beyond. It was undoubtedly the stunning form of these roofs, which covered the building's two main halls, that won Utzon the competition, but they also posed a major problem: Utzon's competition designs had been created without input from structural engineers and did not give enough information to work out exactly what shape the roofs should be.

As a result of the ensuing technical problems, controversies about aspects of the design, and disputes over the budget, the construction of the Opera House was dogged by problems from the start. Work began in 1959 with the design of the roofs still unresolved. Utzon and the structural engineers, Ove Arup and Partners, eventually worked out that the best solution would be to treat the roofs like the sections of a sphere. The concrete structure finally began to rise, but Utzon resigned when the project was put under the control of the Ministry of Public Works and there was a political dispute over control of the work.

After Utzon's resignation the layout of the building's interior was altered to make it more practical. In spite of all the difficulties a stunning building had emerged by the time construction ended, and the Opera House is now a world-class performing arts center. The billowing roofline has become not only a celebrated icon of post-war architecture but also a symbol of the modern, vibrant city of Sydney.

JØRN **UTZON**

1918–2008

The architect of the Sydney Opera House was born in Copenhagen, Denmark. Before setting up his own office in his home city, Utzon worked for the great Swedish architect Gunnar Apslund and spent a year with the influential Finnish modernist Alvar Aalto. He designed houses in Denmark until he won the Sydney competition in 1957. The Opera House became his most famous building, but the controversy surrounding its construction and the huge cost overrun (arguably caused by politicians setting an artificially low budget) meant that few high-profile clients commissioned him. After Sydney, Utzon returned to Europe and designed a memorable church at Bagsværd, Copenhagen, and the National Assembly Building in Kuwait. Both buildings showed his flair for creating sculptural architecture using concrete.

1900–PRESENT

Visual tour

▲ **EXTERIOR STEPS** The imposing approach to the Opera House is up a broad flight of granite steps and across an outside podium to the foyers. These are, therefore, well above ground level, and the service rooms are concealed beneath them.

▼ **ROOF TILES** Chevron-shaped trays containing thousands of white ceramic tiles cover the roofs. Some of the tiles are glazed, while others have a matte finish, and the contrast between the two produces a striking pattern of light and shade across the sculptural roofs.

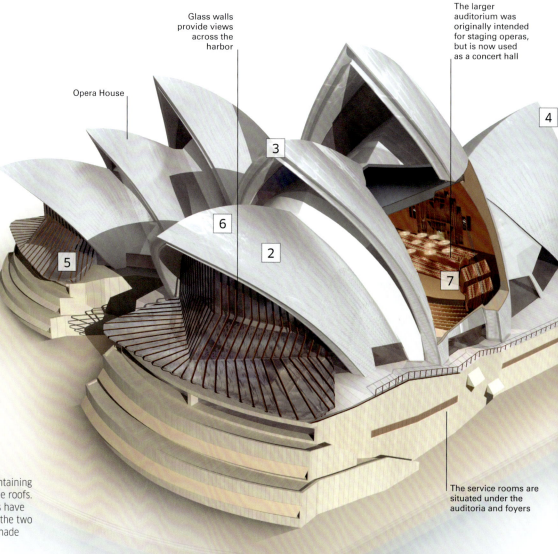

Glass walls provide views across the harbor

The larger auditorium was originally intended for staging operas, but is now used as a concert hall

Opera House

The service rooms are situated under the auditoria and foyers

▲ **ROOF SHELLS** The shape of the roofs was inspired by the sails of boats—Jørn Utzon enjoyed sailing. Their distinctive profile—arching segments standing out against the sky—has made the Opera House the most recognizable building in Australia and has given it iconic status.

▲ **ENTRANCES** Visitors enter the Opera House through soaring "walls" of glass, giving uninterrupted views into the impressive foyers of the twin auditoria. Vertical steel mullions hold the huge sheets of glass in place and anchor the windows directly to the precast concrete structure of the roofs.

SYDNEY OPERA HOUSE ■ AUSTRALIA

A small shell-roofed structure houses the restaurant

▲ **CONCERT HALL INTERIOR** Banks of seating for almost 2,700 people look toward the stage and the organ pipes beyond in this large space originally intended for opera productions. The high, vaulted ceilings are clad in curving panels of plywood and the simple, elegant seat backs in a pale birch veneer.

▲ **GLASS SCREENS** Huge upward-sweeping canopies of glass cover the foyers and bars at the northern end of the building. Each screen consists of a three-layer sandwich of glass held in place by ribs of steel. Utzon is said to have based the design on a bird's wing.

▲ **TAPESTRY** In 1993 Utzon was invited to offer guidance on refurbishing the interiors of the Opera House. In 2004 the Reception Hall, now known as the Utzon Hall, was completed and a stunning, 46ft- (14m-) wide, full-length tapestry, designed by the architect, was hung on the wall opposite the harbor outlook.

ON CONSTRUCTION

Because Utzon's original competition design was short on detail—and because the competition brief itself was somewhat unspecific—the design of the Opera House went through many alterations after Utzon won. Both architect and engineers tried to find a way of working out the geometry of the roofs, trying ellipses, parabolas, and other shapes, before they decided on sections of a sphere. Making the transition from the roofs to the floor was also a major challenge. Utzon achieved this at either end of the building with great walls of glass, which he referred to as glass "curtains." He also redesigned the hall interiors several times, but their final appearance owes most to the team that took over after his resignation.

▲ **Working models**
Utzon and the engineers made numerous cardboard and wooden models of the building to help them with aspects of the design such as the "curtains" of glass (left) and the structural ribs for the roof (right).

IN CONTEXT

In the early part of the 20th century, architects realized that concrete was a material with outstanding sculptural properties. Curves and other unusual shapes that took hard work and skill to achieve in brick or stone could be created relatively easily using concrete. Expressionist architects exploited the malleability of the material in the 1920s and 1930s, and after the end of World War II architects again began to sculpt rounded shapes using concrete.

As well as curving walls, concrete reinforced with steel could be used to create thin-shell structures, as in the roof of the TWA Flight Center, New York, designed by Eero Saarinen, a Finnish architect who was on the judging panel for the Sydney Opera House competition. Jørn Utzon was very much a man of his time in his expressive use of concrete shells.

▲ **TWA Flight Center, New York, 1962**
The outstretched, winglike roofs of Eero Saarinen's building form an obvious symbol for flight. Inside, the concrete structure houses a series of fluid spaces.

Brasília Cathedral

COMPLETED 1970 ■ CATHEDRAL ■ BRASÍLIA, BRAZIL

OSCAR NIEMEYER

Brasília, the capital of Brazil, was built from scratch in the center of the country in the late 1950s. The principal planner was Lucio Costa, and the lead architect was Oscar Niemeyer, who designed not only many government buildings but also the cathedral in the city center. Niemeyer became a master in the use of concrete to produce sweeping sculptural designs, and the cathedral is an outstanding example.

The cathedral is based on 16 identical concrete columns. Each column weighs 90 tons and stretches, in a flowing hyperboloid curve, from the ground to the top of the building. The columns rise and converge, meeting about two-thirds of the way up before splaying outward and upward, creating a crownlike shape topped with a plain cross.

The spaces between the columns are almost entirely glazed so that, from the outside, the concrete stands out from the neutral glass to create one of the most dramatic forms in modern architecture. The vast expanse of glass ensures that the cathedral's interior is bathed in light. There is a strong visual play between the columns, which lead the eye upward, and the swirling patterns of blue, green, and brown stained glass, which converge near the high altar on one edge of the interior. The vast floor can accommodate up to 4,000 worshippers.

This awe-inspiring cathedral is rich in symbolism, with its columns soaring into the sky and metaphorically toward heaven, and its interior a three-dimensional representation of the light of Christianity. The building has, however, had its practical problems. The ventilation proved inadequate and the acoustics were faulty—issues that are being addressed. Despite that, the cathedral remains a stunning design, one that helped to win Niemeyer the prestigious Pritzker Prize in 1988, when the citation praised his buildings for the way they distilled "the colors and light and sensual imagery of his native Brazil."

OSCAR **NIEMEYER**

1907–2012

Centenarian Oscar Niemeyer was born in Rio de Janeiro and, after qualifying, worked for the Brazilian architect and planner Lucio Costa. With Costa he designed the new headquarters of Brazil's Ministry of Education and Public Health (a project on which Le Corbusier was consultant), before working independently on buildings such as the church of St. Francis of Assisi Belo Horizonte, where he developed his flair for curved forms. By the late 1940s he was part of the team designing the new UN headquarters in New York, and his worldwide fame was assured. His work on Brasília began in the 1950s. As a committed Communist he was exiled from Brazil in the 1960s, after which he worked in Europe and North Africa, returning to Brazil in the 1980s. Still working on architectural and sculptural projects after he reached his 100th birthday in 2007, he had the longest career of any modern architect.

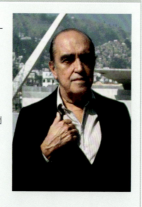

Visual tour

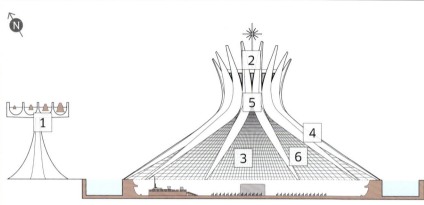

▶ **BELL TOWER** Like medieval and Renaissance cathedrals in Europe, which sometimes have detached campaniles, Brasília Cathedral has a separate bell tower positioned a few feet away from the main building. The tower's main structure is in the same idiom as the cathedral itself, with a single concrete upright tapering to a point at the top. This supports a horizontal concrete beam divided into four sections for the bells, which were donated by Spain.

▲ **CATHEDRAL ROOF** The 16 concrete columns that support the building come to outward-curving points at the top. Here they hold up the concrete disc that forms the central part of the roof. The radiating column tips make the shape of a stylized crown, but they have also been compared to fingers of outstretched hands reaching up toward heaven.

▶ **INTERIOR** The inside of the building consists of a single vast space, about 230ft (70m) in diameter and 246ft (75m) in height. The main architectural feature is the concrete columns. Although large and heavy, they seem light and delicate because they taper toward the floor. The large areas of clear glass between the concrete pillars mean that visitors standing inside the cathedral can look up and see how the columns continue their upward curve on the outside.

BRASÍLIA CATHEDRAL ■ BRAZIL

◀ **STAINED GLASS** A major element of the cathedral, the stained glass fills the elongated triangles between the concrete columns. The glass was designed by the Franco-Brazilian artist Marianne Peretti, who worked on several of Niemeyer's buildings. The irregular pieces of glass contrast with the geometrical grid of dark glazing bars.

▼ **ANGELS** Suspended on steel cables, a group of sculpted angels fly beneath the central ceiling disc. The longest of these is 14ft (4.25m) in length, but it does not look its size as it floats in the large space. The angels are the work of sculptors Alfredo Ceschiatti and Dante Croce, and they were installed in 1970.

◀ **THE HIGH ALTAR** This simple white structure was donated by Pope Paul VI. When the cathedral was built, a change in liturgical fashions led some churches to experiment with "democratically placed" central altars that brought priests and worshippers closer. Although this seemed to work well in round spaces like the one in Brasília, clergy found that a traditional layout, with the altar at one end or edge, was better, enabling the priest to connect with the whole congregation.

IN CONTEXT

The planning of Brasília began in 1956 and by 1960 the city was inaugurated as Brazil's new capital. Niemeyer's contribution to the city was immense. He designed most of the main buildings, including the Brazilian Congress, the president's residence, the deputy's house, the Palace of Justice, and the National Theater. All are in a modern style, with much use of concrete and glass. Many of them have a sculptural quality, revealing Niemeyer's delight in the way concrete can be used to build curves, something unusual in modern architecture before this time. The Congress building, for example, has two curved structures, the dome of the Senate and the dish housing the Chamber of Deputies, separated by a more conventional office tower. The Presidential Palace and Supreme Court are rectilinear, but have curved, tapering columns. The National Museum has a white concrete dome. At Brasília, Niemeyer became a supreme architectural sculptor.

▲ **Brazilian Congress**
With its dome and dish curves, which balance and complement one another as the two legislative chambers are meant to do, the Congress has become one of Niemeyer's most famous buildings.

POMPIDOU CENTRE ■ FRANCE

Pompidou Centre

1971-77 ■ ARTS CENTER ■ PARIS, FRANCE

RICHARD ROGERS AND RENZO PIANO

Located right in the heart of Paris, the Pompidou Centre houses the Musée National d'Art Moderne—one of the largest modern art collections in the world—and an extensive public library, and hosts a wide range of cultural activities. To create the maximum amount of interior space, Richard Rogers and Renzo Piano designed a radical, high-tech structure in which all the services, from the water pipes to the escalators, were suspended on the exterior of the building, leaving the floors and walls inside uncluttered.

Visually, the result of the architects' decision to turn the building inside-out is dramatic. The Pompidou Centre does not have the grand, immaculately finished façades usually found on major galleries but looks more like a giant machine or factory on which an outer structural grid of steel uprights, horizontals, and diagonals is liberally festooned with colorful ducts, tubes, and containers. The rear façade of the building displays a diverse collection of these services, while on the front, which is clad in a less cluttered steel grid, an escalator enclosed in a glazed tube rises in stages, giving visitors views of the bustling piazza below.

The impact of this design approach is, however, more than just visual. By putting the services on display like this, the architects were able to design them too, and they worked closely with the engineers to ensure that everything worked efficiently. The interior of the building is much simpler in comparison, with large windows overlooking both the surrounding streets and the city beyond. The galleries have expansive areas of uninterrupted floor space, including large, flexible spaces that can be reconfigured to suit the specific demands of each exhibition. The network of brightly colored ducts continues across the ceilings, creating a strong visual link with the exterior. A favorite destination for visitors to Paris, the Pompidou Centre is a vibrant space both inside and out.

RICHARD **ROGERS**

1933-2021

The Italian-born architect studied in London and at Yale, where he met Norman Foster. Initially, Foster, Rogers, and their wives, Su Brumwell and Wendy Cheeseman, practiced as Team 4, designing high-tech structures. In 1967 Rogers left the practice to work with Italian architect Renzo Piano, and together they created the Pompidou Centre, which brought both of them international fame. Rogers went on to work all over the world on many high-profile buildings, from the European Court of Human Rights in Strasbourg, to part of the reconstructed World Trade Center site in New York. The practice he founded, RSHP (formerly Rogers Stirk Harbour + Partners), has been involved in several landmark projects, including Madrid's Barajas Airport and the Bordeaux Law Courts. A Pritzker Prize winner, Rogers wrote widely on urbanism and was also influential in European city planning.

Visual tour

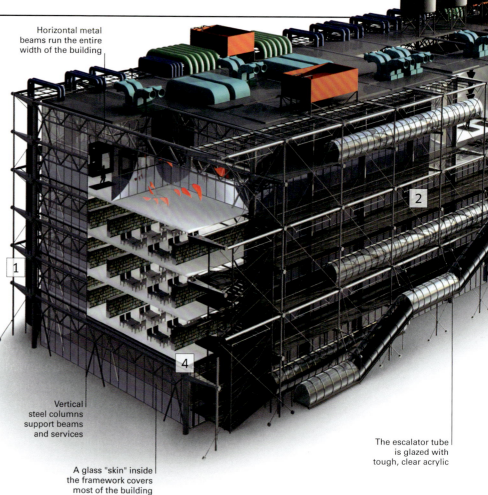

Horizontal metal beams run the entire width of the building

Vertical steel columns support beams and services

A glass "skin" inside the framework covers most of the building

The escalator tube is glazed with tough, clear acrylic

▲ **EXTERIOR DUCTS** The rear wall has the largest collection of service ducts, which run both inside and outside the steel framework of the building. These were color-coded: plumbing was green; the ducts and tubes of the climate-control system were blue; electrical installations were yellow; and the parts of the building used for circulation were red. Although some of the original colors have been modified, the twisting forms of the ducts and pipes still create a vivid splash of color on the building's urban site.

▲ **EXTERNAL FRAMEWORK** Steel columns run all the way up the building, supporting a network of horizontal beams and diagonal struts, some with integrated emergency stairs. The whole system looks as simple as scaffolding, but the structural demands on the framework are much greater. The project's large team of skilled engineers was crucial to its success.

▲ **ESCALATOR TUBE** One of the Pompidou Centre's most distinctive features is a long, glazed tube that projects dramatically from the steel framework of the main façade. The tube encases escalators that snake their way slowly up the building, stopping at the different floors. The red cladding of the rising portions of the tube is just visible at the bottom of each escalator.

POMPIDOU CENTRE ■ FRANCE

▶ **INTERIOR SPACE**
The high and spacious exhibition areas are flooded with natural light from the large windows along the façades. As on the outside, much of the structure is exposed. The white horizontal beams joined by diagonals on the ceilings are the main structural beams that tie the building together, support the floor above, and penetrate the glass wall to join the upright columns outside. The network of blue ducts is part of the building's climate-control system.

IN **CONTEXT**

The high-tech approach adopted by Rogers and Piano for the Pompidou Centre was developed in the 1970s by a number of architects—notably Rogers and Norman Foster, who were interested in technology, materials, and structure and wanted to display these aspects of design openly. As a result, high-tech buildings usually have exposed structures—generally lightweight and made using steel frames, which are sometimes chosen because they are adaptable and easy to assemble. The other key aspect of high-tech architecture is the finish of the exterior, as seen on the Lloyd's Building designed by Rogers, which is typically smooth and immaculate—glass and polished steel are favorite materials.

▲ Lloyd's Building, London, UK, 1978–84

◀ **STRUCTURAL FRAMEWORK** One of the challenges for the engineers was to find a way of hanging the structural elements from the upright columns. They used a design called a gerberette, which consists of a short horizontal casting that swells in the middle where it is joined to the column. Attached to the right-hand end of the gerberette is one of the main structural beams that support the building's roofs and floors; to the left of it are the beams and rods that carry the escalator.

▲ **INTERIOR OF TUBE** Visitors using the escalators travel through tubes glazed with clear acrylic sheets. Unlike interior escalators and elevators, this arrangement offers an interesting visual experience. To one side the building can be seen in close-up; on the other there are views across the neighboring squares and streets. Higher up, the rooftops and church spires of Paris are visible far into the distance. The tubes themselves enhance the building by reflecting the changing colors of the sky.

National Gallery of Canada

1988 ▪ ART GALLERY ▪ OTTAWA, CANADA

MOSHE SAFDIE

When designing Canada's National Gallery, architect Moshe Safdie took an approach that was radically different from that of most art gallery designs. The aim was not only to house the national art collection, library, and archives, but also to provide elegant facilities for special events. Safdie fulfilled this brief with an outstanding building of granite and glass that combines strong, graphic lines and glowing, crystal-like pavilions with a series of spacious galleries that display pictures and sculpture to their best advantage. The corner pavilions have generous interiors flooded with light, as do the exhibition galleries, spaces for social gatherings, and the corridors between them.

The striking building is well-suited to its site, not far from the Ottawa River and with impressive views toward the city's Gothic parliament buildings. The glass lantern roofs of the National Gallery complement the towers on Parliament Hill, and the daring cathedral-like proportions make it an imposing presence.

MOSHE SAFDIE

b.1938

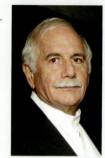

Born in Haifa (then in Palestine), Moshe Safdie moved to Canada when he was 15 years old and studied architecture at McGill University. He became well known when he designed Habitat '67, a housing development based on three-dimensional prefabricated units, which was built for Expo 67 in Montreal. This ground-breaking project, based on work he did while still a student, established Safdie as one of the prominent architects in North America. During the course of a long career he has had many major commissions in Canada, including Ottawa's City Hall and Vancouver's Library Square, as well as designing buildings from museums to university complexes elsewhere. His work is characterized by ingenious geometry and an innovative use of glass and lighting.

NATIONAL GALLERY OF CANADA ■ CANADA

IN CONTEXT

Moshe Safdie designed Habitat '67 to address the problem of how to provide high-density, affordable city apartments with the sense of privacy and access to green spaces common to suburban homes. His brilliant solution was to create 354 prefabricated cubelike living units that could be stacked on top of one another and interlock in an apparently random, yet highly organized way to create 148 separate apartments of varying sizes. Each home has a private terrace and is linked to the others by walkways and communal plazas.

The complex is a striking landmark set within gardens close to the Old Port in Montreal. Safdie had originally intended to make it much bigger, but it is impressive even at its existing size.

▲ **HABITAT '67**
The modular construction and landscaping soften the overall effect of the complex, avoiding the monolithic severity of many other 1960s housing plans.

◀ **GLASS LANTERN** Art galleries are often inward-looking structures, with blank outside walls that give little hint of what lies within. When designing the National Gallery of Canada, Safdie took a different approach, using glass widely and creating a landmark Great Hall with a high glazed roof rising above the granite and glass walls. The Great Hall forms an access point for the galleries and a generous space for special events. When lit up at night, the polygonal roof shines out like a beacon.

▲ **ENTRANCE PAVILION** Situated at one corner of the building, the entrance is a stunning space, roofed and partly walled with glass, designed to attract and to welcome visitors. The complex geometrical forms of its crystalline roof catch the eye, while the glass walls blur the boundary between exterior and interior and admit the maximum amount of light.

▲ **INDOOR COLONNADE** From the entrance, visitors walk the length of this tall passageway. With its soaring granite columns and pitched glass roof the colonnade resembles the nave of a cathedral. The floor slopes gently upward, and walking up this ramp creates a sense of anticipation as visitors approach the Great Hall at the far end.

▲ **EXHIBITION SPACES** One of the key features of the building is the quality of light in the galleries themselves. By using a mixture of skylights and mirrored shafts, Safdie introduced natural light. In some rooms curved ceilings add character. Painted white, they reflect light on to the paintings, making it easier for visitors to pick out details.

Guggenheim Museum, Bilbao

1997 ■ MUSEUM ■ BILBAO, SPAIN

FRANK GEHRY

The undulating, reflective forms of the Guggenheim Museum, Bilbao, make it one of the most famous buildings of recent decades. The museum was designed by California-based architect Frank Gehry, who insisted on situating it in the city's run-down port area rather than on the downtown site originally proposed. Inspired by the scaly, shimmering forms of fish, Gehry created innovative architectural forms using a mix of straight, stone-covered walls and curving shapes clad in titanium over a steel frame. Appearing almost as if piled up at random and about to topple over, these dazzling structures were the result of Gehry's daring imagination combined with his team's mastery of computer-aided design. The bold, rounded shapes catch the sunlight, while the gaps and folds between them create intriguing shadows, which invite exploration.

Inside, the building is equally stunning. A full-height atrium leads to uniquely shaped galleries—a trapezoid, an L-shaped space, and a long, boat-shaped gallery—while on

the upper floor, the galleries are more conventional. The resulting mix of spaces is perfectly suited to displaying the wide range of modern art in the Guggenheim's collection.

The building's resemblance to a collection of fragments and its strong, non-linear geometry have made some design critics suggest that the museum is an example of the architectural movement known as deconstructivism, a style typified by fragmentation and unpredictability that became fashionable in the late 1980s. Gehry, however, refutes such categorization and his buildings work on their own terms, capturing the imagination. The Guggenheim attracts twice as many visitors as the ambitious target of 500,000 per year—a massive influx of people. The city of Bilbao has reaped the economic benefits brought by the museum, with the income aiding the regeneration of the port area—a triumph of urban renewal as well as of architecture.

FRANK **GEHRY**

b.1929

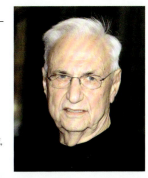

Born in Toronto, Canada, Frank Gehry tried out different careers before studying architecture in Southern California. His first notable designs, however, were not architectural but for a range of furniture made out of cardboard. The building that helped establish his architectural credentials was his own house in Santa Monica, which combines corrugated metal, chain-link fencing, exposed framing, and other materials to create an arresting whole that some found disorienting. The house brought Gehry publicity and a host of commissions, allowing him to experiment with dramatic new forms, often on a large scale. Among his landmark structures are the Vitra Design Museum in Weil am Rhein, Germany; the Chiat/Day Building in Venice, California, which is partly shaped like a pair of binoculars; and the Frederick Weisman Museum of Art in Minneapolis, which has a multifaceted shimmering façade similar to the Guggenheim. In over 50 years as an architect Gehry has continued to push the boundaries of architecture and devise innovative shapes and forms.

Visual tour

WATER GARDEN AND CANOPY Having chosen a site near Bilbao's docks and river, Gehry wanted to bring water close to the building so he created a water garden by the walls of the museum. By extending the canopy out into the water, he further integrated the building and its setting. The structure's complex surfaces are reflected by the gently rippling water, amplifying the shimmering effect of the Guggenheim's titanium cladding.

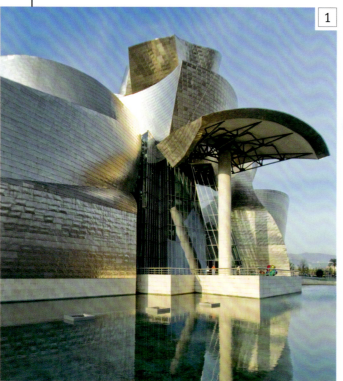

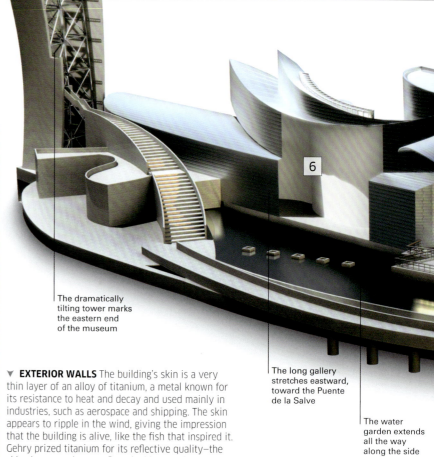

The dramatically tilting tower marks the eastern end of the museum

The long gallery stretches eastward, toward the Puente de la Salve

The water garden extends all the way along the side of the building

EXTERIOR WALLS The building's skin is a very thin layer of an alloy of titanium, a metal known for its resistance to heat and decay and used mainly in industries, such as aerospace and shipping. The skin appears to ripple in the wind, giving the impression that the building is alive, like the fish that inspired it. Gehry prized titanium for its reflective quality—the skin changes color to reflect the blues and grays of the sky, and the glow of sunset or sunrise.

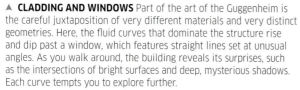

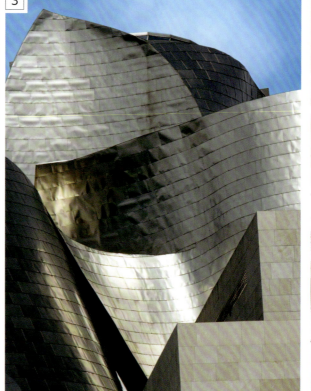

CLADDING AND WINDOWS Part of the art of the Guggenheim is the careful juxtaposition of very different materials and very distinct geometries. Here, the fluid curves that dominate the structure rise and dip past a window, which features straight lines set at unusual angles. As you walk around, the building reveals its surprises, such as the intersections of bright surfaces and deep, mysterious shadows. Each curve tempts you to explore further.

GUGGENHEIM MUSEUM, BILBAO ■ SPAIN 225

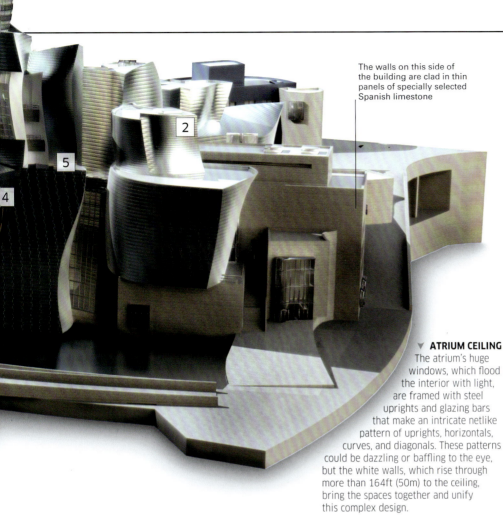

The walls on this side of the building are clad in thin panels of specially selected Spanish limestone

▼ **ATRIUM CEILING**
The atrium's huge windows, which flood the interior with light, are framed with steel uprights and glazing bars that make an intricate netlike pattern of uprights, horizontals, curves, and diagonals. These patterns could be dazzling or baffling to the eye, but the white walls, which rise through more than 164ft (50m) to the ceiling, bring the spaces together and unify this complex design.

IN CONTEXT

Gehry often incorporates the idea of movement into his buildings. A good example is the Nationale-Nederlanden Building in Prague, Czechia. It has been nicknamed the "Dancing House" or "Ginger and Fred Building," because its forms reflect the dancing figures of Fred Astaire (the round corner tower) and Ginger Rogers (the tapering, glass-enclosed form to the left). The rows of windows on the right-hand façade correspond to those of 19th-century apartment houses nearby, but set at varying levels, they look as if they are on the move.

▲ **Dancing House**
The curving shapes of this block seem to be dancing their way toward the nearby River Vltava.

◄ **ATRIUM**
This cavernous space is lit by vast windows that rise from floor to ceiling. Access walks and glass elevators cut across it, while staircases with eccentric bends mirror the curves of walls, windows, and steel frames. The space is partly a tribute to the large atrium at the Guggenheim, New York, a round, top-lit hall designed by Frank Lloyd Wright. Where Wright's space is completely white, Gehry's blends soaring white walls and acres of glass with areas of beautifully finished stone, bringing traditional and contemporary materials together. The spatial geometry, with walls and windows set out at various angles, is as complex and exciting as the building's exterior.

▲ **EXHIBITION SPACE** The museum has around 20 galleries. The largest and most dramatic, at around 425ft (130m) in length and 100ft (30m) across, is the one on the ground floor that extends from the atrium toward the nearby bridge. Although the architecture is bold, it does not distract from the exhibits, and occasional glimpses of Bilbao through a window can enhance the displays by giving them context.

Jean-Marie Tjibaou Cultural Centre

1991–98 ■ MUSEUM ■ NOUMÉA, NEW CALEDONIA, SOUTH PACIFIC

RENZO PIANO

Ten tall, shell-like structures made of upright wooden staves rise up from the trees of the Tinu Peninsula on Grande Terre, the main island of New Caledonia (Kanaky). This arresting complex is the Jean-Marie Tjibaou Cultural Centre, which showcases the culture of the Kanak people and is named after the leader of the Kanak independence movement, Jean-Marie Tjibaou, who was assassinated in 1989.

The structures, often known by the French term, *cases* (huts), are the work of Italian architect Renzo Piano, who won a competition to design the Centre. By combining local building traditions with modern materials and technology, the shell-like *cases* harmonize with their lush surroundings and reflect the Kanak culture. They are also strong enough to withstand the challenging weather conditions in the South Pacific, especially the fierce tropical cyclones that can hit the island.

After spending time with local people to gain a better understanding of their culture, Piano came up with a design that was sensitive to the site—three groups of podlike structures lined up in a row along a forested ridge. Each group of pods—which has adjoining rooms in the buildings behind it—has a particular function and is dominated by a tall pod reminiscent of the great house of a Kanak chief.

The first group houses exhibitions and includes an auditorium; the second contains a multimedia library and conference venue; and the third offers studios for creative artists and an education center where children can learn about Kanak art. The activities all take place in pleasant, light spaces, made comfortable by their ingenious design. Each pod has adjustable timber louvers that filter the wind and sunlight and allow air to flow through the building, keeping it cool.

RENZO **PIANO**

b.1937

Born in Genoa, Italy, Renzo Piano studied architecture in Milan before working in the office of the great American architect, Louis Kahn. In 1971 Piano established a partnership with British architect Richard Rogers. Their most famous collaboration was the Pompidou Centre in Paris (see pp.216–19), but they also produced innovative designs for other buildings, including the headquarters of the furniture firm B&B Italia at Como, Italy. In 1981 Piano set up his own practice, the Renzo Piano Building Workshop, which has offices in Paris, New York, and his native Genoa. He has worked on a wide spectrum of projects, ranging from landmark museums and galleries to major city towers, such as the Shard in London, as well as vast transport buildings, including Japan's Kansai International Airport. In 2013, he was elected into the National Academy of Design.

Visual tour

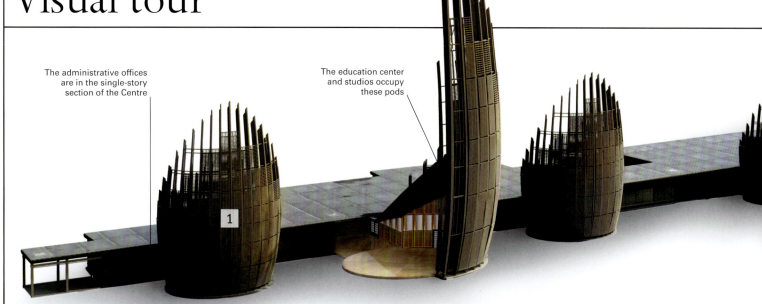

The administrative offices are in the single-story section of the Centre

The education center and studios occupy these pods

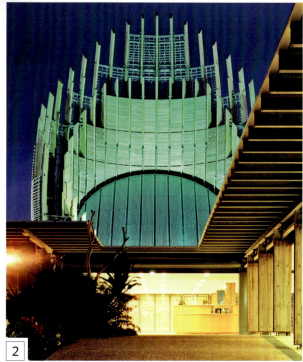

▲ **BEHIND THE SHELLS** Offices, the auditorium, and other rooms stretch behind the convex side of the tall, curved shells. These parts of the Centre are fairly conventional in structure, although a few are open-sided. They are flat-roofed, single-story buildings, and some of the rooms have been built underground to minimize their visual impact. The low-level buildings cannot be seen at all from some places, which means that the overall impression is dominated by the tall shells and the surrounding trees. The trees grow right next to the buildings and even inside some of the open-sided ones, helping the Centre to integrate fully with its setting.

◀ **PODS** The walls of each pod are mainly constructed of horizontal timber louvers that stretch between the rows of upright iroko-wood ribs. These ribs, which rise above the louvers to give the building a distinctive featherlike profile, are all the same distance apart, but the spaces between the louvers vary according to their height. Some of the louvers are adjustable, and the gaps between the slats can be altered to control the flow of air through and around the building.

JEAN-MARIE TJIBAOU CULTURAL CENTRE ■ NEW CALEDONIA

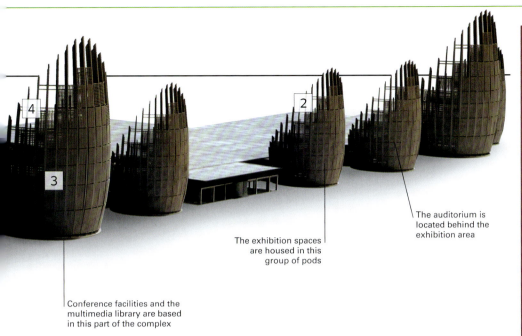

Conference facilities and the multimedia library are based in this part of the complex

The exhibition spaces are housed in this group of pods

The auditorium is located behind the exhibition area

IN CONTEXT

The traditional huts of the Kanak people are round and have thatched roofs. The tallest of them are the great houses, which are reserved for men of high status. These have very tall, conical roofs topped with ornately carved finials. A traditional village would have just one great house and a number of smaller huts. Although the Centre's pods are not exact copies of traditional Kanak buildings, they resemble them in style and shape and have a similar "village" setting. Each group of pods in the Jean-Marie Tjibaou Cultural Centre includes one that has a tall roof and two or three with smaller ones.

▲ Traditional Kanak great house

▲ **LIBRARY** The large pods house exhibition spaces, the education center, and the multimedia library (above). The library is a resource center for the study of the Kanak people and their culture. The roof sweeps down across this tall, imposing space, and a custom-built desk curves around the room, parallel to the outer shell. This shell is lined with a range of standardized units—storage shelves at the bottom, with glass and wooden panels above them. Planted patios, roofed with panels of pierced aluminium, are linked to this pod, helping to make the interior of the library light and airy.

▲ **CLIMATE-CONTROL** The adjustable louvers that line the curved surfaces of the pods are open in normal conditions so that the prevailing trade winds flow through them—the angle can be altered according to the strength of the wind. The air flow can be directed toward the rooms and exhibition areas, helping to keep them comfortably cool, but these areas also have air conditioning to deal with the tropical temperatures.

ON CONSTRUCTION

The tall, vertical ribs of the shells are made from African iroko wood, which was chosen because it is durable and resistant to termite attack. It can also be laminated, a process in which thin layers of the lumber are glued together to make them stronger.

Iroko weathers to a silvery gray color, similar to that of the galvanized steel components used to cap the ribs (to stop water penetration) and attach them to the concrete foundations, as well as in the low buildings set behind the pods. The iroko ribs are joined together by horizontal, galvanized steel tubes, and steel braces keep the pods stable in high winds. The ribs are evenly spaced apart, and Renzo Piano designed a range of different elements—including louvers, fixed windows, wooden panels, and storage units—to fill the spaces between them.

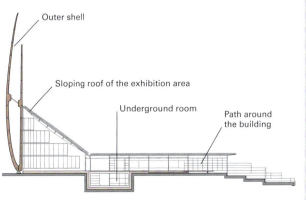

▲ **Cross section**
A slice through one of the buildings shows the huge variation in height between the pod and the building behind it, but both parts are designed to blend in with the surrounding trees.

Jin Mao Tower

1998 ■ COMMERCIAL DEVELOPMENT ■ SHANGHAI, CHINA

ADRIAN SMITH

Since the 1990s no city has seen such dramatic growth as Shanghai. As China developed economically, Shanghai acquired a vast number of new buildings, from shops and banks to office blocks and hotels. The city spread onto land once occupied by farms, but the expansion was vertical as well as horizontal. Among the crop of recent skyscrapers one of the tallest and most spectacular is the 1,380ft (420.5m) Jin Mao Tower.

The tower was designed by a large team under the leadership of Adrian Smith of the firm Skidmore, Owings and Merrill (SOM), an American practice responsible for many of the world's largest and tallest office buildings. In keeping with these origins, the Jin Mao Tower is a high-tech structure of steel, concrete, and glass, but it also has many traditional features. These start with its name, which means "Golden Luxuriance Building," and also relate to its proportions. Many of the tower's measurements and statistics involve the number eight, a number that has traditionally been considered auspicious in Chinese culture. The tower has 88 stories divided into 16 segments, and its height-to-width ratio is 8:1. At the tower's heart is an octagonal concrete core, and the building has two sets of eight structural columns. The dedication ceremony took place on 28 August 1998, but the tower was not fully completed until 1999.

The building is a mixed-use development with many different occupants. The adjoining Podium building contains conference and banqueting facilities and a shopping mall. The main tower has some 50 floors of offices, and floors 53 to 87 are home to the five-star Shanghai Grand Hyatt Hotel, which has 555 rooms and is one of the tallest hotels in the world. Above the hotel on floor 88 is a large, enclosed observation deck, accessed by express elevators, that offers breathtaking views of the expanding city of Shanghai.

ADRIAN **SMITH**

b.1944

The American architect Adrian Smith joined SOM in 1967, when the practice was at the forefront of skyscraper design. Founded in 1936, it designed many of the world's best-known steel-and-glass towers, including Chicago's John Hancock Center (1969) and the Sears Tower (1973). During his time with SOM, Smith designed many award-winning office developments in the US, Britain, and China. He worked on high-profile commercial buildings, such as the Trump International Hotel and Tower in Chicago and London's Canary Wharf and Bishopsgate developments. One of his best-known projects is the Burj Khalifa in Dubai, a super-tall skyscraper with a unique tapering design. When it opened in 2010, it was the tallest building in the world. In 2006 Smith left SOM to set up a new practice, Adrian Smith + Gordon Gill Architecture, where he continues to design prestigious, tall buildings.

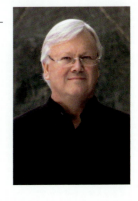

1900 TO PRESENT

Visual tour: exterior

▶ **VIEW FROM STREET LEVEL** This view of the Jin Mao Tower shows how the face of the building works as a series of expanses of metal and glass, stepping back at the edges and anchored with a central vertical "spine" that juts out slightly. The surface is broken at intervals by darker horizontal bands. Each band is set at a slight angle to give the building a profile similar to an understated version of a traditional Chinese pagoda. This is one example of the way in which the architects blended traditional and modern elements in their design.

JIN MAO TOWER ■ CHINA   233

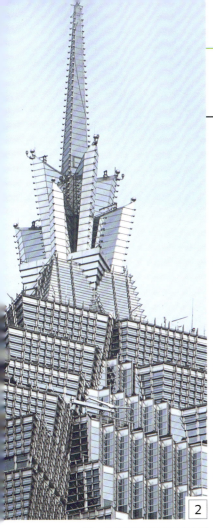

◀ **JAGGED CROWN** The design of the tower becomes more complex as it rises, drawing the eye upward as it undergoes a series of dramatic changes in shape at the top. Here, there are four stories with outward-splaying walls, each slightly smaller than the one below. Above these is the observation deck, and higher still is the crown, a collection of jagged fins terminating in a tapering finial. Gray during the day, the crown of the building is illuminated at night to form a bright, glowing landmark.

IN CONTEXT

During the decades after World War II developers built taller and taller skyscrapers. Most of these were variations on the glass-and-steel box, usually a flat-sided, rectangular structure supported by a metal framework. In the last 20 years, however, skyscraper designs have evolved, their different forms designed with the aid of computers and constructed using the latest materials. Gently curving walls and towers that twist as they rise are now possible; so are skyscrapers based on tubes or shards, or buildings that swell and taper. International firms, such as SOM, Foster and Partners (architects of London's "Gherkin" building), and Kohn Pedersen Fox (the Shanghai World Financial Center), are at the forefront of such innovative designs.

▲ **ENTRANCE** At ground level a series of doors leads into the tower. These openings are surprisingly plain and understated for the entrance to such a prestigious building, but the near-circular window above offers a glimpse into the lobby, increasing the visitor's sense of anticipation and excitement.

▲ **Burj Khalifa, Dubai** This skyscraper by SOM is 2,723ft (830m) tall.

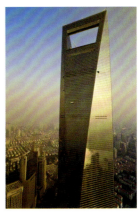

▲ **Shanghai World Financial Center** This is 1,599ft (487m) high.

▲ **PIPING** The metal elements of the building are made of aluminium alloy and various types of steel, including stainless steel. These pipes of stainless steel are part of the structure that supports the glass-roofed arcade at the foot of the tower, through which is the access to the many offices.

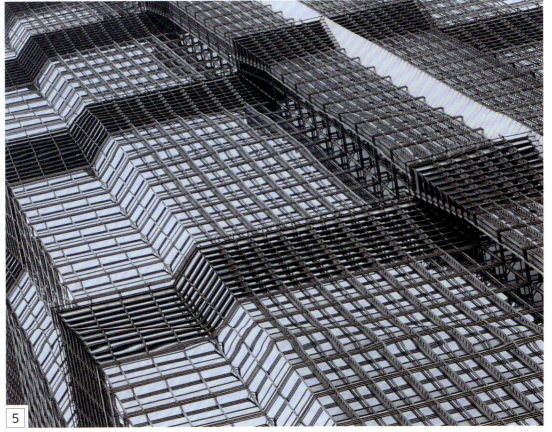

▲ **CLADDING** A close-up of part of the exterior shows how the walls are constructed as a series of setbacks (steplike recessions). These have various advantages: they break up and add interest to the façade, enabling the shape of the building to change as it rises. The windows also face in different directions, which means that more natural light can enter the building as the sun moves around it during the day.

Visual tour: interior

▶ **ATRIUM FROM BELOW** The upper part of the building, from floors 53 to 87, is occupied by the Grand Hyatt Hotel. At the heart of these floors is a cavernous atrium, encircled by a series of corridors. This remarkable space, one of the world's tallest atria, is around 377ft (115m) high and 88ft (27m) across. The stairs from one level to the next are arranged in a spiral, made visible by slight protrusions on the corridors.

▼ **ATRIUM FROM ABOVE** From the observation deck, the view downward shows the difference in treatment between the corridors and the convex wall of the atrium. While the corridors are treated as a series of light and dark rings, the convex wall is much smoother and is articulated with a grid of rectangles. The impression of rich, golden surfaces bathed in light from the corridors recalls the "golden luxuriance" of the tower's name.

▶ **ELEVATOR LOBBY** The sense of opulence, so obvious in the atrium, is also evident in the elevator lobby, where the light and dark materials of the floors and ceilings combine to create a striking pattern. The elevators themselves are decorated in gold, which adds to the luxurious quality of the interior.

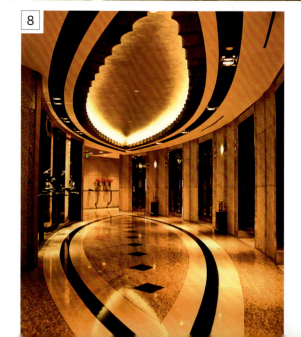

JIN MAO TOWER ■ CHINA

◄ INSIDE THE PODIUM
This six-story building is to one side of the main tower. It offers conference and banqueting facilities for the Shanghai Grand Hyatt Hotel, together with a concert hall, shops, and restaurants. The Podium has a large, top-lit atrium framed with steel and contains a stack of escalators at one end. Suspended glass floors are a feature of this part of the structure, allowing light to pass between levels.

▼ OBSERVATION DECK
This viewpoint is near the top of the tower, immediately below the crown, and can be reached quickly using two express elevators. Although the observation deck looks small from the ground, it has enough space for more than 1,000 people, who can gaze out of the tall glass windows across the city and beyond.

◄ SPIRAL STAIRS The Podium building has stairs as well as escalators. In many similar buildings the stairs are hidden away in corners or behind doors, but in the Podium they are a decorative feature in their own right. The parallel steel rails and treads make an elegant spiral around two structural columns.

► FRAMEWORK STRUCTURE Although the low Podium is in many respects a very different kind of structure from the super-tall skyscraper beside it, the two buildings share a common feature—the use of structural columns and tubes that are exposed to view. This steelwork plays a major part in the visual impact of both buildings.

Seattle Central Library

2004 ■ LIBRARY ■ SEATTLE

REM KOOLHAAS

After detailed analysis of the basic needs of a library building, Rem Koolhaas conceived a radical architectural form to fulfill them. The arresting, multifaceted glass skin of the Seattle Central Library makes a dramatic statement in its city setting, yet the interior spaces work in practical terms. At the bottom of the building are the spacious Living Room and Mixing Chamber, the latter housing the library's information hub. Beyond them rises the Book Spiral, a novel way of displaying the library's collection—in bookcases that spiral upward along a ramp so that volumes do not have to be moved between floors when new ones are added. A bold decorative scheme, marrying strongly patterned carpets with the glass walls, also rewrites the rules of library design.

REM KOOLHAAS

b.1944

Born in 1944, Dutch architect Rem Koolhaas trained in London and New York before founding OMA (Office for Metropolitan Architecture) in 1975. His work includes large public buildings, such as the Nederlands Dans Theater at The Hague, the Kunsthal in Rotterdam, and the China Central Television Headquarters in Beijing. Koolhaas is a Harvard professor, and his books on urbanism have proved highly influential among architects and designers.

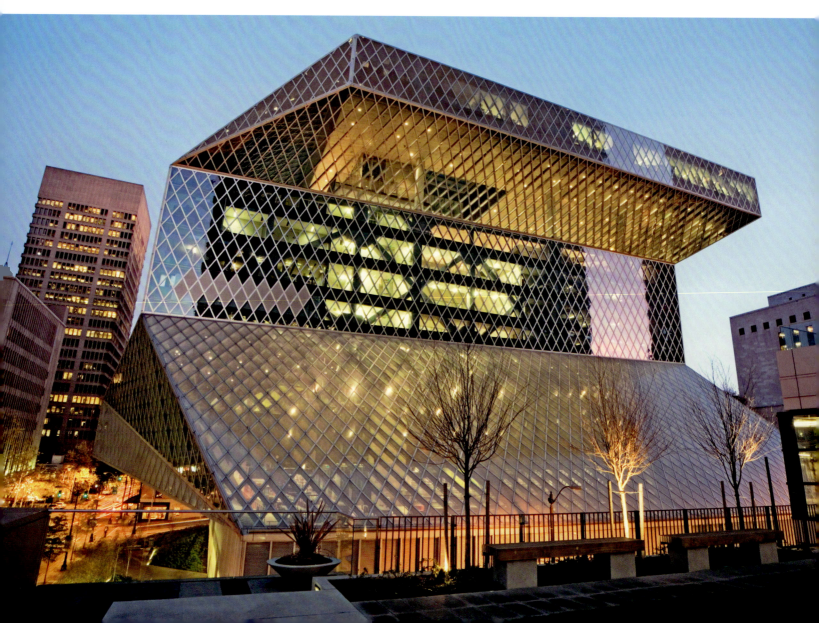

SEATTLE CENTRAL LIBRARY ■ USA

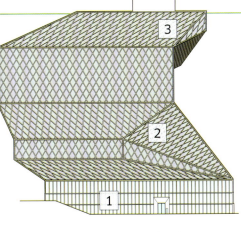

▶ **EXTERIOR WALKWAY** Running along one edge of the library, the walkway is bound on one side by a metal grid that encloses much of the building, and on the other by windows looking into the Living Room. The window glass reflects the diamond network of the grid, making yet more complex patterns of lines, and green plants harmonize with the carpet design, creating a visual link between the interior and exterior.

▲ **LIVING ROOM** Situated at street level, this vast, multi-purpose space contains bookshelves, reading desks, and gathering areas—all lit by an enormous sloping wall of glass. Carpets printed with a bold leaf pattern cover part of the floor. At the rear of the Living Room visitors can access the Book Spiral, which rises to a height equivalent to several stories.

▼ **READING ROOM** This reading and study area is located at the top of the building. Unlike many reference libraries, where rows of desks occupy a somber or neutral space, Seattle's has comfortable chairs for sitting and reading. From the sweeping glass roof to the swirling, purple-patterned carpets, the Reading Room is refreshingly unconventional.

ON DESIGN

The striking design of the library, which might at first appear to be a randomly organized set of shapes, was the result of very practical decisions. The architect conceived the building as a series of boxes (containing offices and rooms), and stacked these elements on top of one another before adjusting their positions. For example, moving an element to one side reduced the glare from sunlight in the Mixing Chamber, while another shift enhanced the view from the Reading Room. The diamond-pattern glazing that clads the main spaces adds to the multifaceted effect.

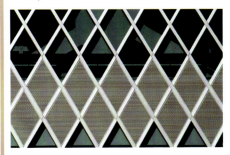

▲ **Glazing**
The huge areas of glass have been triple glazed to save energy. The glazing reduces heat loss in winter and prevents the space from overheating in summer.

IN CONTEXT

Practices such as OMA often produce strikingly unusual buildings. Their radical forms have been developed not merely for effect, but also to solve specific design challenges. To achieve successful results, the architects use computerized design and take advantage of new building technologies. Distorted towers, cubes with irregular windows cutting across them at odd angles, dramatic overhangs, and gigantic structures with little visible means of support have all become features of cities around the world. Breaking the boundaries of traditional architecture, they are helping to create a new urban experience.

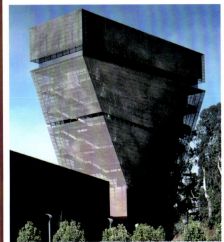

▲ **De Young Museum, San Francisco**
Swiss architects Herzog & de Meuron designed this arts museum in 2005. The bold, wedge-shaped tower is clad in perforated, dimpled copper.

Palace of the Arts

2005 ■ OPERA HOUSE ■ VALENCIA, SPAIN

SANTIAGO CALATRAVA

One of the sensational buildings of the City of Arts and Sciences in Valencia, the Queen Sofia Palace of the Arts is a large, concrete and steel opera house clad in mosaic. It is renowned for its remarkable, soaring white roof, which might be taken for the giant sculpture of a sea creature in motion. At 246ft (75m) high it is the tallest opera house in the world and contains four auditoria—two of them large (one mainly for opera, and the other for multiple uses) and a couple of smaller performance spaces. From the windows of the opera house spectators can look out through the gaps in the sweeping roof and across the surrounding ornamental lakes and verdant gardens to the other equally flamboyant buildings of the City of Arts and Sciences.

SANTIAGO CALATRAVA
b.1951

Born in Valencia, Santiago Calatrava studied architecture before moving to Switzerland to study civil engineering. He began his career as a structural engineer, creating bridges and railway stations that became known for their blend of innovative engineering and elegant design. Calatrava is a sculptor and architect, as well as an engineer. He has designed many high-profile public buildings, such as museums, sports complexes, and cultural centers, most of which display an inventive sculptural quality.

PALACE OF THE ARTS ■ SPAIN

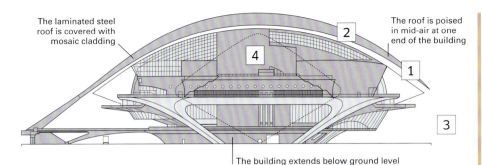

The laminated steel roof is covered with mosaic cladding

The roof is poised in mid-air at one end of the building

The building extends below ground level

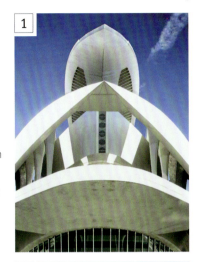

▶ **ROOF SHELLS**
The opera house is covered by two huge, symmetrical, cutaway roof shells, which arch right over the building, and rest on its base with little visible means of support. The roof shells look thin and fragile, but they are in fact made of laminated steel and weigh around 3,000 tons. Numerous openings in the shells let natural light pour into the building.

▶ **CONICAL PAVILION**
Ancillary structures close to the opera house are designed with just as much care as the main building, often taking an unexpected geometric form and creating an element of surprise. This conical roof covers the entrance to a parking garage near the Palace of the Arts. Like the main roof behind, it is clad with glittering white mosaic.

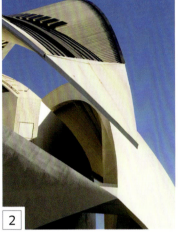

▲ **MOSAIC CLADDING** Calatrava created the roof's shimmering white by cladding it with *trencadís*, a traditional form of mosaic made from fragments of ceramic tile that was popular with earlier Spanish architects, such as Antoni Gaudí. In a gesture of architectural daring the point of the roof shell is suspended in mid-air.

▼ **MAIN HALL** Operas (as well as occasional symphony concerts and plays) are staged in the main hall, the largest auditorium, which seats up to 1,800 people. The unusual curve of the balconies, the lines of the soaring ceiling, and the gleaming white finishes bear a striking resemblance to the features of the building's exterior.

ON DESIGN

Many of Calatrava's bridges are variations on the cable-stayed bridge, in which structural cables usually extend from either side of a central upright pylon down to the bridge deck. Calatrava adapted this design by placing the pylon to one side and slanting it, then running the cables from one side only, to create a structure that looks like a harp. The pylon is filled with cement so that it counterbalances the weight of the bridge deck.

Calatrava has also built other innovative bridges, including tied-arch bridges and a suspension bridge that rotates to allow ships to pass. Their sculptural forms, usually in gleaming white, have become landmarks and are often imitated by other engineers and architects.

▲ **Alamillo Bridge, Seville, Spain**
This bridge, completed in 1992, has a 656-ft (200-m) span. It is held up by a single cantilevered pylon set at an angle of 58 degrees and 13 steel cables.

ON SITE

In 1957 a devastating flood hit Valencia. To prevent further flooding, the Turia River, which ran through the center of the city, was diverted and the former riverbed was made into a huge public park. This later became the site of the City of Arts and Sciences. Construction began in 1996 under the direction of Calatrava. The complex contains several buildings by Calatrava himself, including L'Hemisfèric, which contains an Imax cinema and digital projection, and an interactive Science Museum. L'Oceanogràfic, the largest aquarium in Europe, was designed by Félix Candela, another Spanish architect. These avant-garde buildings all share the curving geometric shapes of the Palace of the Arts.

▲ **L'Hemisfèric**
This building contains a 9,690-sq ft (900-sq m) concave screen. It has a hemispheric dome and, seen from the side, it looks like a huge human eye.

MAXXI

2010 ■ MUSEUM ■ ROME, ITALY

ZAHA HADID

Italy's magnificent national museum of 21st-century visual art is a future-oriented exhibition space that promotes cultural innovation. In responding to the challenges of MAXXI, architect Zaha Hadid has created a building as radical and innovative as the institution itself.

Faced with an awkward L-shaped plot, the architect came up with the concept of a collection of meandering lines that travel up and down while also crossing from one end of the site to the other. These lines became walls, which enclose not simply a single building, but a series of related "suites," treated almost as separate buildings. They contain galleries and other spaces, enabling curators to stage several independent exhibitions at once. Other lines became stairs, walkways, and bridges flowing through and linking the suites. Seen from the outside, this revolutionary structure curves, dips, and rises to create a group of undulating forms and soft outlines that invite exploration. Large windows offer passersby glimpses of the interior, while exterior views set the building in context. Inside, there is a similar sense of gently curving spaces, counterpointed by the system of access ways and bridges, some hugging the sides of the interior spaces, others jumping across voids to create new and energetic lines.

MAXXI achieves its dynamic effect with a very restricted palette of colors. The exterior of the structure is predominantly white, allowing a play of shadows between the curving walls. At night, when the building is lit, partly from ground level, the contrast of dark and light is also emphasized. Inside, a similar effect is achieved through the combination of the pale walls and black lines of stairs and walkways. The result is a spectacular building that is restrained without being neutral, one that is inviting and fascinates the eye without overwhelming the art on display.

ZAHA **HADID**

1950-2016

Iraqi-British architect Zaha Hadid received a degree in mathematics in Beirut before studying architecture in London. She worked with Rem Koolhaas (who had been one of her teachers at London's Architectural Association) at the Office for Metropolitan Architecture before starting her own practice in London in 1980. Her buildings are widely admired and have won many awards. They often have dramatic exteriors (frequently featuring unusual and arresting geometry) and display innovative use of both interior and exterior space. Hadid's career began slowly, partly because the unique shapes she invented seemed difficult or impossible to build. Small-scale projects, however, led to much larger commissions—from the Rosenthal Center for Contemporary Art in Cincinnati to the Guangzhou Opera House. In 2004 she became the first woman to win the prestigious Pritzker Prize, architecture's highest honor.

Visual tour

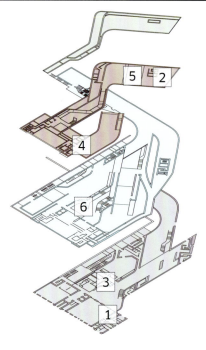

▼ **ENTRANCE** From this point it is clear that the building is made up of different elements that sweep above and past one another. As well as forming interior suites of galleries, these elements also define exterior spaces. This area near the doorway provides shelter and shade to visitors entering and leaving and also allows sculptures to be displayed outside.

▶ **SUITE V WINDOW** This suite sails over the rest of the building and ends in a striking projecting section with a huge floor-to-ceiling window. The drama of this overhang is enhanced because of the unusual geometry, which lends a sense of instability to the otherwise solid-looking structure. This eye-catching feature offers extensive views outside.

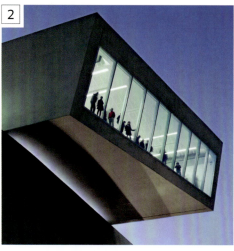

◀ **ROUTES INSIDE**
The pathways through the building create a feeling of adventure, and there is a sense of flowing space rather than the succession of individual rooms that make up most art galleries. In places where there is no art on the walls, the spaces themselves seem like enormous sculptures.

▼ **SUITE V INTERIOR**
The exhibits in Suite V benefit both from artificial light and from light entering the huge window. The architect wanted to integrate the museum with its surroundings, and the window achieves this by offering fantastic views of nearby buildings.

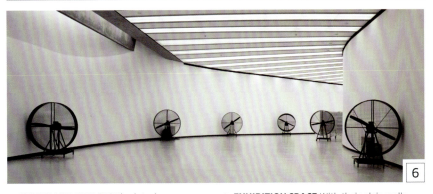

◀ **STAIRS AND BRIDGES** The interior access ways that link the various suites of galleries curve, rise, and fall just like the buildings' walls. They also introduce visual contrasts—the dark sides throw into relief the pale surfaces elsewhere, while the pattern of stair treads echoes on a smaller scale the grid of lines created by the louvers in the glazed roof.

▲ **EXHIBITION SPACE** With their plain walls the galleries provide a fitting home for a variety of different contemporary works of art. The interiors, with their curving spaces, invite visitors to explore further and discover what is around the next corner. Most of the galleries are top lit, and the ceiling pattern contrasts strongly with the plain white walls.

ON DESIGN

Zaha Hadid saw the museum not as a single "object," in the way that a more conventional building might be regarded, but as a collection or "field" of buildings, all equally accessible and with no rigid boundary between the interior and the exterior. The concept was realized by thinking of the museum as a series of sinuous lines, and these lines become clear in the architect's model of the structure (below). Seen from above, the model shows how the lines weave their way through three dimensions, parting and coming together like elevated highways.

▲ **Model of MAXXI**
The architectural models of Zaha Hadid, such as this one of MAXXI, reveal the concepts that underlie her buildings.

IN CONTEXT

Zaha Hadid was known for her ability to find innovative solutions to design challenges, and the results are often dramatic and thought-provoking. Even small buildings, such as the Mobile Art exhibition pavilion designed for Chanel, display these characteristic qualities. The pavilion is compact, uses unusual materials such as PVC and fiber-reinforced plastic, and was designed to be assembled in less than one week so that it could be moved easily from one site to another. Special attention has been given to lighting, both artificial and natural—through the transparent central area of the roof that lights inner courtyard areas.

▲ **Mobile Art exhibition pavilion**
This small building has an unusual form in which the various different components fit together to make a perfectly smooth surface.

Yusuhara Wooden Bridge Museum

2010 ■ MUSEUM ■ KŌCHI, JAPAN

KENGO KUMA

Set against a backdrop of tall evergreens, this striking museum is the work of Kengo Kuma. A celebrated Japanese architect, Kuma uses traditional materials to create distinctive contemporary structures that stand in harmony with their environment. Yusuhara, a township in Kōchi Prefecture, is in a mountainous area with many trees. Kuma had already designed the Town Hall, using locally produced Japanese cedar wood in the walls, floors, and ceilings, and he chose the same material for the museum. Its intricate structure of wooden beams is based on the cantilevers of traditional Japanese temple roofs, but by extending and multiplying the beams Kuma has created a broad and daring span. This is a museum like no other, apparently held up on a slender wooden pillar, from which beams fan out to support a long, bridgelike building containing a hall and rooms. Similar in form to a tree branching out from its trunk, this unusual building harmonizes with the densely forested hillsides that surround the site.

KENGO KUMA

b.1954

Born in Kanagawa, Japan, Kengo Kuma studied architecture in Tokyo and later went to Columbia University, New York, as a researcher. In the early 1990s he embraced postmodernism and designed two buildings in Tokyo– the Doric and M2 Buildings–that pay reference to western classical architecture. Since then, he has adopted many different approaches, including using walls of glass or screens of upright slats to dissolve the edges of buildings and create light, ambiguous spaces. More recently, he has tried to revive some of the flair of traditional Japanese architecture, employing materials such as lumber in buildings that aim for both lightness of touch and sensitivity to site and surroundings.

YUSUHARA WOODEN BRIDGE MUSEUM ■ JAPAN

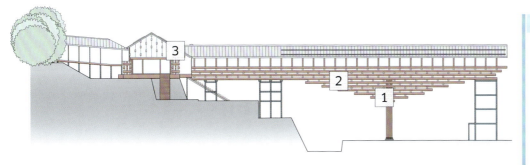

ON SITE

Fitting the museum into a cramped site that was already home to two substantial civic buildings that were divided by a road presented Kuma with a considerable challenge. His solution was to create a design that linked the existing structures with a bridge, entered from a smaller, pavilionlike building at one end. In this way he was able to create an elevated space above the road and give the site a new cohesiveness.

▲ **Aerial view**
The museum blends more successfully into its natural surroundings than the other buildings.

▼ **BEAMS** A close-up of the cantilevered beams shows the meticulous treatment of the timber, which has been carefully selected to display the beautiful grain of the wood and create a satisfying pattern of light and dark shades. Rather than placing one beam directly on top of the other, each is fixed into a shallow groove cut into the beam on which it rests, so that all the components are firmly locked together.

▲ **COLUMN AND LIFT SHAFT** The museum's beams are cantilevered out from the central pillar, each layer slightly wider than the one beneath it, so the building can span the space below. The pillar alone would not be able to bear the huge weight of the lumber, so glass and steel lift-shafts at the ends provide additional support. The dark metal frame and clear walls of the shafts minimize their visual impact, revealing the trees beyond and focusing attention on the wooden structure.

▼ **INTERIOR** Inside, the museum is clad with planks and beams that match the exterior beams. The long central corridor has smooth, polished wooden floors and walls with pitched roof timbers, whose repeated diagonals create visual interest. Rows of glass doors lead off the corridor to the rooms on either side, flooding the interior with light and making the walls appear transparent. They also open up inviting views through the building to the surrounding countryside.

IN CONTEXT

The interlocking structural beams of the museum are inspired by traditional Japanese pagodas, such as the one at Hōryū-ji Temple (below). Beneath the upturned roofs of these pagodas is a network of connected beams that extends from the building and supports the overhang. Inside, there is a single main wooden post–the "spine" of the pagoda. The central column of the museum, which is exposed to view, acts as its key support in much the same way as a pagoda's hidden spine.

▲ **Hōryū-ji Temple, Ikaruga, Japan**
The wooden structure of this famous pagoda was originally built in the 6th century.

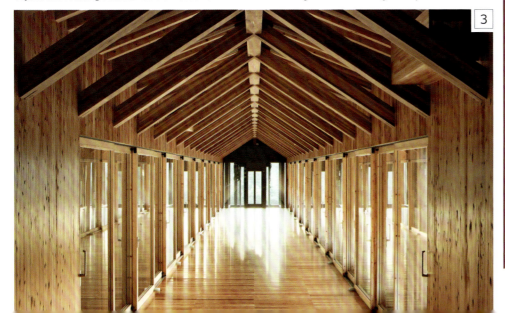

Glossary

ABACUS
A plain, flat slab set on top of a capital.

ACANTHUS
A plant with large, scalloped leaves carved as a decorative feature on classical buildings. Most commonly seen on Corinthian and Composite capitals, but also used on friezes or moldings.

ACRYLIC
Sheets of hard, clear plastic that are used as a flexible, shatter-resistant alternative to glass.

AISLE
The side part of a church or similar building, usually separated from the central nave by a row of columns. Churches and Roman basilicas typically have two aisles, one on either side of the nave, though occasionally there are four.

AMBULATORY
A passageway, usually around the apse of a church, that was originally used for processions.

AMPHITHEATER
A circular or elliptical auditorium surrounded by tiers of seats that was used to stage gladiatorial contests and other events in ancient Rome.

APSE
A semicircular or polygonal area, often at the east end of a church but sometimes around another part of the building, and usually roofed with a vault.

ARCHITRAVE
The lowest part of the entablature in classical architecture. It is a horizontal strip that runs immediately above a row of columns; more generally, a molded strip around a doorway, window, or similar opening.

ART DECO
A style of architecture and decoration popular during the 1920s and 1930s in Europe and North America. It combined bright colors and geometrical decoration with particular motifs from ancient Egyptian art.

ART NOUVEAU
A decorative style that spread throughout Europe from about 1890 to 1910, in which sinuous shapes based on plant tendrils and stems predominate. Its name was intended to show that this was a new style and not a revival.

ATRIUM
In Roman architecture an open courtyard surrounded by rooms forming part of a house; later used to describe a covered courtyard (often glazed) forming part of a large building.

BALUSTER
A short post supporting a rail, often forming part of a staircase or balcony.

BANDED RUSTICATION
Masonry made of massive blocks in which the horizontal joints are deeply cut to suggest that the wall is made up of horizontal bands.

BAPTISTERY
A building or room used for Christian baptisms; baptisteries are often circular or polygonal spaces with the font placed in the center.

BAROQUE
A style of architecture, popular in churches and grand palaces during the 17th and 18th centuries, especially in Spain, Italy, and central Europe. Baroque buildings were massive structures that featured curvaceous walls and shapes, and exuberant decoration.

BARREL VAULT
A vault with a semicircular cross section, like a half-cylinder in form; also called a tunnel vault.

BARTIZAN
A small turret that projects from the top or corner of a structure, such as a castle or tower.

BASILICA
A type of structure usually consisting of a long nave flanked by aisles and terminating in an apse. It was commonly used in ancient Rome for administrative buildings, and the form was later adopted for Christian churches.

BATTLEMENT
A parapet in which raised sections alternate with gaps, often used on the walls of castles and other fortifications; also called crenellation.

BEAM
The horizontal part of a framework, such as a roof timber or a piece of horizontal steelwork in a modern frame structure.

BEAUX ARTS
An ornate form of classical architecture, fashionable in France in the late 19th century and imitated elsewhere in Europe and the US. Named after the École des Beaux-Arts in Paris, where many architects were trained.

BOSS
An ornamental projecting stone or knob, placed at the intersection of ribs in a vault.

BUTTRESS
A mass of masonry, projecting from the outside of a building, designed to strengthen the structure. *See also* Flying buttress.

BYZANTINE
Relating to the civilization based in Constantinople (modern Istanbul), the capital of the eastern Roman empire in the 4th century. Byzantine churches were centrally planned, often with domes, and became the greatest monuments of early Christian architecture.

CAMPANILE
A bell tower, usually detached from the building to which it belongs.

CAPITAL
The structure that crowns a column. In classical architecture the design follows one of the orders; in Egyptian buildings, capitals are often stylized lotus flowers; in Gothic architecture, they often bear foliate carving or plain moldings.

CASEMATE
A vaulted room, forming part of a fortification. Casemates that are used for artillery have openings through which guns may be fired.

CAST IRON
Iron that has been cast in a mold. Widely used since the 17th century for railings, gates, street furniture, and decoration, it was first used to construct the frameworks of factories and warehouses during the Industrial Revolution.

CASTLE
In medieval architecture the fortified residence of a lord or monarch, with defensive features and containing spacious living quarters. In post-medieval architecture the term can refer to large country houses, especially those in the Gothic revival style.

CELLA
The main inner room of a Greek temple containing the statue of the deity.

CLASSICAL
Relating to the tradition of ancient Greek or Roman architecture. Classical architecture generally involves the use of the orders combined with an emphasis on symmetry. The purest form of this type of architecture is seen in temples.

CLASSICISM
A revival of the classical style. Many revivals took place from the Renaissance onward.

CLERESTORY
A row of windows above an arcade, often in the nave of a church.

CLOISTER
An open space or courtyard, usually in a monastery, surrounded by a vaulted passage that is open on the inner side.

COFFER
A decorative sunken panel in a vault or ceiling.

COLONNADE
A row of columns that supports an entablature or arches.

COLUMN
A circular upright support consisting of a base, a shaft, and a capital. *See also* Order.

COMPOSITE
One of the orders of classical architecture, identifiable by its capitals, which combine the acanthus leaves of the Corinthian order with the spiral volutes of the Ionic.

CORBEL
A projecting block used to support part of a structure, such as a roof beam or part of a vault, and often decoratively carved.

CORINTHIAN
One of the orders of classical architecture. Corinthian columns have ornate capitals decorated with acanthus leaves.

CORNICE
A projecting horizontal molding running along the top of a building; specifically, the upper, projecting part of the entablature in classical architecture.

COVE or COVING
A concave molding, especially where a wall joins a ceiling.

CRENELLATION
See Battlement.

CROCKET
A decorative carving in the form of a leaf, projecting at intervals along the edge of a spire or pinnacle. Crockets were especially fashionable in the ornate late phase of Gothic architecture.

CROSSING
The space formed by the junction of the nave, choir, and transepts in a church. A crossing is often crowned by a tower, spire, or dome.

CUPOLA
A small dome that roofs a tower or turret.

CURTAIN WALL
In medieval architecture the outer defensive wall of a castle, usually punctuated with towers and topped with battlements. In modern architecture the outer non-load-bearing wall of a skyscraper or other framework-based building.

DECONSTRUCTIVISM
A term used to refer to a concept in architectural theory and practice from the 1980s onward, relating to architecture that exploits notions of dislocation, disruption, deflection, and distortion.

DENTILS
Rectangular blocks, arranged in rows along classical cornices or along a building's eaves.

DIOCLETIAN WINDOW
A semicircular window divided by a pair of horizontal bars, first used in Roman architecture, notably in the baths of Diocletian, Rome, and often a feature of classical revival buildings.

DONJON
The great tower, also called the keep, at the heart of a medieval castle. The donjon was designed with enough accommodation to provide a secure refuge for the household and retainers during times of war.

DORIC
One of the orders of classical architecture, typified by very plain capitals and the lack of a base to the column.

DRUM
A vertical wall, usually round or polygonal in plan, supporting a dome.

ECLECTIC
Works of architecture and design (especially of the 19th or 20th centuries) that combine elements from more than one style.

ELEVATION
The external face of a building; a drawing showing more than one external façade.

ENTABLATURE
The upper part of a classical order, consisting of the complete horizontal band running above the columns and made up of three strips—the architrave at the bottom, the frieze in the center, and the cornice at the top.

FAÇADE
The front or face of a building.

FAN VAULT
A type of vault used in late medieval English architecture, in which the ribs form patterns resembling opened fans. In a fan vault, unlike other medieval types of vaulting, the ribs are purely decorative rather than structural.

FINIAL
The ornament at the top of a pinnacle or gable, or in a similar elevated position on a building.

FLUTE
A shallow, concave groove running down the surface of a classical column or pilaster.

FLYING BUTTRESS
A buttress in the form of an arch that carries the lateral thrust of a roof or vault toward a support on the outside of a building. Flying buttresses are one of the key components in Gothic architecture, especially in large buildings such as cathedrals.

FRAMEWORK BUILDING
A structure in which the weight is carried by a frame of wood, metal, or some other material, rather than by the external walls.

FRESCO
A wall painting, strictly one in which the pigment is applied when the plaster is still damp.

FRIEZE
The central part of the entablature in classical architecture, sometimes decorated with relief carving or moldings. A decorated band along the upper part of an internal wall (below the cornice) is also known as a frieze.

GABLE
The upper part of the end wall of a building with a pitched roof, usually triangular in shape.

GALLERY
In churches an upper level built over the aisle, which opens on to the nave; in large houses a long room on an upper floor for recreation.

GAZEBO
A small tower, pavilion, or summerhouse, designed to provide a place from which to admire the view in a park or garden.

GERBERETTE
A type of structural component made of cast steel that makes the connection between an upright post and a horizontal beam.

GOTHIC
The dominant style of architecture in Europe during the Middle Ages, featuring ribbed stone vaults, flying buttresses, pointed arches, and large stained-glass windows. The style was revived in the 18th and 19th centuries, especially for churches and public buildings.

GROINED VAULT
A vault resulting from the intersection of two barrel vaults, in which the elements join at a sharp edge, without ribs.

HAMMER BEAM
A horizontal, projecting roof bracket carrying a beam that allowed the creation of wide spans in medieval wooden-framed roofs.

HERM
A square stone pillar topped with a carved head or bust, used as decoration on some classical buildings and in gardens.

HIGH-TECH
An approach to building and design developed in the 1970s. The structure of high-tech buildings, as well as their services, is usually exposed, and immaculate exterior finishes tend to be favored.

ICONOSTASIS
A screen bearing icons erected in churches of the Orthodox tradition.

INTARSIA
A form of inlay, made by building up patterns or images in different colored woods. Intarsia was popular in Renaissance Italy, especially for the decoration of small rooms, such as studies, in palaces and country houses.

IONIC
One of the orders of classical architecture characterized by its capitals, which have pairs of spiral volutes.

ISLAMIC ARCHITECTURE
A term used for both the religious and secular architecture of the Muslim world, including western and central Asia, northern Africa, Spain, and India. Many Islamic buildings feature decoration in abstract or foliate patterns with extensive use of ceramic tiles.

IWAN
A portal consisting of an arch recessed in a wall, used in some types of Islamic architecture.

GLOSSARY

JALI
A pierced screen used in Islamic architecture.

KEEP
See Donjon.

KEYSTONE
A central wedge-shaped stone at the top of an arch or in a vault rib.

LANCET
A tall, narrow window with a pointed top, used in early Gothic architecture.

LANTERN
A small circular or polygonal structure, often with windows, on top of a roof or dome.

LIERNE VAULT
A ribbed vault incorporating small ribs that start neither from the central boss nor from one of the main springers of the vault. The patterns of ribs in a lierne vault can be intricate and highly decorative.

LINTEL
A supporting horizontal beam that spans an opening in a wall or between columns.

LOGGIA
A gallery, balcony, or room, open on one side.

LOOP
A small, unglazed opening in a wall, often in a castle or fortification and used by defenders to shoot through.

LOUVERS
Overlapping boards or strips of glass, slanted so that they will admit light and air while excluding rain, and sometimes adjustable so that the degree of ventilation can be varied.

MACHICOLATION
A projecting parapet on a castle wall or tower, which has holes in the floor, through which missiles or boiling liquids can be dropped on to enemies below.

MANSARD
A form of roof with a double slope, the lower slope being steeper than the upper.

METOPE
A square panel, either carved or plain, in a classical frieze, set between two triglyphs.

MIHRAB
A niche in the prayer hall of a mosque, which is positioned to indicate the direction of Mecca and is often elaborately decorated with tiles or mocarabe ornament.

MINARET
In Islamic architecture a tall tower, usually forming part of a mosque, from which the call to prayer is given.

MOCARABE
A form of ornament used in Islamic architecture, in which miniature arches and stalactitelike forms adorn ceilings and vaults.

MODERNISM
A movement in architecture originating in the early 20th century, concerned with adapting architecture to social needs. Modernist architects were influenced by the idea of functionalism (the form a building takes should be dictated by its function). They built with steel, concrete, and glass, and rejected ornamentation. Modernist buildings tend to be asymmetrical, have flat roofs, and be lit by long strips of windows.

MOSQUE
In Islamic architecture a building that is used for prayer and oriented toward Mecca. A mosque may incorporate a school as well as a prayer hall.

MOLDING
A decorative edging or band, often of carved stone, projecting from a wall or other surface.

MUGHAL
An elegant style of architecture with intricate decoration that developed in India under the Mughal emperors (early 16th to the early 18th centuries). It incorporated Persian and Asian elements, such as onion-shaped domes.

MULLION
A vertical upright dividing a window into sections.

MULTIFOIL ARCH
An arch in which the curved sides are broken by a series of projections, creating a number of miniature indentations.

NARTHEX
In Byzantine architecture an entrance vestibule at the west end of a church.

NAVE
The main central space in a church or basilica, often flanked by aisles; the main part of the church set aside for the congregation.

NEOCLASSICAL
A style based on the architecture of classical Greece and Rome that developed in the mid-18th century. Neoclassical buildings are typically plain and geometric in form.

OCULUS
A round window or opening, usually in a dome.

OGEE
An arch in which each side consists of two curves, one concave and one convex. Ogee arches were used widely in the late, ornate phase of Gothic architecture.

ORDER
In classical architecture an order is a way of designing an arrangement of a column, capital, and entablature. There were five classical orders. Greek architecture used three: Doric, Ionic, and Corinthian; Roman architecture added two more: Tuscan and Composite.

ORGANIC ARCHITECTURE
Used to describe the architecture practiced by Frank Lloyd Wright and his followers. Organic buildings are closely integrated with their site and sensitive to the processes of nature. The term is also used more widely to describe structures that are planned in a way that reflects natural forms.

PAGODA
A tower of a Chinese or Japanese temple, usually multi-story in structure, with an overhanging roof for each story, and topped with a tall finial.

PALLADIAN
A style of architecture influenced by the work and writings of the Italian architect Andrea Palladio and drawing on classical (especially Roman and Italian) models. Palladianism was particularly widespread during the 18th century in Italy and England, from where it also spread to the US. Generally, the Italian proponents of the style stuck more closely to Palladio's careful proportions than architects elsewhere.

PARAPET
A low wall surrounding a structure such as a roof or bridge to protect people from a sudden drop.

PARTERRE
A part of a garden near the house laid out in a formal fashion, with carefully arranged flower beds, paths, and low hedges. It was designed to create a striking pattern when viewed from the house windows or a terrace.

PAVILION
A small ornamental building, often a decorative feature in a garden, and usually of lightweight construction.

PEDIMENT
A low-pitched gable, sometimes ornately carved, placed above a portico in classical architecture; or a similar triangular feature above a door, window, or other opening.

PENDENTIVE
A concave structure that forms the link between two straight walls and the curved lower edge of a dome.

PIANO NOBILE
The first floor of a Renaissance or classical house, containing the principal rooms. It usually features larger windows than those of the floors above and below.

PIER
A mass of masonry used to support a structure such as an arch.

PILASTER
A projecting vertical band of masonry, designed, like a column, to conform to one of the orders.

PILE
A structure of wood, metal, or concrete driven into the ground to support the foundations of a building.

PILOTIS
Narrow columns used to support buildings and raise them above the ground in modernist architecture. They were used most famously by Le Corbusier.

PLINTH
A slab beneath the base of a column, or the projecting base of any other structure.

PORTCULLIS
A gate of wood, strengthened by iron, designed to slide up and down; used as a defensive feature in medieval castles.

PORTICO
A covered entrance porch to a classical temple or other building, fronted by columns, topped with a pediment, and usually becoming the central feature of a façade.

PUTTI
The representations in paint or sculpture of naked, winged children (including cherubs or cupids) widely used in Renaissance and Baroque decorative art.

QUATREFOIL
A circular opening subdivided around the edge into four lobelike shapes.

QUOINS
The dressed stones at the corners of a building (from *coin*, the French for corner).

REINFORCED CONCRETE
Concrete that has been given greater tensile strength by pouring it over a metal mesh or a network of metal rods. Since its introduction in the 19th century, reinforced concrete has been widely used, especially in tall buildings, where its fireproof quality is valued. It is also sometimes known as ferro-concrete.

RELIEVING ARCH
An arch built into a wall, above an opening or window, in order to reduce the effect of the weight of the masonry above.

RENAISSANCE
In architecture the term is applied first to Italian architecture from c.1420 to c.1550, when the orders and the proportions of ancient Roman architecture were revived. In other countries Renaissance architecture involved copying and adapting the style of the Italian Renaissance, often with the addition of decorative motifs.

RIBBED VAULT
A vault in which the individual compartments are separated by projecting bands of masonry known as ribs.

ROCOCO
A style of architecture and decoration popular in 18th-century Europe and characterized by pale colors and the use of motifs such as shells, scrolls, and coral-like forms—often arranged asymmetrically. Although often seen as the final phase of baroque, rococo design has a lightness of touch, in contrast to the massive nature of many baroque buildings.

ROMANESQUE
Partly inspired by Roman building, this style of architecture was prevalent in Europe between the 10th and 12th centuries. Romanesque buildings usually have round-topped arches, massive walls, and relatively small windows. Where buildings were vaulted, the types generally used were barrel or groined.

ROSE WINDOW
A circular window divided up with tracery, like the spokes of a wheel, and used in Gothic churches and cathedrals.

ROTUNDA
A building or room with a circular plan and usually with a domed roof.

ROUNDEL
A small round opening or window that is usually ornamental.

RUSTICATION
Masonry arranged in large blocks with deep joints between them.

SALON
A large reception room found in a palace or country house.

SANCTUARY
The space at the east end of a church where the high altar is housed.

SARCOPHAGUS
A coffin, made of stone or terra-cotta, and often decorated with relief carvings.

SASH WINDOW
A window made up of two or more vertically sliding sections supported in grooves and counterbalanced with weights.

SEGMENTAL
A term used to describe an arch shaped like the shallow arc of a circle, and which is less than a semicircle in extent.

SETBACK
The upper part of a tall building, such as a skyscraper, that is stepped back from the lower façade to admit more natural light at street level.

SHAFT
A slender column that is attached to a doorway or window or arranged in a group around a larger column or pier.

SHINGLES
Wooden tiles cut to standard shapes and used to cover roofs, spires, and sometimes walls.

SKYSCRAPER
A tall, multistory building supported by a steel frame and equipped with high-speed elevators.

SPANDREL
A triangular space adjacent to an arch.

SPRINGING LINE or **SPRINGER**
The line or level from which an arch or vault rises from its supports.

STAVE
A wooden upright plank forming part of a wall in an early Scandinavian church or hall.

STONE-DROPPING WINDOW
In Japanese castles a window built with an overhang so that stones or other missiles could be dropped on to enemies below.

STUCCO
A form of plaster applied to both the inside and outside walls of buildings, designed to set slowly and make it easy to create molded decoration.

STUPA
A form of Buddhist shrine, originally consisting of a moundlike structure, and later sometimes taking the form of a bell-like structure.

SUPERSTRUCTURE
The part of a building above the foundations.

SWAG
An ornamental detail consisting of a carved or molded length of cloth or a garland of fruit or flowers. Both cloth and garland are draped over two supports and tied with ribbons.

TALUS
The sloping base of a wall in a fortification.

TESSERA
A small cube of glass, marble, or other stone used in the creation of mosaics.

TRACERY
A system of ornamental glazing bars, usually made of stone, dividing up the top of a window into a series of small compartments. Tracery was used widely in Gothic architecture to make a range of delicate patterns.

TRANSEPT
The arms of a church, running from side to side and at right angles to the nave and sanctuary.

TRIGLYPH
The grooved blocks separating the metopes in a classical frieze.

TROMPE L'OEIL
A style of illusionistic decorative painting that was especially popular in buildings of the baroque style.

TUSCAN
An order of architecture introduced by the Romans, characterized by plain unfluted columns and very simple capitals and bases.

TYMPANUM
The area between the horizontal lintel of a doorway and the arch above it, often containing a stone panel carved in relief.

VAULT
An arched ceiling built of stone, brick, or concrete.

VESTIBULE
A passage or space between a building's entrance and its interior.

VOLUTE
A spiral scroll used as part of the decoration on an Ionic or Composite capital.

Index

A

Abbaye de Ste-Madeleine, Vézelay 11, 60-63
Ahmad, Ustad (architect)
   Mumtaz Mahal's mausoleum 137, 140
   Red Fort, Delhi 137
Alamillo Bridge, Seville 239
Albanese, Giovanni Battista (sculptor),
   Villa La Rotonda, Vicenza 126
Alhambra, Granada 88-93
   Comares Tower 90, 92
   Court of Lions 91
   Court of Myrtles 90
   Daraxa's *mirador* 93
   Gilded Room 90, 92
   Halls 90, 91, 92-93
Amalienburg Pavilion, Nymphenburg 164-67
Angkor Wat, Cambodia 12, 56-59
Anthemius of Tralles (architect),
   Hagia Sophia, Istanbul 33
Arnolfo di Cambio (architect),
   Florence Cathedral 83
Art Deco style 246
   Chrysler Building, New York 194-97
Art Nouveau style 246
   Grand Palais, Paris 188-91
   Hôtel Tassel, Brussels 186-87
   Sagrada Familia, Barcelona 180-85
Athena Nike temple, Athens 21
Australia, Sydney Opera House 208-11
Austria
   Garsten Abbey 155
   Melk Abbey 154-57
   St. Florian, Linz 155
Autun Cathedral, France 61

B

B&B Italia HQ, Como 226
Bagsværd church, Copenhagen 209
Barajas Airport, Madrid 217
Barcelona Pavilion 201
Baroque architecture 246
   Blenheim Palace, UK 158-63
   Melk Abbey 154-57
   Palace of Versailles, Paris 146, 147, 151
Barry, Charles (architect), Houses of
   Parliament, London 172-75
basilicas 33, 61, 246
Bayon, Angkor, Cambodia 59
Beaux Arts style 246
   Grand Palais, Paris 188-91
Beduzzi, Antonio (architect), Melk Abbey 157
Belém Tower, Lisbon 9, 112-15
Belgium
   Central Station, Brussels 186
   Cinquantenaire Arch, Brussels 189
   Congo Palace, Brussels 189
   Hôtel Tassel, Brussels 186-87
   Hôtel van Eetvelde, Brussels 187
Benedetto di Maiano (artist), Ducal Palace,
   Urbino 109
Bishopsgate, London 231
Blenheim Palace, UK 8, 158-63
   gardens 161
   Great Hall 162
   Green Writing Room 162
   Long Library 163
   Red Drawing Room 163
   Saloon 162
Bon, Giovanni and Bartolomeo (architects),
   Doge's Palace, Venice 94
Bordeaux Law Courts 217
Borgund stave church, Norway 68-71
Borobudur, Java 9, 50-53
   Arch of Kala 52
bosses 76, 105, 246
Brasília Cathedral, Brazil 11, 212-15
Brazil
   Brasília Cathedral 212-15
   Congress Building, Brasília 215
   Ministry of Education HQ 212
   St. Francis of Assisi, Belo Horizonte 212
Bridge of Sighs, Venice 97
bronze doors
   Florence Cathedral 83, 87
   Hagia Sophia, Istanbul 34-35
   Pantheon, Rome 30
Brown, "Capability" (landscape gardener) 161
Brunelleschi, Filippo (sculptor)
   Ducal Palace, Urbino 108
   Florence Cathedral 83, 85, 86-87
   Palazzo di Parte Guelfa, Florence 83
   San Lorenzo, Florence 83
   San Spirito, Florence 83
   Spedale degli Innocenti, Florence 83
Brussels Central Station 186
Buddhism
   Angkor Wat, Cambodia 58-59
   Bayon, Angkor 59
   Borobudur, Java 50-53
   see also Bulguksa Temple
Bulguksa Temple, South Korea 42-45
   Dabotap pagoda 45
   Daeungjeon 44
   Gwaneumjeon shrine 45
   Museoljeon 44-45
   Seokgatap pagoda 45
Burghausen Castle, Germany 78-81
   Chapel of St. Elisabeth 81
   Georg's Gate 80, 81
   Knights' Hall 80, 81
Burj Khalifa, Dubai 231, 233
Byzantine architecture 11, 246
   Hagia Sophia, Istanbul 32-37
   Palatine Chapel, Aachen 47
   St. Basil's Cathedral, Moscow 121
   San Vitale, Ravenna 49

C

Ca' d'Oro, Venice 94
Caen, abbeys at 61
Calatrava, Santiago (architect)
   Alamillo Bridge, Seville 239
   L'Hemisfèric, Valencia 239
   Palace of the Arts, Valencia 238-39
Cambodia
   Angkor Wat, Cambodia 56-59
   Bayon, Angkor 59
Canada
   Habitat '67 housing, Montreal 220, 221
   National Gallery, Ottawa 220-21
Canary Wharf, London 231
Candela, Felix (architect), L'Oceanogràfic,
   Valencia 239
Capua Vetere Amphitheatre, Italy 27
Caracalla, Baths of, Rome 31
Cartellier, Pierre (sculptor), Palace of
   Versailles, Paris 148
Casa Milá and Casa Batlló, Barcelona 180
Chambers, William (architect), Blenheim
   Palace, UK 163
Chandigarh, India 199
Chanel, Mobile Art exhibition pavilion 243
Chartres Cathedral, France 9, 13, 72-77
Château de Chambord, Loire Valley 116-19
Château de Marly, Paris 147
Château de Pierrefonds, France 177, 178
Chiat/Day Building, Venice, California 223
China
   Forbidden City, Beijing 101
   Jin Mao Tower, Shanghai 230-35
   Podium, Shanghai 234-35
   Temple of Heaven, Beijing 98-101
   World Financial Center, Shanghai 233
Chiswick House, London 127
Chrysler Building, New York 9, 194-97
Cigoli, Ludovico (artist), Florence Cathedral 85
Cinquantenaire Arch, Brussels 189
classicism 246
   Amalienburg Pavilion 164-67
   see also Golden Age classical style;
   neoclassicism; Renaissance architecture
Colosseum, Rome 24-27
columns
   Composite order 118, 247
   pilotis, Villa Savoye 198-201, 248
   Sagrada Familia, Barcelona 184-85

see also Corinthian, Doric, Ionic, and Tuscan columns
computer-aided design 237
    Guggenheim Museum, Bilbao 222
Congo Palace, Brussels 189
Congress Building, Brasília 215
Contino, Antonio (architect), Bridge of Sighs, Venice 97
Corinthian columns 23, 247
    Blenheim Palace, UK 160
    Colosseum, Rome 26, 27
    Ducal Palace, Urbino 108
    Palace of Versailles, Paris 149
    Palatine Chapel, Aachen 49
    Pantheon, Rome 30, 31
Costa, Lucio (architect), Ministry of Education HQ, Brazil 212
Cotte, Robert de (architect), Palace of Versailles, Paris 149
Coypel, Antoine (artist), Palace of Versailles 151
Crystal Palace, London 191
Cuvilliés, François (architect), Amalienburg Pavilion, Nymphenburg 164, 165
Czechia, Dancing House, Prague 225

D

Da Sangallo family (architects) 117
    Florence Cathedral 86
Dancing House, Prague 225
De Young Museum, San Francisco 237
deconstructivism 247
    Guggenheim Museum, Bilbao 223
Deglane, Henri (architect), Grand Palais, Paris 189, 190
Denmark, Bagsværd church, Copenhagen 209
Dietrich, Joachim (woodcarver), Amalienburg Pavilion, Nymphenburg 165, 167
Doge's Palace, Venice 12, 94-97
    Bridge of Sighs 97
    Porta della Carta 96
    Sala del Maggior Consiglio 97
    Scala dei Giganti 97
domes
    Alhambra, Granada 92, 93
    Congress Building, Brasília 215
    Florence Cathedral 82-83, 85, 86-87
    Grand Palais, Paris 190, 191
    Hagia Sophia, Istanbul 32-37
    Hôtel Tassel, Brussels 185
    L'Hemisfèric, Valencia 239
    Masjid-i-Shah, Isfahan 132-35
    Melk Abbey, Austria 157
    Monticello, Charlottesville 169, 170
    Palatine Chapel, Aachen 47, 48-49
    Pantheon, Rome 29, 30-31
    St. Basil's Cathedral, Moscow 120-23
    St. Peter's, Rome 83
    Taj Mahal, Agra 136-37, 138, 141
    Villa La Rotonda, Vicenza 126
Dom-ino House, Le Corbusier 201
Domenico da Cortona (architect)
    Château de Chambord, Loire Valley 116-19
    St.-Eustache, Paris 117

Doric Building, Tokyo 244
Doric columns 247
    Monticello, Charlottesville 170
    Parthenon, Athens 21, 22-23
Dubai, Burj Khalifa 231, 233
Ducal Palace, Urbino 106-09
    Chapel of Redemption 109
Durham Cathedral 61

E

Egypt, Great Pyramid 16-19
Ely, Reginald (architect), King's College Chapel, Cambridge 102-05
Empire State Building, New York 197
Erechtheion, Athens 21
European Court of Human Rights, Strasbourg 217

F

Fallingwater, Mill Run 202-07
Fanti, Gaetano (artist), Melk Abbey 157
Florence Cathedral, Italy 82-87
Flower, Barnard (artist), King's College Chapel, Cambridge 105
flying buttresses 35, 62, 74, 75, 247
Forbidden City, Beijing 101
Foster, Norman (architect) 217, 219
France
    Abbaye de Ste-Madeleine, Vézelay 60-63
    Autun Cathedral 61
    Bordeaux Law Courts 217
    Caen abbeys 61
    Chartres Cathedral 72-77
    Château de Chambord, Loire Valley 116-19
    Château de Marly, Paris 147
    Château de Pierrefonds 178
    European Court of Human Rights, Strasbourg 217
    Grand Palais, Paris 188-91
    Hôtel de Choudens, Paris 189
    Longchamps racecourse, Paris 189
    Louis Pasteur tomb, Paris 189
    Palace of Versailles, Paris 146-51
    Pompidou Centre, Paris 216-19
    Ronchamp Chapel 199
    St.-Eustache, Paris 117
    Villa Savoye, Poissy 198-201
Francisco de Arruda (architect), Belém Tower, Lisbon 112-15
Frederick Weisman Museum of Art, Minneapolis 223
frescoes
    Doge's Palace, Venice 97
    Florence Cathedral 86-87
    Melk Abbey 157
    St. Basil's Cathedral, Moscow 122
    Villa La Rotonda, Vicenza 124, 127

G

gardens 248
    Blenheim Palace, UK 161
    Palace of Versailles, Paris 149

gargoyles 75, 197
Garsten Abbey, Steyr 155
Gaudí, Antoni (architect)
    Casa Milá and Casa Batlló, Barcelona 180
    Park Güell, Barcelona 180
    Sagrada Familia, Barcelona 180-85
Gehry, Frank (architect)
    Chiat/Day Building, California 223
    Dancing House, Prague 225
    Frank Gehry house, Santa Monica 223
    Frederick Weisman Museum of Art, Minneapolis 223
    Guggenheim Museum, Bilbao 222-25
    Vitra Design Museum, Weil am Rhein 223
Germany
    Amalienburg Pavilion 164-67
    Burghausen Castle 78-81
    Neuschwanstein Castle 176-79
    Palatine Chapel, Aachen 46-49
    Speyer Cathedral 61
    Wartburg Castle, Eisenach 177, 179
    Worms Cathedral 61
Ghiberti, Lorenzo (sculptor), Florence Cathedral 83, 87
Gibbons, Grinling (carver) 162
Giotto (architect), Florence Cathedral 83, 84, 85
Girault, Charles (architect)
    Cinquantenaire Arch, Brussels 189
    Congo Palace, Brussels 189
    Grand Palais, Paris 188-91
    Hôtel de Choudens, Paris 189
    Longchamps racecourse, Paris 189
    Louis Pasteur tomb, Paris 189
glass construction
    Barcelona Pavilion 201
    Brasília Cathedral 212-15
    Crystal Palace, London 191
    Fallingwater, Mill Run 205, 207
    Grand Palais, Paris 188-91
    Jin Mao Tower, Shanghai 230-35
    National Gallery of Canada, Ottawa 220-21
    Seattle Central Library 236-37
    Sydney Opera House 210-11
Golden Age classical style, Royal Palace, Amsterdam 142-45
Gothic architecture 27
    Abbaye de Ste-Madeleine, Vézelay 62-63
    Belém Tower, Lisbon 112-15
    Burghausen Castle 78-81
    Ca' d'Oro, Venice 94
    Chartres Cathedral 72-77
    Doge's Palace, Venice 94-97
    Florence Cathedral 82-87
    Houses of Parliament, London 172-75
    King's College Chapel, Cambridge 102-05
    Krak des Chevaliers, Syria 64-67
    Palatine Chapel, Aachen 49
    Sagrada Familia, Barcelona 180-85
    St.-Eustache, Paris 117
    Woolworth Building, New York 197
    see also Perpendicular Gothic style
Grand Palais, Paris 13, 188-91
Great Pyramid, Giza 16-19

INDEX

Greece
   Athena Nike temple, Athens 21
   Erechtheion, Athens 21
   Parthenon, Athens 20-23
   Propylaea Gateway, Athens 21
Guggenheim Museum, Bilbao 222-25
Guggenheim Museum, New York 202, 225

H

Habitat '67 housing, Montreal 220, 221
Hadid, Zaha (architect)
   MAXXI museum, Rome 240-43
   Mobile Art exhibition pavilion 243
Hagia Sophia, Istanbul 11, 32-37
   Empress's Loge 37
Hardouin-Mansart, Jules (architect)
   Château de Marly, Paris 147
   Palace of Versailles, Paris 146-51
Hawksmoor, Nicholas (architect), Blenheim Palace 158, 159, 163
Heddal stave church, Norway 69
Herland, Hugh (carpenter), Houses of Parliament, London 175
Herzog & de Meuron (architects), De Young Museum, San Francisco 237
high-tech design 247
   Jean-Marie Tjibaou Cultural Centre 226-29
   Pompidou Centre, Paris 216-19
Himeji Castle, Japan 128-31
Hindu architecture and influence
   Angkor Wat, Cambodia 56-59
   Borobudur, Java 52
Hone, Galyon (artist), King's College Chapel, Cambridge 105
Horta, Victor (architect)
   Central Station, Brussels 186
   Hôtel Tassel, Brussels 186-87
   Hôtel van Eetvelde, Brussels 187
Hōryū-ji temple, Ikaruga 245
Hôtel de Choudens, Paris 189
Hôtel Tassel, Brussels 186-87
Hôtel van Eetvelde, Brussels 187
Houses of Parliament, London 172-75
   Big Ben clock tower 174
   Central Lobby 175
   House of Lords 175
   Victoria Tower 174
   Westminster Hall 174-75
Humayun's Tomb, Delhi 137, 139

I

Iktinos (architect), Parthenon 20-23
Imperial Hotel, Tokyo 202
India
   Chandigarh 199
   Humayun's Tomb, Delhi 137, 139
   Red Fort, Delhi 137
   Taj Mahal, Agra 136-41
Indonesia, Borobudur 50-53
Ionic columns 23, 26, 27, 247
Iran, Masjid-i-Shah 132-35
Isidorus of Miletus (architect), Hagia Sophia 33

Islamic architecture 247-48
   Alhambra, Granada 88-93
   Belém Tower, Lisbon 113, 114
   Hagia Sophia, Istanbul 34, 37
   Masjid-i-Shah, Isfahan 132-35
   Taj Mahal, Agra 136-41
Italy
   B&B Italia HQ, Como 226
   Baths of Caracalla, Rome 31
   Bridge of Sighs, Venice 97
   Ca' d'Oro, Venice 94
   Capua Vetere Amphitheatre 27
   Colosseum, Rome 24-27
   Doge's Palace, Venice 94-97
   Ducal Palace, Urbino 106-09
   Florence Cathedral 82-87
   MAXXI museum, Rome 240-43
   Palazzo di Parte Guelfa, Florence 83
   Pantheon, Rome 28-31
   St. Peter's, Rome 83
   San Lorenzo, Florence 83
   San Spirito, Florence 83
   San Vitale, Ravenna 49
   Spedale degli Innocenti, Florence 83
   Teatro Olimpico, Vicenza 125
   Temple of Claudius, Rome 24
   Temple of Peace, Rome 24
   Villa La Rotonda, Vicenza 124-27

J

Jank, Christian (designer), Neuschwanstein Castle 177
Japan
   Doric Building, Tokyo 244
   Himeji Castle 128-31
   Hōryū-ji temple, Ikaruga 245
   Imperial Hotel, Tokyo 202
   Kansai International Airport 226
   M2 Building, Tokyo 244
   Yusuhara Wooden Bridge Museum, Kōchi 244-45
Jean-Marie Tjibaou Cultural Centre, New Caledonia 226-29
Jefferson, Thomas (architect), Monticello, Charlottesville 168-71
Jehan de Beauce (mason), Chartres Cathedral 72, 74, 77
Jerónimos Monastery, Lisbon 113
Jin Mao Tower, Shanghai 230-35
John Hancock Center, Chicago 231
Johnson Wax HQ, Racine 202

K

Kallikrates (architect), Parthenon 20-23
Kansai International Airport, Japan 226
Khan, Amanat (calligrapher), Taj Mahal 139
Kim Daeseong (architect), Bulguksa Temple 43
King's College Chapel, Cambridge 10, 102-05
Kohn Pederson Fox (architects), World Financial Center, Shanghai 233
Koolhaas, Rem (architect), Seattle Central Library 236-37

Krak des Chevaliers, Syria 64-67
   Tower of the King's Daughter 66
Kuma, Kengo (architect)
   Doric Building, Tokyo 244
   M2 Building, Tokyo 244
   Yusuhara Wooden Bridge Museum 244-45
Kuwait National Assembly Building 209

L

Laguerre, Louis (artist), Blenheim Palace 162
Laurano, Luciano (architect), Ducal Palace, Urbino 107
Le Brun, Charles (artist), Palace of Versailles, Paris 146, 150-51
Le Corbusier (architect)
   Chandigarh, India 199
   Dom-ino House 201
   Ronchamp Chapel 199
   Villa Savoye, Poissy 198-201
Le Nôtre, André, (landscape gardener) 149
Le Vau, Louis (architect), Palace of Versailles, Paris 146
Leonardo da Vinci (artist), Château de Chambord, Loire Valley 119
L'Hemisfèric, Valencia 239
Lloyd's Building, London 219
L'Oceanogràfic, Valencia 239
Lombardo, Pietro (architect), Ducal Palace, Urbino 109
Longchamps racecourse, Paris 189
Louis Pasteur tomb, Paris 189
Louvet, Albert (architect), Grand Palais, Paris 189

M

M2 Building, Tokyo 244
Maganza, Alessandro (artist) 127
Manueline architecture
   Belém Tower, Lisbon 112-15
   Jerónimos Monastery, Lisbon 113
Masjid-i-Shah, Isfahan 13, 132-35
Maso di Bartolomeo (architect), Ducal Palace, Urbino 108-09
Mauritshuis, The Hague 142, 145
MAXXI museum, Rome 11, 240-43
Mayan architecture, Temple of the Inscriptions, Palenque 38-41
Melk Abbey, Austria 154-57
Mereworth Castle, UK 127
Mexico, Temple of the Inscriptions 38-41
Michelino, Domenico di (artist), Florence Cathedral 87
Mies van der Rohe, Ludwig (architect), Barcelona Pavilion 201
minarets 248
   Hagia Sophia, Istanbul 34-35
   Masjid-i-Shah, Isfahan 132, 134, 135
   Taj Mahal, Agra 138-39
moats
   Angkor Wat, Cambodia 56-57
   Burghausen Castle 78, 80
   Château de Chambord, Loire Valley 116

INDEX

Forbidden City, Beijing 101
Krak des Chevaliers 66-67
Mobile Art pavilion (Chanel) 243
modernist architecture 248
    Barcelona Pavilion 201
    Villa Savoye, Poissy 198-201
Monticello, Charlottesville 168-71
mosaics
    Florence Cathedral 86-87
    Hagia Sophia 33, 35, 36, 37
    Masjid-i-Shah, Isfahan 135
    Palace of the Arts, Valencia 239
    Palatine Chapel, Aachen 49
    Sagrada Familia, Barcelona 180, 182
Mughal architecture 248
    Humayun's Tomb, Delhi 137, 139
    Taj Mahal, Agra 136-41
Mungenast, Josef (architect), Melk Abbey 155

N

National Gallery of Canada, Ottawa 220-21
neoclassicism 248
    Blenheim Palace 163
    Monticello, Charlottesville 168-71
    see also classicism
Netherlands
    Mauritshuis, The Hague 142, 145
    Paleis Noordeinde, The Hague 142
    Royal Palace, Amsterdam 142-45
Neuschwanstein Castle, Bavaria 176-79
    Palas (residential block) 178
    Royal Bedroom 179
    Singers' Hall 179
    swan imagery 179
    Throne Room 178
New Caledonia (Kanaky), Jean-Marie Tjibaou Cultural Centre 226-29
Niemeyer, Oscar (architect)
    Brasília Cathedral 212-15
    St. Francis of Assisi, Belo Horizonte 212
    Congress Building, Brasília 215
    Ministry of Education HQ, Brazil 212
Norman architecture 61
    see also Romanesque architecture
Norway
    Borgund stave church 68-71
    Heddal stave church 69

O

Odo of Metz (architect), Palatine Chapel, Aachen 46-49
OMA (architects), Seattle Central Library 236-37
organic architecture 248
    Fallingwater 202-07

P

Palace of the Arts, Valencia 238-39
Palace of Versailles 8, 10, 146-51
    Grand Trianon 147, 149
    Hall of Battles 150
    Hall of Mirrors 150-51
    King's Bedroom 150-51
    Royal Chapel 149, 151
    Salon d'Apollon 151
Palace of Westminster *see* Houses of Parliament, London
Palacio Güell, Barcelona 180
Palatine Chapel, Aachen 46-49
Palazzo di Parte Guelfa, Florence 83
Paleis Noordeinde, The Hague 142
Palladian architecture 248
    Royal Palace, Amsterdam 142-45
Palladio, Andrea (architect) 168
    Teatro Olimpico, Vicenza 125
    Villa La Rotonda, Vicenza 124-27
Pantheon, Rome 12, 28-31
Park Güell, Barcelona 180
Parthenon, Athens 20-23
Paxton, Joseph (architect), Crystal Palace, London 191
Peretti, Marianne (artist), Brasília Cathedral 215
Perpendicular Gothic style
    Houses of Parliament, London 172-75
    King's College Chapel, Cambridge 102-05
    see also Gothic architecture
Perret, Auguste (architect), Dom-ino House 201
Peterborough Cathedral, UK 61
Petitot, Louis (sculptor), Palace of Versailles, Paris 148
Phidias (sculptor), Parthenon, Athens 22, 23
Piano, Renzo (architect)
    B&B Italia HQ, Como 226
    Jean-Marie Tjibaou Cultural Centre 226-29
    Kansai International Airport, Japan 226
    Pompidou Centre, Paris 216-19
Pisano, Andrea (sculptor), Florence Cathedral 85, 87
Podium, Shanghai 234-35
Pompidou Centre, Paris 216-19
Pontelli, Baccio (artist), Ducal Palace, Urbino 109
Portugal
    Belém Tower, Lisbon 112-15
    Jerónimos Monastery, Lisbon 113
Prairie houses, US 205
Prandtauer, Jakob (architect)
    Garsten Abbey, Steyr 155
    Melk Abbey 154-57
Pritzker Prize 212, 217, 241
Propylaea Gateway, Athens 21
Pugin, A. W. N. (architect), Houses of Parliament, London 172-75

Q

Quellien, Artus (sculptor), Royal Palace, Amsterdam 144

R

Red Fort, Delhi 137
Renaissance architecture 249
    Belém Tower, Lisbon 112-15
    Blenheim Palace 163
    Château de Chambord, Loire Valley 116-19
    Doge's Palace, Venice 94-97
    Ducal Palace, Urbino 106-09
    Florence Cathedral 82-87
    King's College Chapel 103, 104-05
    Monticello, Charlottesville 168-71
    Palace of Versailles, Paris 151
    St.-Eustache, Paris 117
    see also classicism
Riedel, Eduard (architect) Neuschwanstein Castle, 177
Robie House, Chicago 205
rococo style 249
    Amalienburg Pavilion 164-67
Rogers, Richard (architect)
    Barajas Airport, Madrid 217
    Bordeaux Law Courts 217
    European Court of Human Rights, Strasbourg 217
    Lloyd's Building, London 219
    Pompidou Centre, Paris 216-19
    World Trade Center site, New York 217
Romanesque architecture 249
    Abbaye de Ste-Madeleine, Vézelay 60-63
    Neuschwanstein Castle 176-79
    Speyer Cathedral 61
    Worms Cathedral 61
Ronchamp Chapel 199
rose windows 249
    Chartres Cathedral 74
    Sagrada Familia, Barcelona 183
Rosselli, Domenico (sculptor), Ducal Palace, Urbino 109
Rottmayr, Johann Michael (artist), Melk Abbey 157
Royal Palace, Amsterdam 142-45
    Citizens' Hall 144-45
Rubini, Agostino (artist), Villa La Rotonda 127
Russia, St. Basil's Cathedral 120-23

S

Saarinen, Eero, TWA Flight Center, New York 211
Safavid architecture, Masjid-i-Shah 132-35
Safdie, Moshe (architect)
    Habitat '67 housing, Montreal 220, 221
    National Gallery of Canada, Ottawa 220-21
Sagrada Familia, Barcelona 180-85
St. Basil's Cathedral, Moscow 120-23
St.-Eustache, Paris 117
St. Florian, Linz 155
St. Francis of Assisi, Belo Horizonte 212
St. Peter's, Rome 83
San Lorenzo, Florence 83
San Spirito, Florence 83
San Vitale, Ravenna 47, 49
Sears Tower, Chicago 231
Seattle Central Library 236-37
Shard, London 226
Shaykh Bahai, Ostad (architect), Masjid-i-Shah, Isfahan 132-35

INDEX

Smith, Adrian (architect)
  Bishopsgate, London 231
  Burj Khalifa, Dubai 231, 233
  Canary Wharf, London 231
  Jin Mao Tower, Shanghai 230-35
  Trump International Hotel and Tower, Chicago 231
SOM (architects)
  Burj Khalifa, Dubai 231, 233
  Jin Mao Tower, Shanghai 230-35
  Johnson Wax HQ, Racine 202
  Sears Tower, Chicago 231
South Korea, Bulguksa Temple 42-45
Spain
  Alamillo Bridge, Seville 239
  Alhambra, Granada 88-93
  Barajas Airport, Madrid 217
  Barcelona Pavilion 201
  Casa Milá and Casa Batlló, Barcelona 180
  Guggenheim Museum, Bilbao 222-25
  L'Hemisfèric, Valencia 239
  L'Oceanogràfic, Valencia 239
  Palace of the Arts, Valencia 238-39
  Park Güell, Barcelona 180
  Sagrada Familia, Barcelona 180-85
Spedale degli Innocenti, Florence 83
Speyer Cathedral 61
stained glass
  Brasília Cathedral 212, 215
  Chartres Cathedral 72, 76-77
  Hôtel Tassel, Brussels 187
  Houses of Parliament, London 175
  King's College Chapel, Cambridge 103, 104, 105
  Neuschwanstein Castle, Bavaria 179
  Palatine Chapel, Aachen 49
  Sagrada Familia, Barcelona 180, 184
steel, use of
  Chrysler Building, New York 196-97
  Fallingwater, Mill Run 202, 204
  Guggenheim Museum, Bilbao 222, 225
  Jin Mao Tower, Shanghai 230-35
  Lloyd's Building, London 219
  Palace of the Arts, Valencia 238-39
  Pompidou Centre, Paris 216-19
  Sydney Opera House 210, 211
Subirachs, Josep Maria (sculptor), Sagrada Familia, Barcelona 182, 183
Sydney Opera House 208-11
Syria, Krak des Chevaliers 64-67

T

Taj Mahal, Agra 136-41
Taoism, Temple of Heaven, Beijing 98-101
Teatro Olimpico, Vicenza 125
Temple of Claudius, Rome 24
Temple of Heaven, Beijing 98-101
  Circular Mound Altar 99, 100, 101
  Hall of Prayer for Good Harvests 99, 100-01
  Imperial Vault of Heaven 99, 100
  Vermillion Steps Bridge 99
Temple of the Inscriptions, Palenque 38-41
Temple of Peace, Rome 24

Thomas, Albert (architect), Grand Palais, Paris 189
Thornhill, James (artist), Blenheim Palace 162
Tintoretto (artist), Doge's Palace 97
trompe l'oeil 249
  Ducal Palace, Urbino 109
  Melk Abbey 157
  Parthenon, Athens 21
  Villa La Rotonda, Vicenza 124, 127
Trump International Hotel and Tower, Chicago 231
Türkiye, Hagia Sophia, Istanbul 32-37
Tuscan columns 26, 27, 249
TWA Flight Center, New York 211

U

UK
  Bishopsgate, London 231
  Blenheim Palace 158-63
  Canary Wharf, London 231
  Chiswick House, London 127
  Crystal Palace, London 191
  Durham Cathedral 61
  Houses of Parliament, London 172-75
  King's College Chapel, Cambridge 102-05
  Lloyd's Building, London 219
  Mereworth Castle 127
  Peterborough Cathedral 61
  Shard, London 226
US
  Chiat/Day Building, Venice 223
  Chrysler Building, New York 194-97
  De Young Museum, San Francisco 237
  Empire State Building, New York 197
  Fallingwater, Mill Run 202-07
  Frank Gehry house, Santa Monica 223
  Frederick Weisman Museum of Art, Minneapolis 223
  Guggenheim Museum, New York 202, 225
  John Hancock Center, Chicago 231
  Johnson Wax HQ, Racine 202
  Monticello, Charlottesville 168-71
  Prairie houses 205
  Robie House, Chicago 205
  Sears Tower, Chicago 231
  Seattle Central Library 236-37
  Trump International Hotel and Tower, Chicago 231
  TWA Flight Center, New York 211
  Woolworth Building, New York 197
  World Trade Center site, New York 217
Utzon, Jørn (architect)
  Bagsværd church, Copenhagen 209
  Kuwait National Assembly Building 209
  Sydney Opera House 208-11

V

Van Alen, William (architect), Chrysler Building, New York 194-97
Van Campen, Jacob (architect)
  Mauritshuis, The Hague 142, 145

  Paleis Noordeinde, The Hague 142
  Royal Palace, Amsterdam 142-45
Vanbrugh, John (architect), Blenheim Palace 158-63
Vasari, Giorgio (artist), Florence Cathedral 83, 86-87
Vellert, Dierick (artist), King's College Chapel, Cambridge 105
Veronese, Paolo (artist), Doge's Palace 97
Vila-Grau, Joan (artist), Sagrada Familia 184
Villa La Rotonda, Vicenza 8, 124-27
Villa Savoye, Poissy 198-201
Viollet-le-Duc, Eugène-Emmanuel (architect), Abbaye de Ste-Madeleine 60-63

W

Wagner, Richard (composer) 179
Wartburg Castle, Eisenach 177, 179
Wassenhove, Joos van (artist), Ducal Palace, Urbino 109
Wastell, John (stonemason), King's College Chapel, Cambridge 103, 104
water, use of
  Alhambra 90, 91
  Fallingwater 202-07
  Masjid-i-Shah 134
  Melk Abbey 156
  Taj Mahal 136-37, 139
Wise, Henry (landscape gardener), Blenheim Palace 161
wood, use of
  Borgund Stave Church 68-71
  Bulguksa Temple 42-45
  Forbidden City, Beijing 101
  Jean-Marie Tjibaou Cultural Centre 226-29
  Temple of Heaven, Beijing 98-101
  Yusuhara Wooden Bridge Museum 244-45
Woolworth Building, New York 197
World Financial Center, Shanghai 233
World Trade Center site, New York 217
Worms Cathedral, Germany 61
Wright, Frank Lloyd (architect)
  Fallingwater, Mill Run 202-07
  Guggenheim Museum, New York 202, 225
  Imperial Hotel, Tokyo 202
  Johnson Wax HQ, Racine 202
  Prairie houses 205
  Robie House, Chicago 205

Y

Yakovlev, Postnik (architect), St. Basil's Cathedral 120-23
Yevele, Henry (stonemason), Houses of Parliament, London 175
Yusuhara Wooden Bridge Museum 244-45

Z

Zimmermann, Johann Baptist (artist), Amalienburg Pavilion, Nymphenburg 165
Zuccaro, Federico (artist), Florence Cathedral 83

The author

Philip Wilkinson has written many books about architecture and history. His titles include the award-winning *Amazing Buildings*, the ground-breaking *English Buildings Book*, *The Shock of the Old*, and *Turn Back Time: The High Street*, written to accompany the recent successful BBC television series. Passionate about everything to do with architecture, Philip gives talks and teaches classes on historic buildings, appears on the radio, and regularly blogs about English buildings (at www.englishbuildings.blogspot.com). He lives in the Cotswolds in the UK and Southern Bohemia in Czechia.

The illustrator

Dotnamestudios produces iPad apps and 3D visualizations. It has contributed to over 50 print titles, has had apps featured in Gizmodo and 3d Arts, and broadcast on New York 1 News "Appwrap".

Acknowledgments

Dorling Kindersley would like to thank the following for their assistance with this book: Anna Fischel and Kajal Mistry for editorial assistance, Yenmai Tsang for design assistance, and Margaret McCormack for compiling the index. DK Delhi would like to thank Vagisha Pushp for picture research assistance, and Raman Panwar and Jagtar Singh for pre-production assistance.

The publisher would like to thank the following for their kind permission to reproduce their photographs:

(Key: a-above; b-below/bottom; c-center; f-far; l-left; r-right; t-top)

1 SuperStock: Cosmo Condina (cl); TAO Images (c). **Alamy Stock Photo:** Inigo Bujedo Aguirre-VIEW (cr). **2 Shutterstock.com:** Alberto Masnovo. **3 Getty Images:** Ian Cumming. **4-5 Corbis:** Christopher Pillitz. **6 Alamy Images:** Joshua Murnane (tr); Mark Sunderland (bc). **Corbis:** Charles Lenars (tl); George Hammerstein (bl). **Getty Images:** Carma Casula / Cover (br); H P Merten (tl). **Lonely Planet Images:** Izzet Keribar (cl). **SuperStock:** Fancy Collection (tc); Marka (cr). **7 Alamy Images:** hemis.fr (bl). **Corbis:** Paul Souders (tl). **SuperStock:** Photononstop (cl). **8-9 Getty Images:** Marco Simoni (b). **8 Corbis:** Yann Arthus-Bertrand (bl). **Photolibrary:** (bc). **9 akg-images:** Andrea Jemolo (br). **Getty Images:** Marc Garanger (tr); Philippe Bourseiller (tl). **10 Alamy Stock Photo:** Album (crb). **SuperStock:** Universal Images Group (bl). **11 Corbis:** Jane Sweeney (br); Max Rossi / Reuters (tc). **Mary Evans Picture Library:** Aisa Media (clb). **12 Alamy Images:** Arcaid Images (bc). **Corbis:** Jake Warga (br). **Masterfile:** Zoran Milich (bl). **13 Corbis:** Abu'l Qasim (bl). **Photolibrary:** Keith Levit (tl). **Sonia Halliday Photographs:** (br). **14-15 Corbis:** Mike Burton / Arcaid. **16-17 SuperStock:** imagebroker.net. **17 Getty Images:** DEA / A. Jemolo (br). **18 Alamy Images:** Jim Henderson (tl). **The Trustees of the British Museum:** (clb). **19 Getty Images:** (cr); Patrick Chapuis / Gamma-Rapho (bc, bl); Richard Nowitz (br). **Jim Henderson / Crooktree Images:** (tc). **SuperStock:** Robert Harding Picture Library. **20-21 Alamy Images:** nagelestock.com. **21 4Corners:** Reinhard Schmid / Huber (br). **22 Alamy Images:** Bill Heinsohn (tl). **Sites & Photos:** Samuel Magal (br). **Werner Forman Archive:** (bl). **23 Corbis:** Vanni Archive (tr). **Werner Forman Archive:** (fbl, cr). **24 Photo Scala, Florence:** Courtesy of the Ministero Beni e Att. Culturali (bc). **24-25 SuperStock:** age fotostock. **26 4Corners:** Giovanni Simeone / SIME (bl). **Getty Images:** Photoservice Electa (tr). **SuperStock:** Ingram Publishing (br). **Travel Pictures:** (tl). **27 Alamy Images:** Yannick Luthy (tr). **Lonely Planet Images:** Linda Ching (cl). **Photo Scala, Florence:** Courtesy of the Ministero Beni e Att. Culturali (c). **Werner Forman Archive:** (bl). **28-29 Masterfile:** Bryan Reinhart. **29 Corbis:** Alinari Archives (br). **30 Alamy Images:** Gary Hebding Jr. (cl). **Corbis:** Vanni Archive (bl). **SuperStock:** Fotosearch (tl). **31 4Corners:** Luigi Vaccarella / SIME (tl). **Alamy Images:** Joshua Murnane (c). **Getty Images:** Image Source (bc). **SuperStock:** age fotostock (cr); (br). **32-33 Corbis:** Tolga Bozoglu / Epa. **33 Werner Forman Archive:** (br). **34 akg-images:** Electa (tl); Gerard Degeorge (bl). **Getty Images:** Pete Ryan (cl). **Photolibrary:** (bc). **35 Alamy Images:** Melvyn Longhurst (br). **Corbis:** Bob Krist (cr); Mike McQueen (bl). **36 Corbis:** Atlantide Phototravel (bl); Bob Krist (r). **Lonely Planet Images:** Izzet Keribar (cl). **37 Alamy Images:** Gezmen (tl); Michele Burgess (br). **Getty Images:** Ayse Topbas (cra); Kimberley Coole (tl). **Lonely Planet Images:** Izzet Keribar (bl). **38-39 4Corners:** Fridmar Damm / Huber. **38 Corbis:** Danny Lehman (bc). **40 Mary Evans Picture Library:** Aisa Media (bl, br). **41 Alamy Images:** Carver Mostardi (cr). **The Art Archive:** Gianni Dagli / National Anthropological Museum MexicoOrti (br). **Mary Evans Picture Library:** Aisa Media (bl). **42-43 Corbis:** Steven Vidler / Eurasia Press. **43 Ancient Art & Architecture Collection:** EuroCreon (br). **44 De Agostini Editore:** W. Buss (tr). **SuperStock:** Eye Ubiquitous (bl); Fotosearch (br). **45 Alamy Images:** David Parker (br). **SuperStock:** JTB Photo (tl, cr, br); Pixtal (bc). **46-47 akg-images:** Bildarchiv Monheim. **47 Lebrecht Music and Arts:** RA (br). **48 Photolibrary:** (tr). **SuperStock:** imagebroker.net (bl, br). **49 4Corners:** Guido Baviera / SIME (br). **Alamy Images:** Bildarchiv Monheim GmbH (bl). **Photolibrary:** (c, tc, cra). **50-51 Getty Images:** Philippe Bourseiller. **52 Corbis:** Charles Lenars (b). **Photolibrary:** (c). **SuperStock:** Clover (cl). **52-53 Photolibrary:** (t). **53 Corbis:** Albrecht G. Schaefer (bl). **SuperStock:** age fotostock (br). **Thinkstock:** iStockphoto (cr). **54-55 Alamy Images:** Matt Botwood. **56-57 Corbis:** Joson. **56 Lebrecht Music and Arts:** Leemage (tr). **58 Alamy Images:** Andrew Morse (bc). **Corbis:** Jake Warga (bl). **Photolibrary:** (tl). **58-59 Alamy Images:** Cathy Topping (b). **59 akg-images:** Bildarchiv Monheim (bl). **Ancient Art & Architecture Collection:** Barry Crisp (br). **Wolfgang Kaehler Photography:** (tc). **SuperStock:** Pixtal (cr); Robert Harding Picture Library (c). **60-61 Getty Images:** Herve Champollion / Gamma-Rapho. **61 SuperStock:** Universal Images Group (br). **62 Corbis:** Gianni Dagli Orti (br). **Getty Images:** Herve Champollion / Gamma-Rapho (bl). **SuperStock:** (tl). **63 Mary Evans Picture Library:** Aisa Media (bl). **Photolibrary:** (c). **SuperStock:** Photononstop (cr). **64-65 Corbis:** Michael Jenner / Robert Harding World Imagery. **65 Ancient Art & Architecture Collection:** Richard Ashworth (tr). **66 akg-images:** Tarek Camoisson (bl). **Ancient Art & Architecture Collection:** Prisma (tl). **Getty Images:** Manuel Cohen (br). **Photolibrary:** (cl). **67 Getty Images:** DEA / C. Sappa / De Agostini (tr). **Photolibrary:** (bl). **SuperStock:** age fotostock (br). **68-69 Mariusz Petelicki. 69 4Corners:** Günter Gräfenhain / Huber (br). **70 Alamy Images:** Aivar Mikko (tr); David Robertson (bl); Rob Watkins (tc). **71 akg-images:** Nadine Dinter (tc). **Arcaid Images:** Bildarchiv Monheim (bl). **Lonely Planet Images:** Grant Dixon (tl). **Photolibrary:** (br). **72 Sonia Halliday Photographs:** (bc). **72-73 SuperStock:** Tetra Images. **74 Alamy Images:** Scott Hortop Images (tl). **SuperStock:** Photononstop (bl, tc). **75 Sonia Halliday Photographs:** (tc, bl). **76 Sonia Halliday Photographs:** (r). **77 Art History Images:** Holly Hayes (br). **Sonia Halliday Photographs:** (fbl, bc, cb, crb). **SuperStock:** Peter Willi (tl); Photononstop (bl). **78 Alamy Images:** Blickwinkel (bc). **78-79 Thinkstock:** Salih Kuelcue. **80 Alamy Images:** imagebroker (ca); Peter Widmann (cb, tr). **80-81 SuperStock:** imagebroker.net (b). **81 akg-images:** Erich Lessing (cla). **Alamy Images:** imagebroker (cra); Pieder (b). **Bayerische Schlösserverwaltung, München, www.schloesser.bayern.de:** (cb). **82-83 Masterfile:** Larry Fisher. **83 Corbis:** Michael Nicholson (br). **84 Corbis:** Justin Foulkes / SOPA (tl); Mike Burton / Arcaid (tr). **85 4Corners:** Giovanni Simeone / SIME (tc). **Photo Scala, Florence:** Courtesy of the Ministero Beni e Att. Culturali (cra); Photo Spectrum / Heritage Images (b). **86 Alamy Images:** Ian Dagnall (b). **86-87 Alamy Images:** Arcaid Images (t). **87 Dorling Kindersley:** John Heseltine / Courtesy of Opera Di S. Maria del Fiore Di Firenze (bl). **88-89 4Corners:** Richard Taylor. **90 4Corners:** Giovanni Simeone / SIME (bl). **Alamy Images:** Bill Heinsohn (br). **Getty Images:** Maurizio Borgese (tl). **Photolibrary:** (bc). **91 4Corners:** Massimo Ripani / SIME (bl). **Mary Evans Picture Library:** Aisa Media (br). **Photolibrary:** (tr). **92-tc Alamy Images:** HP Canada. **92-93 Photolibrary:** (t). **92 4Corners:** Massimo Ripani / SIME (bl). **Photo Scala, Florence:** White Images (bc). **93 4Corners:** Massimo Ripani / SIME (br). **Getty Images:** Image Source (cr). **Photolibrary:** (bl). **SuperStock:** imagebroker.net (c). **Thinkstock:** Alfredo Maiquez (tc). **94-95 SuperStock:** De Agostini. **94 TipsImages:** Francesco Reginato (bc). **96 Corbis:** Angelo Hornak (br); Danny Lehman (tl). **97 4Corners:** Guido Baviera / SIME (br). **Photoshot:** (tc). **Robert Harding Picture Library:** Mel Longhurst (cr). **TipsImages:** Mark Edward Smith (bl). **98-99 Photolibrary. 99 TopFoto.co.uk:** The Granger Collection (b). **100 Getty Images:** Shi Wei (br). **101 4Corners:** HP Huber / Huber (br). **Photolibrary:** (cra). **SuperStock:** imagebroker.net (cl); TAO Images (bl). **102-103 Getty Images:** Andrew Holt. **103 Alamy Images:** Bhandol (crb). **104 Getty Images:** Peter Packer (cr). **Lonely Planet Images:** Jon Davison (tc). **SuperStock:** imagebroker.net (bl); Universal Images Group (br). **105 Alamy Images:** Matt Botwood (br). **Art History Images:** Holly Hayes (bl). **With permission by The Provost and Scholars of King's College, Cambridge:** (cr). **106-107 Corbis:** Miles Ertman. **107 Corbis:** The Gallery Collection (b). **108 Alamy Images:** Christine Webb (bc). **Photo Scala, Florence:** Courtesy of the Ministero Beni e Att. Culturali (tl, br). **Eva Suba:** (bl). **109 Corbis:** Alfredo Dagli Orti (br). **Getty Images:** De Agostini (tc). **Photo Scala, Florence:** Courtesy of the Ministero Beni e Att. Culturali (bl, tr). **110-111 TipsImages:** Tomasinelli Francesco. **112-113 4Corners:** Giovanni Simeone / SIME. **113 Mary Evans Picture Library:** Aisa Media (br). **114 Robert Harding Picture Library:** Wojtek Buss (tr). **SuperStock:** age fotostock (cl, bc). **114-115 SuperStock:** Photononstop (b). **115 Corbis:** Sylvain Sonnet (tc, bc). **Robert Harding Picture Library:** Sylvain Grandadam (br). **116-117 Getty Images:** Panoramic Images. **117 akg-images:** (tr). **118 akg-images:** Hervé Champollion (clb). **Photolibrary:** (tl). **119 Alamy Stock Photo:** MB_Photo (bc). **120-121 Photolibrary. 121 TopFoto.co.uk:** RIA Novosti (br). **122 4Corners:** Matteo Carassale / SIME (tc). **Depositphotos Inc:** pedro2009 (clb). **SuperStock:** Igor Sinitsyn (tr); Pixtal (br). **123 Getty Images:** Ludovic Maisant (tr).

256 ACKNOWLEDGMENTS

Photolibrary: (bl). **TopFoto.co.uk:** RIA Novosti (br). **124–125 TipsImages:** Mark Edward Smith (b). **125 Bettma/Corbis** (tr). **126 Arcaid Images:** Fabio Zoratti (tr). **Corbis:** Yves Talensac / Photononstop (tl). **TipsImages:** Mark Edward Smith (cb, br). **127 4Corners:** Massimo Ripani / SIME (br). **Corbis:** Yann Arthus-Bertrand (cra). **TipsImages:** Mark Edward Smith (cb). **128–129 Corbis:** Ocean. **128 Lebrecht Music and Arts:** Tottori Prefectural Museum / Haga Library (bc). **130 Alamy Images:** Andy Smy Travel (bc). **Mary Evans Picture Library:** Aisa Media (tl, bl). **131 Alamy Images:** JTB Photo Communications, Inc. (cr); Malcolm Fairman (bc). **Corbis:** Charles & Josette Lenars (bl). **Werner Forman Archive:** (tr). **132-133 Alamy Stock Photo:** imageBROKER.com GmbH & Co. KG / Egmont Strigl. **132 Corbis:** Roger Wood (bc). **134 Science Photo Library:** George Holton (tr). **Alamy Images:** JTB Photo Communications, Inc. (bl). **The Bridgeman Art Library:** Julian Chichester (bc). **Mary Evans Picture Library:** Aisa Media (br). **135 Corbis:** Abu'l Qasim (br). **Getty Images:** Andrea Thompson Photography (bc). **SuperStock:** Robert Harding Picture Library (cr). **TipsImages:** Tomasinelli Francesco (tl). **136–137 SuperStock:** George Hunter. **137 The Art Archive:** Victoria and Albert Museum London / Sally Chappell (br). **138 Dorling Kindersley:** Amit Pasricha (c, bl, br); Amit Pasricha (tl, cl). **139 Dorling Kindersley:** Amit Pasricha (c, bl); Ram Rahman (br). **SuperStock:** imagebroker.net (bc). **140 Dorling Kindersley:** Amit Pasricha. **140–141 Dorling Kindersley:** Dinesh Khanna (b). **141 Dorling Kindersley:** Amit Pasricha; Dinesh Khanna (br). **142–143 Royal Palace Foundation Amsterdam**. **142 Amsterdam City Archives:** (bc). **144–145 Alamy Stock Photo:** imageBROKER.com GmbH & Co. KG / Hans Zaglitsch (c). **144 Alamy Stock Photo:** Mark Davidson (ca); imageBROKER / R. Kiedrowski (bc). **eyevine:** Thomas Schlijper / Hollandse Hoogte (clb). **145 Alamy Stock Photo:** Zoonar / Anastasy Yarmolovich (br). **Royal Palace Foundation Amsterdam:** Erik & Petra Hesmerg (tr, c). **146–147 hemis.fr:** Bertrand Gardel. **147 Photo Scala, Florence:** White Images (tr). **148 Shutterstock.com:** agsaz (tr); The Image Bank Unreleased / Marc Dozier (bl). **hemis.fr:** Bertrand Rieger (br). **149 Corbis:** Bertrand Rieger / Hemis (cra). **Dorling Kindersley:** Courtesy of CNHMS, Paris (tl); Courtesy of l'Etablissement Public du Musee et du Domaine National de Versailles (cb). **SuperStock:** Cosmo Condina (br). **150–151 4Corners:** HP Huber / Huber (t). **150 Alamy Stock Photo:** AuthorsImage / Bernard Dupont (c); AuthorsImage / Mickael David (bl); Hemis.fr / Bertrand Rieger (br). **151 Alamy Stock Photo:** AuthorsImage / Bernard Dupont (c). **Corbis:** Philippe Lissac / Godong (br). **Mary Evans Picture Library:** Aisa Media (bl). **152–153 The Art Archive:** Keenpress / NGS Image Collection. **154–155 The Art Archive:** Keenpress / NGS Image Collection. **155 akg-images:** ullstein bild (br). **156 Alamy Stock Photo:** Image Professionals GmbH / Andreas Strauss (tc, bc). **Getty Images:** Godong (cl). **156–157 Corbis:** Massimo Listri (b). **157 akg-images:** Rainer Hackenberg (cr). **Corbis:** Arcaid (c); Doug Pearson / JAI (tc). **TipsImages:** J-C.& D. Pratt / Photononstop (br). **158–159 Photolibrary**. **159 Getty Images:** Hulton Archive (cla). **159–161 Photolibrary:** (t). **160 Photolibrary:** (bc); (cl). **SuperStock:** Andrew Michael / age fotostock (br). **161 akg-images:** Sambraus (br). **Photolibrary:** (bl). **SuperStock:** Andrew Michael / age fotostock (cra). **162 Reproduced with the kind permission of His Grace the Duke of Marlborough, Blenheim Palace Image Library:** Jarrald Publishing (bl). **Getty Images:** VisitBritain / Britain on View (br). **Mary Evans Picture Library:** Aisa Media (c). **163 Reproduced with the kind permission of His Grace the Duke of Marlborough, Blenheim Palace Image Library:** Jarrald Publishing (bl, t). **164–165 Alamy Images:** AM Stock (b). **165 Mary Evans Picture Library:** D.H. Teuffen / Interfoto (tr). **166 akg-images:** Erich Lessing (cl); Paul M.R. Maeyaert (br). **Alamy Images:** Bildarchiv Monheim GmbH (tr). **167 Alamy Images:** Bildarchiv Monheim GmbH (cb). **Camera Press:** Christian Kerber / Laif (cra). **Corbis:** Hugh Rooney (br). **Getty Images:** Leemage (tl). **168–169 Alamy Images:** Pat & Chuck Blackley (b). **168 Corbis:** (tr). **170 Archivision Inc.:** Scott Gilchrist (tr, bl). **Thomas Jefferson Foundation, Inc. at Monticello:** (br). **171 Alamy Images:** Buddy Mays (bl, br); Pat & Chuck Blackley (tc). **172–173 4Corners:** Massimo Ripani / SIME (b). **173 Alamy Images:** Mary Evans Picture Library (cra, tr). **174 Shutterstock.com:** Circumnavigation (bc); cooperman (bl). **174 Alamy Stock Photo:** Coy St. Clair (cl). **175 Corbis:** Adam Woolfitt (bl). **Photolibrary:** (br). **SuperStock:** G.R. Richardson (c). **176–177 4Corners:** Reinhard Schmid / Huber. **177 akg-images:** (br). **178 4Corners:** HP Huber / Huber (br). **178 Alamy Stock Photo:** Gibson Outdoor Photography (c); Prisma by Dukas Presseagentur GmbH / Luthy Yannick (tl); Craig McAteer (bl). **179 Getty Images:** DEA / A. Dagli Orti (br). **Bayerische Schlösserverwaltung, München, www.schloesser.bayern.de:** (tr). **Corbis:** Adam Woolfitt (bl). **180 Getty Images:** Apic (crb). **181 Getty Images:** Sylvain Sonnet. **182 Corbis:** Sylvain Sonnet (r). **Dorling Kindersley:** Based on a plan supplied courtesy of Junta Constructora del Temple de la Sagrada Familia (tl); Max Alexander (bl). **183 Alamy Stock Photo:** Danita Delimont (c). **Corbis:** Jeremy Horner (tr). **Fotolia:** Jenny Solomon (tl); Mario Savoia (bl). **184 Alamy Images:** Shirley Kilpatrick (br). **Mary Evans Picture Library:** Aisa Media (bl). **184–185 Corbis:** Sylvain Sonnet (t). **185 Corbis:** Alan Copson / JAI (tc). **Fotolia:** kevin14 (bl). **Getty Images:** Nick Servian (br). **Mary Evans Picture Library:** Aisa Media (bc). **186 Archives du Musée Horta, Saint-Gilles, Bruxelles:** (bl). **Ookaboo.com:** Karl Stas (r). **187 akg-images:** Hilbich (tr). **Bastin & Evrard sprl:** (cl, bl). **Alastair Carew-Cox:** (ca, br). **188–189 Corbis:** Arnaud Chicurel / Hemis. **189 Roland Smithies:** (br). **190 Corbis:** Bertrand Rieger / Hemis (cra); (tl). **SuperStock:** hemis.fr (clb); Photononstop (br). **191 Alamy Images:** Schütze / Rodemann (cr, clb). **Corbis:** Bettmann (cra). **SuperStock:** hemis.fr (bl). **192–193 Getty Images:** Carma Casula / Cover. **194 Corbis:** (bl). **195 Photolibrary:** John Frechet. **196 Alamy Stock Photo:** Forray Didier / Sagaphoto.com (bl); imageBROKER.com GmbH & Co. KG / Michael Szönyi (ca). **Corbis:** Vince Streano (c). **196–197 Corbis:** George Hammerstein. **197 Alamy Stock Photo:** George Thiel (br). **Alamy Images:** Eric Bechtold (ca). **Corbis:** Nathan Benn (cb). **198-199 Alamy Stock Photo:** Bildarchiv Monheim GmbH / Schütze / Rodemann / Le Corbusier / FLCI ADAGP, Paris / © DACS 2025 (b). **199 Corbis:** Keystone (tr). **200 Alamy Stock Photo:** Arcaid Images / Le Corbusier / FLCI ADAGP, Paris / © DACS 2025 (bc); Bildarchiv Monheim GmbH / Schütze / Rodemann / Le Corbusier / FLCI ADAGP, Paris / © DACS 2025 (tl). **Dreamstime.com:** Gilles Bizet / Le Corbusier / FLCI ADAGP, Paris / © DACS 2025 (cl). **200-201 Alamy Stock Photo:** Bildarchiv Monheim GmbH / Schütze / Rodemann / Le Corbusier / FLCI ADAGP, Paris / © DACS 2025 (b). **201 Alamy Stock Photo:** Bildarchiv Monheim GmbH / Schütze / Rodemann / Le Corbusier / FLCI ADAGP, Paris / © DACS 2025 (cb); imageBROKER / Moritz Wolf / Le Corbusier / FLCI ADAGP, Paris / © DACS 2025 (br); Paul Raftery / Le Corbusier / FLCI ADAGP, Paris / © DACS 2025 (c). **202-203 Alamy Stock Photo:** H. Mark Weidman Photography / Wright Frank Lloyd / ARS, NY / © DACS 2025. **202 Corbis:** Bettmann (bc). **204 Science Photo Library:** Spencer Grant / Wright Frank Lloyd / ARS, NY / © DACS 2025 (bl). **Shutterstock.com:** Taras Vovchuk / Wright Frank Lloyd / ARS, NY / © DACS 2025 (br). **204 Alamy Stock Photo:** Simone Celeste / Wright Frank Lloyd / ARS, NY / © DACS 2025 (tl). **205 Alamy Stock Photo:** Art Directors & TRIP / Wright Frank Lloyd / ARS, NY / © DACS 2025 (bl). **Rex by Shutterstock:** Courtesy Everett Collection / Wright Frank Lloyd / ARS, NY / © DACS 2025 (br). **Photo Scala, Florence:** The Frank Lloyd Wright Fdn, AZ / Art Resource, NY (cra). **206 Getty Images:** Laura Farr / Wright Frank Lloyd / ARS, NY / © DACS 2025 (bc). **SuperStock:** age fotostock / Wright Frank Lloyd / ARS, NY / © DACS 2025 (br). **Alamy Stock Photo:** Peter Cook-VIEW / Wright Frank Lloyd / ARS, NY / © DACS 2025 (bl). **206-207 Alamy Stock Photo:** Peter Cook-VIEW / Wright Frank Lloyd / ARS, NY / © DACS 2025 (t). **207 akg-images:** VIEW Pictures Ltd / Wright Frank Lloyd / ARS, NY / © DACS 2025 (tr). **Alamy Stock Photo:** Peter Cook-VIEW / Wright Frank Lloyd / ARS, NY / © DACS 2025 (bc, crb). **208–209 SuperStock:** View Pictures Ltd. **209 Rex Features:** Barry J. Peake (br). **210 Getty Images:** Ian Cumming (bl); Wilfried Krecichwost (tl). **SuperStock:** age fotostock (bc); Prisma (br). **211 Alamy Images:** Aurora Photos (bl). **Getty Images:** Dennis Hallinan (br). **Newspix / News Ltd:** (cra, fcra). **Photolibrary:** David Messent (tl). **Sydney Opera House:** (bc). **212 Corbis:** Stephanie Maze (bc). **212–213 Fotolia:** snaptitude. **214–215 Corbis:** Jane Sweeney (c). **214 Dreamstime.com:** Bevan Ward (c). **SuperStock:** imagebroker.net (clb). **215 Getty Images:** Fernando Bueno (tc); Mauricio Simonetti (br); SambaPhoto (cl). **SuperStock:** imagebroker.net (cr). **216 Corbis:** Hulton-Deutsch Collection (br). **216–217 Photolibrary:** Photoservice Electa. **218 Alamy Images:** Prisma Bildagentur AG (bc). **SuperStock:** Bryan Reinhart / Mauritius Images (bl); Photoservice Electa (tl). **218–219 SuperStock:** Photoservice Electa (b). **219 Dreamstime.com:** Makukolj (crb). **Getty Images:** VisitBritain / Britain on View (cra). **SuperStock:** Photoservice Electa (tl). **220 Getty Images:** Evan Agostini (cra). **National Gallery of Canada / Musée des beaux-arts du Canada:** (b). **221 Alamy Images:** AA World Travel Library (cr); JTB Photo Communications, Inc. (br); Wolfgang Kaehler (bc); Prisma Bildagentur AG (bl). **Dreamstime.com:** Nantela (c). **222–223 Getty Images:** Mark R. Thomas (b). **223 Getty Images:** Andreas Rent (tr). **224 Corbis:** Bob Krist (cl). **Getty Images:** Altrendo Travel (bc); Cristina Arias / Cover (br); Carma Casula / Cover (bl). **225 © FMGB Guggenheim Bilbao Museoa, 2012:** Erika Barahona-Ede (bl). **Getty Images:** LatitudeStock - TTL (cra). **Mary Evans Picture Library:** Aisa Media (br). **226–227 Alamy Images:** Author's Image Ltd. **226 Corbis:** James Leynse (bc). **228 Alamy Images:** Arcaid Images (cr). **Corbis:** Franck Guiziou / Hemis (bl). **229 Alamy Images:** Jon Arnold Images Ltd (cr). **Rpbw, Renzo Piano Building Workshop:** Michel Denancé (cl); William Vassal (c). **230–231 Getty Images:** Nikada. **231 Adrian Smith + Gordon Gill Architecture:** (br). **232–232 Dorling Kindersley:** Chen Chao (t). **232 Corbis:** Inmagine Asia. **233 Getty Images:** David Trood (cra); Michael DeFreitas (fcra). **234 Corbis:** Christopher Pillitz (br, bl). **234–235 Photolibrary:** (t). **235 Corbis:** Christopher Pillitz (tc); James Leynse (br). **236 Alamy Stock Photo:** Paul Christian Gordon / Koolhaas Rem / OMA / © DACS 2025 (b). **Corbis:** Kevin P. Casey / Koolhaas Rem / OMA / © DACS 2025 (cra). **237 Alamy Stock Photo:** Ron Buskirk / Koolhaas Rem / OMA / © DACS 2025 (cl). **Corbis:** Michael Robinson / Beateworks / Koolhaas Rem / OMA / © DACS 2025 (tc); Ramin Talaie / Koolhaas Rem / OMA / © DACS 2025 (bl); John Edward Linden / Koolhaas Rem / OMA / © DACS 2025 (br). **Dreamstime.com:** Brian Walters (cra). **238 Corbis:** Jose Fuste Raga (b). **Getty Images:** Cover (cra). **239 Corbis:** Atlantide Phototravel (br); Inigo Bujedo Aguirre / View (bl); Fernando Alda (cra). **Getty Images:** De Agostini (ca); Jose Jordan / AFP (cla). Getty Images: Universal Images Group / View Pictures (cl). **240–241 SuperStock:** View Pictures Ltd. **241 Getty Images:** Jeff J. Mitchell (br). **242 Corbis:** Atlantide Phototravel (cl); Max Rossi / Reuters (r). **Masterfile:** Siephoto (bl). **243 Corbis:** Richard Bryant / Arcaid (cl); Victor Fraile / Reuters (br). **Courtesy of Zaha Hadid Architects:** (cra). **SuperStock:** Marka (tl); View Pictures Ltd (bl). **244 Courtesy of Kengo Kuma & Associates:** Takumi Ota Photography (b). **Getty Images:** Torin Boyd / Bloomberg (cra). **245 Courtesy of Kengo Kuma & Associates:** Takumi Ota Photography (tr, ca, cla, bl). **Dorling Kindersley:** Demetrio Carrasco (br)

Cover images: *Front:* **Alamy Stock Photo:** Chronicle clb, Felix Lipov fcra, NiKreative cl; **Dreamstime.com:** Atanasbozhikov fcrb, Roman Sakhno cr, Trudywsimmons fbr; **Getty Images:** Jodie Bell fcl, Tibor Bognar fcr, Alex Dissanayake / Lonely Planet RF crb, Peter Zelei Images fcla, Artie Photography (Artie Ng) bl, Bo Zaunders cla; **Getty Images / iStock:** EricFalco fbl, haoliang fclb, Vincent_St_Thomas cra, tunart br; *Back:* **Alamy Stock Photo:** Felix Lipov fbl; **Dreamstime.com:** Atanasbozhikov cla, Roman Sakhno bl, Trudywsimmons fcl; **Getty Images / iStock:** EricFalco clb, haoliang fcla, Vincent_St_Thomas cl, tunart fclb; *Spine:* **Getty Images:** Bo Zaunders t

Illustrations created by **Dotnamestudios © Dorling Kindersley:** 26tr, 66-67c, 70br, 105tl, 108-109t, 114tr, 118-119t, 127tl, 174-175t, 178-179t, 191tl, 201tl, 218tr, 224-225t, 228-229t; **3D Illustrations: Visualisation Services:** 18cr, 22-23t, 31-31c, 34-35c, 74cr, 138tr, 204-205t, 210tr